Late Adulthood: Perspectives on Human Development

Second Edition

Life-Span Human Development Series

Series Editors: Freda Rebelsky, Boston University, and Lynn Dorman

Infancy
Kathryn Sherrod, George Peabody College for Teachers
Peter Vietze, National Institutes of Health
Steven Friedman

Early Childhood
Donald L. Peters, The Pennsylvania State University
Sherry L. Willis, The Pennsylvania State University

The Middle Years of Childhood
Patricia Minuchin, Temple University

Adolescence
Kathleen M. White, Boston University
Joseph C. Speisman, Boston University

Early and Middle Adulthood
Lillian E. Troll, Rutgers University

Late Adulthood: Perspectives on Human Development, Second Edition
Richard A. Kalish, Albuquerque, New Mexico

Cross-Cultural Human Development
Robert L. Munroe, Pitzer College
Ruth H. Munroe, Pitzer College

Life-Span Developmental Psychology:
Introduction to Research Methods
Paul B. Baltes, The Pennsylvania State University
Hayne W. Reese, West Virginia University
John R. Nesselroade, The Pennsylvania State University

Biological Perspectives in Developmental Psychology
George F. Michel, Boston University
Celia L. Moore, University of Massachusetts

Cognitive Development: A Life-Span View
George E. Forman, University of Massachusetts
Irving E. Sigel, Educational Testing Service

Personality Development through the Life Span
Barbara M. Newman, Ohio State University
Philip R. Newman

Perceptual Development
Richard D. Walk, George Washington University

Late Adulthood: Perspectives on Human Development

Second Edition

Richard A. Kalish

BROOKS/COLE PUBLISHING COMPANY
MONTEREY, CALIFORNIA

This book is dedicated to my mother, Alice Neuman Kalish, whose career as a gerontologist did not begin until she was 72 years old, and who now, at 78, gives talks, leads workshops, and attends meetings of the Western Gerontological Society.

Brooks/Cole Publishing Company
A Division of Wadsworth, Inc.

Printed in the United States of America

10 9 8 7 6 5 4 3 2 1

Library of Congress Cataloging in Publication Data

Kalish, Richard A.
Late adulthood.

(Life-span human development series)
Bibliography: p.
Includes index.
1. Aged—Psychology. 2. Aging. 3. Retirement.
I. Title. II. Series.
HQ1061.K33 1981 305.2′6 81-10182
ISBN 0-8185-0473-0 AACR2

Cover. Photo courtesy of Jeroboam, Inc. © 1979 by Ilka Hartmann.
Reprinted by permission.

Subject Editor: *C. Deborah Laughton*
Manuscript Editor: *Grace Holloway*
Production Editor: *Marlene Thom*
Series Design: *Linda Marcetti*
Cover Design: *Vicki Van Deventer*
Typesetting: *Computer Typesetting Services, Inc., Glendale, California*

Series Foreword

What are the changes we see over the life span? How can we explain them? And how do we account for individual differences? The Life-Span Human Development Series provides a new way to look at these questions. It approaches human development from three major perspectives: (1) a focus on basic issues related to the study of life-span developmental psychology, such as methodology and rescarch design, cross-cultural and longitudinal studies, age-stage phenomena, and stability and change; (2) a focus on age divisions—infancy, early childhood, middle childhood, adolescence, young and middle adulthood, and late adulthood; and (3) a focus on developmental areas such as physiology, cognition, language, perception, sex roles, and personality.

There is some overlap in the content of these volumes. We believe that it will be stimulating to the reader to think the same idea through from the viewpoints of different authors or from the viewpoints of different areas of development. For example, language development is the subject of one volume and is also discussed in the volume on cross-cultural development, among others.

Instructors and students may use the entire series for a thorough survey of life-span developmental psychology or, since each volume can be used independently, may choose selected volumes to cover specific concept areas or age ranges. Volumes that focus on basic issues can be used to introduce the student to the life-span concept.

No single author could adequately cover the entire field as we have defined it. Our authors found it exciting to focus on their areas of specialization within a limited space while, at the same time, expanding their thinking to encompass the entire life span. It can be beneficial to both author and student to attempt a new integration of familiar material. Since we think it also benefits students to see ideas in development, we encouraged the authors not only to review the relevant literature but also to use what they now know to point up possible new areas of study. As a result, the student will learn to think about human development rather than just learn the facts of development.

Freda Rebelsky

Lynn Dorman

Preface

Growing older is a process experienced by everyone, and birthdays are reminders that this process is indeed ongoing. People in their 20s and 30s can draw very real insights from their own experiences into what it means to be aging. There is room for optimism and a little sadness, for the awareness that some behavior may change, for marshaling and using your own resources, for reminiscing about the past, and for looking with hope into the future. Those who are not yet old have had ample experiences to gain some empathy for those who are.

Through this book I hope to enable the not-yet-old to expand their understanding of aging and their empathy for the elderly by examining the issues, the ideas, and the information available on the psychology of later maturity and old age. In so doing, I have attempted to provide a realistic picture of older people, avoiding the temptation to gain sympathy for them by emphasizing their health and economic problems, their limitations, and their loneliness and lack of power, while simultaneously avoiding the pollyannaish notion that old age is a period of comfortable ease and pleasure, without important worries or cares.

This book was written for several audiences. First, I believe it would fit in well with the last weeks of a life-span development course. Second, in combination with a good book of readings or with a well-designed reading list, it would serve as the basic text for a full course on aging. Third, there are many continuing-education programs, workshops, and seminars on human aging that might find this book useful. Fourth, students who wonder whether they wish to probe deeper into the psychology of aging could begin by reading or even skimming this book. And fifth, I very much hope that nonstudents who are interested in the psychology of aging and the elderly themselves who wonder what the academics have to say about them would pick up this book to browse through.

The book is written primarily so that you can learn a little more about older people and what it means to age, but another kind of awareness is inevitable. Each of you will probably wonder about yourself as you grow older: Does this sentence apply to me? Will I suffer this loss, have this capacity reduced, become more of this or less of that? If so, will I cope successfully, or will I become lonely, depressed, unhappy? Speaking only for myself, I firmly believe that my own involvement in the field of aging has offered me more options as I get older, has helped me to understand some of the changes I see in myself as being anticipated and normal, and has permitted me greater perspective and even a touch of humor about getting old. I feel strongly that an awareness of the human aging process will enable each of us to cope much more effectively with the aging of those we love, with the aging of our friends and associates, and with the aging that will inevitably come to each of us.

Interest in the field of human aging has grown incredibly in the past few years, with popular and professional books and articles virtually tumbling off the presses. The actual increase in knowledge, which always falters far behind the quantity of writing on any topic, has also burgeoned, so that it is difficult to keep a brief book like this one brief.

So this book has changed to keep up with the new information and changing understanding of the aging process and of older people. The demography of aging, which changes constantly, has been updated and expanded. Theories of aging are now included. New material on cognitive changes with age is discussed. A new chapter on physical and mental health builds on what was presented earlier, but now has substantially more material on physical and mental illness, including organicity. Information on educational gerontology, criminal victimization, and the media has been added.

While keeping the style and the orientation of the previous edition, the present book has expanded in both breadth and depth, represented by more than 100 new references, almost all of which were written during the past six years. It is the same book, yet it is a very different book.

As always, a number of people have contributed to the making of this book. I would especially like to thank Herman Brotman, private consultant, Washington, D.C., and Falls Church, Virginia; Donna Cohen, University of Washington; Sally Fitts, University of Washington; and Mary Mokler, Albuquerque, New Mexico. I would also like to thank the instructors who reviewed the manuscript for their valuable comments: Harry J. Berman, Sangamon State University; Leonard Cain, Portland State University; John Colen, California State University, Sacramento; Jeff Elias, Texas Tech University; Joseph Richard Heller, California State University, Sacramento; and Victor W. Marshall, University of Toronto. Last but not least, I would like to thank Anna Poole for her swift and accurate typing.

Richard A. Kalish

Contents

Chapter One Human Aging: An Orientation 1

The Meaning of Life-Span Development 2
Why Study the Later Years? 3
Specialists in Aging 4
Research in Gerontology 6
The Meaning of *Old* 8
The Demography of Aging 12
Personal Growth in the Later Years 15
The Advantages of Being Old 17

Chapter Two Basic Processes and the Aging Individual 19

Biological Changes with Age 19
Sensory Processes 23
Psychomotor Performance 27
Learning, Memory, and Intelligence 31
Cautions in Interpreting the Data 39
Coping with Aging 40

Chapter Three Physical and Mental Health 43

Maintaining Good Health 44
Health Changes in the Later Years 50
Caring for Health Problems 59
The Meaning of Death and the Process of Dying 65
A Last Caution and Some Last Thoughts 68

Chapter Four The Older Individual: Personality and Role 70

The Changing Self-Concept 71
Personality Changes and Aging 75
Successful Aging 79
Adult Socialization and Roles 86
Last Comments 92

Chapter Five Relating to Others 93

Husbands and Wives 95
Parenthood, Grandparenthood, and Great-Grandparenthood 100
Other Family Members 107
Friends and Neighbors 108
Two Issues in Relating to Others: Independence and Sexuality 111
A Concluding Comment 114

Chapter Six Practical Issues: Money, Retirement, and the Living Environment 115

Income and Outgo 115
Work and Retirement 119
Life after Retirement 124
The Physical Environment 129
A Last Comment 134

Chapter Seven Community Responses to Older Persons 135

Attitudes toward Older People 135
Social Services and Social Programs 142
The Elderly and Criminal Victimization 146
Legal Services 148
Religion and the Aging 148
Educational Gerontology 151
Ethnicity and Aging 153
The Rural Aged 156
Aging in the Future 157

References 159

Author Index 171

Subject Index 175

Chapter One

Human Aging: An Orientation

In the time that it took you to read the first 12 words of this sentence, you have aged: you have partaken of the universal phenomenon occurring in humans and other animals, in animate and inanimate objects, in ideas and cultures. You have aged; you have changed; you have gone one more step along the path to your eventual death. True, you may prefer to use the concept of development rather than the notion of aging, since you may view the one as implying an unlimited future while viewing the other as a decremental process. But the concept that you prefer does not alter the fact that you are changing with time, that you are *aging.*

Aging is a process that is sometimes favorable and sometimes unfavorable, but it is natural and inevitable. Being old, elderly, aged, a "senior citizen," a "golden ager," is a stage in this process, occurring just as naturally and just as inevitably as infancy and childhood. Neither the process of aging nor the state of being old is pathological, strange, or deviant except as the result of certain unpleasant occurrences that tend to be age related, much as other unpleasant occurrences are associated with the preschool years, such as being under adult control, or the middle years of life, such as having financial responsibility for children.

My purpose in this abrupt beginning is not to distress you or frighten you into or out of reading further. Rather, I wish to stress that human existence is a continuum with conception at one end and death at the other, and that the later years, even the terminal days, need to be seen as part of this continuum. Later life should be viewed not as a social or psychological problem, although for many it is, but as the final stages of a span of development that is continuous with earlier stages.

Like people of any age group, those in their later years share certain qualities, feelings, experiences, roles, and changes with their age mates; but, like people of any age group, the elderly are also immensely variable in their qualities, feelings, experiences, roles, and changes and are immensely different from others in their age group.

The Meaning of Life-Span Development

At one time, psychologists and others believed that people did not basically change after the age of, say, 5 or 11 or 18. Unless they underwent intensive psychotherapy or have a deeply moving experience, their behavior was essentially set. Human development was seen as ending early in life—the rest was simply a playing out of what was set up in childhood.

Life-span developmentalists, while recognizing the significance of childhood experiences, don't accept the view that development and change end with childhood. They see personal growth as possible at any age and change as occurring at every age. In understanding a 70-year-old woman, it is just as important to know about her life at 60 as it is to know about her life at 16—and in some ways it is more important.

Some of the life-span developmental changes of later life are well known. For example, we are influenced by shrinking futurity. At 30 we usually see our future as extending almost indefinitely. If you think about a limited future at all, it is likely to be in terms of several decades. You may decide to study French, even though you know it may take at least three or four years to become proficient; you may develop a career plan to enable you to be independent in 12 or 15 years; you may decide to work your way up the political ladder to run for a seat on the city council.

At 60 the options have begun to close down. You need to establish priorities, and you may decide that learning French would not be a good use of your time; you may no longer be able to contemplate any career plan that requires a lengthy period; starting to work your way up to run for city council may no longer appear feasible.

The effects of limited futurity differ greatly from person to person. Some older people appear overwhelmed by these time limits and become depressed; some ignore them almost completely and go ahead with long-term plans; and some accommodate themselves to shrinking futurity by focusing more on the moment and less on the years ahead, without diminishing their enjoyment of life at all.

Finitude is only one factor that changes over the life span, although it is faced by each of us. Life-span developmentalists are also likely to look at other aspects of our lives that change over time. Our relationship with our parents is much different when we are in our 20s and they are in their 50s from what it is 20 years later; reading habits change over the years; sleep patterns and the need for sleep are different for 70-year-olds and 30-year-olds.

Sometimes life-span changes occur slowly and fairly regularly, such as the slowing down of reaction time; other characteristics remain stable for many years, then change rapidly, such as the use of leisure time after retirement; sometimes the nature of changes is less predictable, such as the relationship with one's spouse or feelings about living alone. Nevertheless, although individual differences always occur in life-span developmental changes, there are still predictable trends.

Right now, however, I would like to encourage you to view human behavior in a life-span development context, with the later years as simply a later period of development. You might want to apply this concept to your own personal development by considering some characteristic of yours that has changed over your life span. Some possibilities are your athletic involvements, your career aspirations, your sex life, or your income. Then you can project this quality into the future, contemplating how it is likely to change every few years. Doing so will also give you the opportunity to understand the impact of shrinking futurity on your own anticipated future.

Why Study the Later Years?

"Old people are on their way out. We need to focus on those who will be around awhile and can help build a better world." "Getting old just isn't relevant for me. It's simply too far away." "Old people are beyond change and beyond meaningful interventions. Their best years are behind them. Too much input for too little output." "Their values and ideas and habits are so different from mine that I can't really deal with them." "I just don't want to think about getting old and dying. It's too depressing." Yet anyone who is truly concerned with the dignity of all human beings, who really wishes to understand humanity in its entirety, who desires more than a segmentalized view of life, needs to understand the later years. For me, there are three basic reasons to study the psychology of the later years and issues concerning the elderly:

1. To participate in providing resources for those who are old today and for those who will be old tomorrow (that is, you and me), so that they—and we—lead a more satisfactory life during the later years.
2. To enable us to better understand our own relationships to older persons and to our own aging process, so that we can lead a more satisfactory life ourselves today.
3. To place the earlier years of the life span in proper perspective and to perceive individual development as a lifelong process.

These reasons might be labeled service, insight, and theory. I will attempt to provide a balance among these approaches in the coming pages.

We all have a personal stake in the process of aging because it is happening to us all the time. It is obviously also happening to people we love—and to those we don't love; it is happening to our parents, our politicians, our friends, and our coworkers, to everyone. We also have a personal stake in the status of being elderly because the chances are that we and most people we know either are elderly now or will become elderly.

In addition to the personal stake, however, you may have a vocational stake. Your past, present, or future work may involve either the aging process or older persons. If it involves the aging process, you will probably be teaching, counseling, or doing research because few other kinds of employment involve the aging process itself. However, numerous possibilities emerge if your vocational stake is in those people who are elderly. You may be concerned with programs (planning, conducting, evaluating), with policy formation, with direct interactions, with advocacy, with research, or with some combination of these. Or your interest in older people may be as a novelist, as an artist, as a furniture designer, as an architect, as a politician, or as an advertising-agency project director.

Specialists in Aging

Tens of thousands of people have become specialists in aging, either through their studies or through their work. Formal training in gerontology for most of these people has been limited to an occasional workshop or university-extension course, although some have academic degrees with specialization in aging in such diverse fields as recreation, medicine, anthropology, or architecture. A relatively few have studied in undergraduate or graduate programs that offer degrees in gerontology. However, recognition that older people require specially planned services and programs has grown so rapidly that the academic world has not been able to produce enough specialists through the usual college and university programs. Therefore, many specialists in aging have learned their skills on the job, with only a minimal background in more formal education and training.

Programs to provide services for the elderly have absorbed many of these specialists. Work roles include planning and development, program evaluation, administration, and direct services. Specialists in aging work in senior centers, long-term care facilities, adult education, housing for the elderly, nutrition programs that bring older people together for a hot lunch and some social contacts, and such special programs as the Retired Senior Volunteer Program.

Specialists in aging need to integrate their particular work skills with a background in aging. A public administrator might manage a government-subsidized housing development for low-income older people; a social worker might provide both counseling and practical help in a senior center; a health educator might plan and develop a special program for older people through the local school district's adult-education branch, and then teach the courses as well; a dietician might be a consultant for a group of nursing homes; a government worker might oversee the disbursement of county funds for worthwhile projects for the elderly, and then make certain that the funds are being used effectively; a psychologist might develop and administer a questionnaire to determine the effectiveness of an innovative, community-wide, geriatric day-care program, and then evaluate the findings. The possibilities are endless.

Another role for specialists in aging is that of advocacy. This role involves pressing the case for improved conditions for older people with members of Congress, state legislators, county and city elected and appointed officials, and any others who make policy, determine how funds are to be spent, or otherwise influence the conditions under which older people live. An advocate might also encourage local merchants to give older people reduced rates on purchases or try to persuade television networks to portray older characters more frequently and more favorably. Actually, a great deal of advocacy, perhaps the most effective advocacy, is performed by older people themselves, but many specialists in aging devote a portion of their time to this task.

Gerontologists and Geriatricians

Specialists in aging often refer to themselves as gerontologists or geriatricians. *Gerontology* means the study of the elderly (literally, the study of old men, from the Greek word *geros*). *Geriatrics,* the system of treatment of the elderly, initially referred solely to treatment for health problems, but the term is now applied to other fields, such as social work and recreation, as well.

Very few people, however, consider themselves simply as gerontologists, since the study of the elderly and the aging process is a subspecialty of many different fields. A biologist may study the aging process of tissues or of one-celled animals; a sociologist may study housing for the elderly; an anthropologist may focus on the role of the older person in a preliterate community or on the social structure of a retirement community; an educator may be concerned with devising continuing-education programs for preretirees and recent retirees; an economist may investigate the ways in which Social Security and pension programs lead to income redistribution among different age groups.

Even within one discipline a gerontologist's potential range of interest is immense. For example, the psychological gerontologist may be concerned with age-related changes in memory, perception, reaction time, or creativity; or marital roles and family relationships in the later years; or the psychological impact of retirement, the meaning of impending death, the psychological consequences of various living arrangements, loneliness, or mental illness in the later years. In short, if it has some application to later life, anything that a psychologist normally studies can be part of gerontology.

Research in Gerontology

"Research is the only way to provide answers to important questions." "Research is dehumanizing, an invasion of privacy." "Research is meaningless because each individual is unique." "Research takes dollars away from much more important services." "Research is necessary for progress." Each of these statements is familiar, is based to some degree on a valid notion, and is a gross oversimplification of the actual circumstances.

Gerontological research can be divided into three categories: basic, applied, and action or evaluation. Basic research is conducted to develop theories and principles of aging and of the behavior and functioning of older people. Although the person conducting basic research may be deeply and personally concerned about the human condition of the elderly, the practical application of the research is usually left to others.

Applied research is much more practical, though it still has theoretical implications. The results of these studies are more limited to the time and place in which the studies were conducted; that is, the results are less generalizable because they are more affected by the specific situation in which the research was conducted. Examples would be the attitudes of adult children in Atlanta toward their parents and the preferred living arrangements among the healthy elderly in rural areas of Kansas.

The goal of action or evaluation research is the solution of practical problems. One study might evaluate whether a new method of delivering health care to the elderly provided services equivalent to those provided by previous methods but at a reduced cost. Another would be to assess the housing needs of Native American elderly in the Chicago area.

Research Methods in Gerontology

Each gerontologist uses the research methods of his or her own discipline, adapting them as necessary to the special conditions imposed by studying aging or the elderly. Since this book emphasizes the psychological and social components of aging, most of the research discussed depended on behavioral-science methodology: controlled observations, laboratory experiments, field research, participant/observer research, a variety of objective and projective tests, epidemiological studies and other uses of census data and large-scale survey research, interviews and questionnaires, analyses of social and organizational structure, phenomenological research, and whatever innovative methods the most creative gerontologists could devise.

Although it shares basic methodological procedures with research on other age groups, research with persons in their later years entails some unique opportunities and some unique difficulties. This fact is particularly evident when we try to differentiate age changes, generational differences, and accidents of history.

If we want to understand what happens between the ages of 55 and 75, for instance, we have two basic options. We can study a group of 55-year-olds and a group of 75-year-olds, note the significant differences between the two groups, and assume that these differences have arisen because one group has lived longer than the other. *Or* we can begin to study a group of 55-year-olds, follow them up at regular intervals until they reach the age of 75, and assume that the changes taking place have resulted from having lived for 20 years. The former is termed *cross-sectional* research; the latter is known as *longitudinal* research. Both have important advantages; both have major pitfalls. (Readers wishing to probe ways of integrating these two methods should read Schaie & Strother, 1968.)

The cross-sectional approach has some obvious benefits. It can be done fairly quickly: you don't need to wait 20 years to obtain meaningful data. For that reason it also takes much less time, effort, and money than longitudinal research. Moreover, because it is conducted in a brief time span, it is much less affected by the accidents of history. For example, a longitudinal study of changes in physical health and health needs of the elderly begun in 1963 would have immense difficulty in determining the impact of the initiation of Medicare in 1966. Increased rates of visits to physicians and hospitals between 1960 and 1970 might have resulted from the greater availability of low-cost medical services, from increased health problems, from better health education, or from all of these factors.

Longitudinal studies also suffer from attrition. In all age groups a portion of those who begin as participants in longitudinal research drop out before the end of the study. Perhaps they leave the area; they may become bored with the project or irritated with the investigators; or their schedules may make it inconvenient for them to continue. In working with the elderly, an even more difficult problem occurs: attrition through illness and death. A separate problem arises when those who do become too ill to continue or who die during the project differ in some important way from those who remain. Assume that to learn about changes in immediate memory over a ten-year period, we begin in 1970 with 30 persons born in 1900, 30 more born in 1905, and an additional 30 born in 1910. We then administer various memory tests over a 15-year period and, in 1985, we trace the individuals still alive back across the previous decade to see what has occurred.

Some of those who were part of the original sample will have died, and this part of the sample will contain a disproportionately large number of those who had lower memory scores when initially tested (Riegel & Riegel, 1972). We also know that a drop-off in certain kinds of cognitive behavior may predict health problems that can lead to death. Therefore, those who remain at the end of 15 years were probably quite different at the beginning of the project from those lost through illness or death.

We have, of course, learned something about changes in memory over time. Because we could compare three age groups in 1970, we have cross-sectional information on age differences in memory ability. We can compare the same groups of people again in 1975, 1980, and 1985, and we are able to reexamine the data longitudinally to see what changes occurred over time.

When we find cross-sectional differences, there are two possible explanations: either people change as they get older, or people who were born in different decades have had different experiences that reflect when they lived, not how old they now are. The latter explanation is referred to as the *age-cohort effect:* an age cohort consists of those individuals who were born at approximately the same time, such as around the turn of the century or during World War I.

Remaining aware of the age-cohort effect is very important in studying gerontology. Another example may provide emphasis. Extremely reliable data show that older people are shorter than younger people. There are three possible explanations: taller people die sooner; people get shorter as they get older; or the older a person is today, the less likely he or she was to have ever been tall. You may know enough about the aging process and age cohorts to recognize that both the second and third explanations are valid.

When we find longitudinal differences, there are also two possible explanations: either people change as they get older, or the particular conditions of the time period under study lead to the changes. If we had measured attitudes toward women's rights among college students in 1950 and questioned the same individuals in 1980, we would probably have found a significant change in the direction of greater approval. This does not mean, however, that the process of aging causes people to favor women's rights.

Whichever methodology is used, we need to be cautious in interpreting gerontological research data, but not so cautious that we find reasons to discount most research findings.

The Meaning of *Old*

When is a person defined as *old*? As you might expect, there is no one correct answer to that question. Several different approaches are used, each justifiable and each open to criticism. *Old* can be defined strictly in chronological terms: people become old on their 65th birthday. There are legal and economic bases for this definition, although they seem to have become less important during the past decade or so. Age 65 as the determination of old age was once supported by rules on mandatory retirement, by changes in income-tax deductions, by Social Security requirements, and to an appreciable degree by popular consent. With mandatory retirement on its way out, with changes in Social Security age requirements, and with much popular protest against the arbitrary nature of a rigid age boundary, our society has moved one step toward a society in which chronological age has less significance than it does today.

In spite of this trend, we still use chronological age to define *old* in many situations, but it is not our only alternative. We can define *old* in terms of physical changes. These might include changes in posture, gait, facial features, hair color and hairline, voice, skin resiliency, general body contour, and ability to hear and see. Perhaps health is a part of your definition. You have a general physical image of *old*, and the closer an individual approximates your image, the more likely you are to perceive that person as old.

Since some organic changes become translated into behavior, you might think of *old* in terms of forgetfulness (most likely the result, at least in large part, of organic brain changes), slower reaction time, altered sleeping patterns, slower motor behavior, and so forth. Or perhaps you have thought of *old* in terms of ideas, concepts, and reactions to others. Some common stereotypes of the elderly are that they are conservative, hostile to the younger generation, resistant to social change, and easily irritated.

Old can also be defined in terms of social roles. Old is when an individual is retired, in a convalescent facility, a grandparent. Again, this is too simplistic, since hundreds of thousands of people retire, with a pension, before they are 50; younger people can be placed in convalescent facilities; and grandparents in their 40s are hardly unusual. Conversely, 60-year-olds occasionally return to college to complete degrees begun four decades earlier; reports of men (but virtually never women) becoming parents in their 60s and beyond are unusual but not unheard-of. Although the concept of social age or of being socially old is useful, it is hardly a sufficient definition by itself.

So we might settle for self-report. Old is when the individual says "I guess I'm old." That definition solves some problems and creates others. Thus, in a 1960 study, people over the age of 60 (many of them were in their 70s) were asked whether they saw themselves as middle-aged, elderly, or old; the investigators then repeated the study with the same participants in 1970. Of the 235 persons who participated in both studies, 70% declared themselves middle-aged in 1960, and 32% continued to think of themselves as middle-aged in 1970, when all were over 70 years of age. Those who thought of themselves as elderly or old were also less likely to see themselves as better off than others their own age in terms of their need for help, interaction with siblings, group participation, and health (Bultena & Powers, 1978). It would appear that self-report reflects health, functional capacity, and the opportunity for social relationships. A 67-year-old professor represented this position well when he commented to me after we had played two sets of vigorous tennis, "Now that I'm semiretired, I no longer resent being referred to as middle-aged."

In practice, most of us shift our definition of *old* to suit the occasion, often without fully realizing what we are doing. We judge one person old because she behaves in ways we judge old, but in another conversation we refer to older people as all those over 65. Most important, perhaps, is that both the speaker and the listener share the same definition at the same time.

A matter related to definitions of *old* is what terms are most appropriate to use when talking about people of this age. *Old, elderly, aged, aging, senior citizen, senior, golden ager, senescent, older adult, older person, older American* are all possible choices. I usually use *elderly* or *older person,* but I have noticed that many people who work in social agencies use *the seniors.* Preferences vary a great deal, both among specialists in aging and among older people themselves.

Individual Differences in Aging

If we use the arbitrary definition of *old* based on chronological age—more specifically, based on being 65 or older—approximately 25 million residents of the United States are old, some 11% of the entire population (Brotman, 1980). Therefore, generalizations about the entire group are hazardous. Essentially, when we say "Older persons are . . ." we are saying one of five things:

1. All older persons are . . .
2. Almost all older persons are . . .
3. Most older persons are . . .
4. Compared to other age groups, older persons are . . .
5. Relative to their younger days, older persons are . . .

We are encompassing an age group that spans 40 or more years, with members who range from excellent physical and emotional health to imminent death or severe psychosis, from extreme levels of intellectual and cultural awareness to extreme limitations in such awareness, from being actively employed to being actively (or passively) retired, and on and on.

Behavior and performance among a randomly selected group of 100 newborns are not highly variable. There will be some differences (such as in the frequency and duration of crying, the intensity of sucking, and the amount of bodily movement), but we can make highly accurate predictions about newborns if we know only how old they are and whether they are basically normal. As people become older, our ability to predict behavior simply from knowing a person's chronological age diminishes. For the middle-aged, predictions are quite difficult to make: some are already performing in ways we associate with old age, whereas others are behaving in ways we associate with adolescence. If we know that an individual is 3 years old, we can make fairly accurate estimates about ability to walk a mile, to fix dinner, to read and understand a newspaper article, and to memorize a poem. For someone who is 75, however, the accuracy of the prediction is reduced substantially. In brief, older adults vary immensely in biological and behavioral functioning (Botwinick & Thompson, 1968).

We can make certain general statements about older persons: "Older people are much more likely to be hurt by falling than younger people." "Most older persons are not presently employed for income." "Learning a new psychomotor task takes an older person longer than it takes a younger person." "Older adults include a much higher proportion of widows or widowers than any other age group." "Most Americans and Canadians will be over age 65 when they die." But even the most casual look at the statistics responsible for these statements will bring the immediate realization that great variability in both physical change and personal appearance exists within the population over age 65.

To some extent, we can sharpen our predictions by specifying a particular subgroup of elderly. Women are much more likely to be living without a spouse than men. Those over 80 are much more likely to reside in an extended-care facility than those under 75. Black Americans are less likely to be over age 65 when they die than White Americans or Asian Americans. The elderly with incomes below average for the age group are much more likely to have housing or transportation problems than the elderly with above-average incomes.

Even within the cruder classifications of age (for example, 60–69, 70–79), sex, ethnicity, health status, income, or marital status, other demographic distinctions can be made. True, many elderly Blacks are poor, but some are not; it is vital to recognize simultaneously both the concept of most and the existence of variability, so that we don't fall into the trap of stereotyping all elderly Blacks as poor or all elderly women as widows or all elderly couples as grandparents.

Older People Are Senescent

The first time I heard older people referred to as senescent, I was outraged to think that even a gerontologist would be so deprecating. Later I learned that, in spite of having a similar stem, *senescence* has no implication of *senility,* a term that in fact has been discarded by most gerontologists. Senescence is simply that period of life in which people are growing old, with some implication of declining capacity. It does not mean that the individual is confused or incapacitated. Not only are there great individual differences in the onset of general senescence, as just discussed, but intraindividual differences are also great. That is, your body does not age in a unitary fashion; certain organs or systems may show decrement sooner than others. A woman of 70 may, for instance, have a perfectly smooth, unwrinkled face, a full head of brown hair, and a heart performing like that of a woman in her 50s, while her renal functioning maybe comparable to that of an 80-year-old.

The Demography of Aging

As 1981 began, more than 25 million persons, or more than 11% of the population of the United States, were 65 years of age or older; when the census began in 1790, it was barely 2%; by 1900 it was only 4%. So the proportion of elderly in the population doubled in our first century of existence and has almost tripled in the first 80 years of this century. If we have zero population growth for the next 20 years, the then-elderly will number some 32 million, up from the roughly 25 million today, and will constitute slightly more than 12% of the population. By 2030, however, the figures are projected as 55 million and more than 18% (Brotman, 1980, 1981). Elderly Canadians constituted 9.3% of the population in 1981, compared to 5.0% in 1901 (Denton & Spencer, 1980).

The proportion of elderly in a population derives from a combination of birthrate, deathrate, in-migration, and out-migration. If the birthrate goes down, as it has over the past decade, and the deathrate also goes down, as it has over the past decade, the proportion of elderly goes up. And it has over the past decade. This generalization assumes that persons migrating into the country are not numerous, since most immigrants are usually younger people and children. Other industrialized nations have the same low birth- and deathrates, while poorer nations frequently have just the opposite. (See Table 1-1 for life-expectancy data.)

The lower birthrate has meant that not only has the proportion of elderly in the population increased rapidly, but the average age of the population has also increased. In 1790 the median age of Americans (the first count was limited to White males) was about 16; by 1900 it had jumped to nearly 23; in 1980 the median age was just over 30 (Brotman, 1980). We definitely have an aging population, sometimes referred to as the graying of America. The median age in Canada is also rising, now just a shade under 30 and expected to go up to the middle 30s or beyond in 20 years (Spencer, 1981).

Table 1-1. Life expectancies of men and women in selected countries.

Country	*Date*	*Men*	*Women*
Algeria	1970–1975	52.9	55.0
Belgium	1968–1972	67.8	74.2
Canada	1970–1972	69.3	76.4
Chile	1969–1970	60.5	66.0
China	1970–1975	60.7	64.4
Costa Rica	1972–1974	66.3	70.5
Egypt	1960	51.6	53.8
France	1976	69.2	77.2
Gambia	1970–1975	39.4	42.5
Kuwait	1970	66.4	71.5
Mexico	1975	62.8	66.7
Morocco	1970–1975	51.4	54.5
Netherlands	1977	72.0	78.4
Pakistan	1962	53.7	48.8
Peru	1960–1965	52.6	55.5
Poland	1976	66.9	74.8
Senegal	1970–1975	39.4	42.5
Switzerland	1968–1973	70.3	76.2
United States	1975	68.7	76.5

From *Demographic Yearbook, 1978*, by the Statistical Office of the United Nations, Department of Economic and Social Affairs. New York: United Nations, 1979.

Life expectancy has also increased, from 48 years in 1900 to 73 years in 1978, and more than 75% of all the people born today are expected to reach age 65, as opposed to just 40% in 1900. Most of the improvement in life expectancy, however, has resulted from eliminating the health conditions that caused death at early ages, so that the future life expectancy of a person who turned 65 in 1978 is an additional 16 years, only four years longer than his or her 1900 counterpart (Brotman, 1981).

Age, Sex, and Ethnicity

Although the data for the entire population are certainly relevant information, relatively few policies and programs can be based on the knowledge that there are 25 million older Americans. For many purposes demographic data on various subgroups are what matters. A great deal of such information is available in the Bureau of the Census documents in public libraries—for example, the age breakdown of households in the state of Texas or the proportion of elderly Blacks in San Bernardino County, California.

Some of the statistical breakdowns, however, have more than local significance. For example, between 1976 and the year 2000, the population between the ages of 65 and 74 will increase by almost 23%, but those between 75 and 84 will increase by 57%, and those 85 and over will increase by a substantial 91% (Brotman, 1981). This projection suggests that the greatest proportionate increases will take place among those persons who will need the most extensive health, social, and financial support services. And since all those people are living today, unless unexpected epidemics or disasters bring death to larger than normal numbers of elderly, the projection is very likely to be accurate, unlike many projections of birthrates, which are influenced by the technology and social values that affect the numbers of women who become pregnant.

The statistics for men and women are not identical. In 1980 there were 147 older women for every 100 older men. In Canada in 1976, the ratio was 129:100 (Denton & Spencer, 1980). When we look across the life span of the aging, the U.S. ratios are 130:100 among those 65 to 74, 178:100 for the next decade, and 224:100 for people over 85 (Brotman, 1981). Life-expectancy data confirm these numbers. Women born in 1978 can anticipate living until they are 77 years old, while men are likely to die nearly eight years sooner. Even those women already 65 years old have an even chance of living until after their 83rd birthday, while 65-year-old men have the same chance of living until just before their 79th birthday (Brotman, 1980). Canadian statistics are very similar (Sheppard, 1979).

The social implications of these data are important. They mean that older women are much more likely to be widows than older men are to be widowers. Since women normally marry men a few years their senior, women are also probably going to take care of their husbands' last illness and dying process. The statistics further suggest that older women have a reduced opportunity for remarriage, limited access to heterosexual relationships, and greater need for geriatric-health and other specialists who are particularly alert to the needs of older women.

Are older women fortunate in that they live longer than men? Or are they unfortunate because they have to deal with the death of their spouses, with a greater span of probable loneliness, and with more years of diminished income? The issue can be argued both ways.

The aging of the larger ethnic-minority groups differs from that of the general population. Black Americans, for example, have a life expectancy at birth of under 69 years, some five years less than the life expectancy of Whites (Brotman, 1981). However, the life expectancy of those Black men and women who do live into their 70s is the same as or greater than that of Whites of the same age. This phenomenon has been described as the demographic ethnic crossover (Jackson, 1980).

While in 1978 some 7.8% of all Blacks were over age 65, the proportion for Hispanics was much lower, about 4%. Although some of the difference reflects lower life expectancy, much of it results from both a high birthrate and the rapid in-migration of younger Hispanic people together with the return of some of the elderly to their land of birth or family origin for their last years. Fewer than 6% of Native Americans are over 65, primarily because the deathrate is high. And between 6% and 8% of the major Asian-American communities are elderly, with the variation resulting from each

Asian nation's unique patterns of immigration to this country, their health practices and deathrates, and their birthrates.

On the other side of the scale are the people referred to as White ethnic groups. Of those of English or Irish background, 15% are elderly; elderly Americans of French or German ancestry are 13% of their communities; Italians are only 11%. These figures result from a combination of low in-migration and low birth- and deathrates.

Population by States

Florida has the highest proportion of older people of any state in the country, with 18%, while Alaska has the lowest proportion, with slightly more than 2.5%. These figures have resulted from a large migration of elderly to Florida and a large migration of young persons to Alaska, together with a substantial out-migration of elderly who seek a warmer climate and a lower cost of living.

Those states with the most rapidly increasing number of elderly are all Sun Belt states (Nevada, where the elderly population almost doubled during the 1970s; Arizona; Florida; Hawaii; and New Mexico), where many elderly people have gone to retire, plus Alaska (Brotman, 1981), which has made a concentrated effort to encourage its older residents to remain rather than to leave at retirement.

Although the Sun Belt states have shown the most rapid growth in numbers of elderly, the five states with the largest proportion of elderly after Florida are Midwestern agricultural states: Arkansas, Iowa, South Dakota, Missouri, and Nebraska, all with more than 13% (Brotman, 1981). These high proportions have resulted from younger people's leaving the states while the elderly have tended to remain.

The Human Side of Numbers

The previous pages are filled with numbers, life-expectancy rates, and other statistics that you can easily perceive as having no personal meaning. I hope you have not done so. Each time a statistic was presented, vast numbers of human beings were represented. These kinds of information can greatly improve policy development and program planning. You may need to know about comparable data for your state, county, community, or neighborhood to develop policies for your agency or local government or to plan programs for the elderly in your community today or for those residents who will be elderly in the future.

Personal Growth in the Later Years

Much of the work in gerontology and geriatrics has emphasized losses and decrements, so that the initial research findings and general attitudes were bleak. It seemed as though getting old meant becoming worse off in virtually every way. But when you talk with individual older people, they may complain about their arthritis or their loneliness or their reduced income, but many still seem not only cheerful but positively enthusiastic about their lives.

One reason is that these older people have learned to cope effectively with the unpleasant changes in their lives by overcoming them, working around them, or ignoring them. A second reason is that they paid no attention to those people who were telling them that they could no longer learn new things or be stimulated by new ideas and went right ahead exploring the world, enjoying themselves, and finding stimulation and challenge.

Models of Aging

At one time most gerontologists and nongerontologists alike viewed older people through either a *pathology model* or a *decrement model.* Then these were replaced by a more optimistic *minimal-change model,* which presumed only small degrees of decrement, and subsequently by a *normal-person model.* In the last model it isn't that aging itself is causing these changes, but that health changes, the loss of loved ones, or reduced functional capacity produces decrements. These decrements can occur at any age, and they do not inevitably occur with old age, but they are more likely, often much more likely, to be found among the elderly than among younger people (Kalish, 1979a).

Now the *personal-growth model* is becoming more prominent. The later years can be a time of substantial personal growth, sometimes because of the losses that lead to growth, sometimes in spite of the losses, and sometimes without regard for the losses. And, of course, sometimes the losses are minimal or nonexistent. For some older people, as for some younger, personal growth is difficult or impossible: personal stress, a destructive childhood, major health or disability problems, and overwhelming losses can all provide insurmountable obstacles (although I'm constantly impressed by those older persons who confront all these difficulties and still find pleasure and excitement in their lives). Individual differences in these regards are immense.

We all view ourselves at least to some extent as we believe others view us. This is true not only of how we think others perceive us as individuals but of how we think others perceive the groups to which we belong. Therefore, when older people in general are seen through the decremental model, they are treated as deteriorating and may tend to view themselves as such—it takes great personal strength to see yourself as competent, growing, and "whole" when others view you as incompetent, static or constricting, and unwhole. To escape this self-concept, many elderly take the *that-old-person-over-there* position; they accept the general-population view of the elderly but apply it to other older people, seeing themselves as exceptions.

Now it seems that more and more elderly and nonelderly are taking an optimistic position, viewing the elderly as having the potential to grow, improve, learn, be stimulated, and gain pleasure from life. Programs and policies for older people are changing to reflect this position, and older people are increasingly viewed as individuals who can do things for themselves rather than as those who need to have things done for them.

The Advantages of Being Old

So much of the popular and professional literature on aging looks at the difficulties of the later years that I would like to address some of the advantages of aging for the older person:

1. Many responsibilities have ceased. The children of the older generation are usually self-sufficient, and elderly parents have frequently (but not always) died; repetitive and fatiguing work demands no longer occur; stressful competitive needs are no longer strong.
2. Many of the constraints based on what other people think have been shed.
3. Many older people have worked through much of their fear of their own death.
4. Older people realize that the future is finite, and this knowledge often allows them to attend only to matters that have a truly high priority, permitting them, if they wish, to ignore the minutiae of life.
5. There is tremendous discretionary time that can be used to satisfy the high-priority needs. However, there is sometimes so much time available that it is not used effectively, which is a danger in retirement (Kalish, 1979a).

To this list can be added a few more practical advantages: older people are less frequently victimized by criminals than any other adult age group; they suffer fewer accidents; they receive a certain amount of income and health care without working; and they have some tax advantages and free or reduced-rate services (Palmore, 1979).

One survey of older persons found that increased leisure time was mentioned by 43% as one of the best things about being over 65; freedom from responsibility was cited by 31%; financial support and security were mentioned by 22%; and not having to work was listed by 18% (Harris & Associates, 1975).

In the final analysis, then, you and I and everyone else are faced with two alternatives: to live old or to die young. When phrased in such abrupt terms, neither alternative seems appealing; yet those who have had contact with a wide variety of old people—both in institutions and out, both in good health and in less than adequate health—come away impressed by their ability to live with their difficulties and to enjoy life as much as, and often more than, younger persons. In the film *Gigi,* Maurice Chevalier sings a ballad called "I'm Glad I'm Not Young Anymore." The lyrics remind us that people in their later years are no longer susceptible to the anxieties and vanities and social pressures of their youth and middle age, that they can be more free to be themselves and to do what is important to them. If income, health care, such facilities as transportation and housing, and general opportunities and options continue to become more available for the elderly, the later years can indeed be a time of personal growth and satisfaction.

Chapter Two

Basic Processes and the Aging Individual

Why do people (and, indeed, all other organisms) age? Is aging really a natural process? An inevitable process? What can be done to slow the pace of aging or to eliminate it altogether? If a crash program in biomedical research showed promise of adding 30 healthy years to life, as has been proposed (Comfort, 1969), should the government provide substantial financial support for it? Both the benefits and the hazards of a significant increase in life expectancy are considerable, and relevant issues have been explored in recent books (for example, Veatch, 1979).

Biological Changes with Age

Aging, it is generally although not universally believed, is not a disease. Some scholars assume that it is genetically based; others assume that non-genetic factors are primarily responsible. Therefore, as scientists debate the most promising approach to influencing the course of aging, some emphasize intervening at the genetic level or in the physiology of the body, while others look to changing the physical or social environment.

Theories of Biological Aging

In the final analysis all theories about the causes of aging end up with a biological basis that is genetic in origin. That means that we all inherit from our parents not only the inevitability that we will age but the inevitability, given present knowledge, that our maximum life span has been established. The differences in the theories revolve around the particular factors that produce the aging process and the ways to affect these factors so that aging can be slowed down. There are three major groupings of such theories (Shock, 1977).

The first group has been termed *genetic theories.* Advocates of this position recognize that "information is transferred from DNA molecules through a variety of steps to the ultimate formation of proteins (enzymes) which are critical for the continued function of specific cells in the animal" (Shock, 1977, p. 104). To support their position, they turn to studies suggesting that some body cells can divide only a certain number of times before they die (Hayflick, 1974). The assumption is that cells are genetically programmed to die, perhaps from damage to the cellular DNA, perhaps from even very low levels of radiation that always exist in the atmosphere, perhaps from other causes (Shock, 1977).

Second are the *nongenetic cellular theories.* These assume that the passage of time produces changes in the cells that reduce their effectiveness. These changes might arise from insufficient nutrients and oxygen delivered to the cells or from the introduction of chemical substances to the cells that impede their capacity to function properly (Shock, 1977).

The third grouping, the *physiological theories* of aging, considers aging as the result of "the breakdown in the performance of a single organ system or more reasonably in terms of impairments in physiological control mechanisms" (Shock, 1977). Thus, it is assumed that aging comes about because of the deterioration of, for example, the cardiovascular system or the endocrine or the immunological system. Physiological stress may be a factor in this breakdown (Selye, 1976).

Each of these theories has implications for interfering in the aging process. According to the genetic theories, scientists must intervene directly in the genetic programming and improve the ability of cells to divide more times, perhaps through altering the DNA molecules. The nongenetic cellular theories look to the possibility of affecting the durability of the cells during the person's lifetime or to eliminating factors that lead to cellular death. And the adherents of the physiological theories would attempt to improve the capabilities of the various organs whose breakdown they believe leads to aging. Nathan Shock (1977), one of the foremost experts in this field, urges that scientists examine the likelihood that the interrelationships among cells, tissues, and organs interact to produce aging. He opposes the search for a single mechanism and encourages recognition that "aging is a highly complex phenomenon which may require different explanatory principles for different aspects of the process" (p. 113).

It's important that we not confuse the mechanisms that cause aging with those that cause death, although the two are related. To live longer, we are encouraged to eat properly, get adequate rest, avoid tobacco, drink no more than a moderate amount of alcohol, obtain adequate medical care, get appropriate exercise, and learn to handle inevitable psychological and social stresses while avoiding chronic, excessive stress. Considerable evidence has accumulated to establish each of these factors as increasing our chances for a longer and healthier life.

The Meaning of Biological Aging

Two questions arise when we consider the meaning of biological aging. First, we don't always know whether the biological changes we associate with aging are the results of primary aging (hereditary factors), secondary aging (results of disease or injury that is not genetic in origin), or tertiary aging (changes resulting from degeneration of or damage to the central nervous system) (Busse, 1969; Cohen & Wu, 1980). For example, we know that loss of teeth is a biological change that occurs with age, but we don't know whether dental problems are induced by genetic mechanisms that also cause other parts of the organism to age or whether they are caused by other processes occurring over time. The development of caries and the deterioration of the gums may be the outcome of environmental factors that accumulate over the years, such as diet or wear and tear, rather than of the primary aging process.

Second, with our present limited knowledge, we cannot be certain whether a particular change is inevitable in the aging process or whether available or potentially available forms of social, psychological, or medical intervention might slow down the process, stop it altogether, or even reverse it. We know that the interaction between biological changes in aging and psychological and social processes is great, but we don't know how great in specific situations. For example, baldness is associated with aging, and we have not been successful in stopping or reversing most baldness (except through transplants), but diminished lung capacity can be slowed down or reversed by increased exercise, by deep-breathing exercises, or by stopping smoking.

Describing the kinds of decrements that occur with aging, especially those that become most evident during the 60s, is only the first step in ascertaining their meaning to the individuals themselves. We must ask a series of questions that are generally applicable to all forms of age-related change:

1. Does it matter? Granted that we can accurately measure innumerable age-related changes: do these changes necessarily have a meaningful impact on the lives of the persons affected? Substantial hearing loss obviously does; so does severely reduced short-term memory. But how important is reduced olfactory capability? Or sensitivity to temperature change?
2. Does it imply other changes of a more serious nature? A relatively rapid decline in certain types of cognitive capacities may indicate cardiovascular or other health problems, perhaps prognosticating more serious illness or even death. Another change may signify little of importance for the future.
3. Will an intervention alter the path of the decrement? Will a surgical procedure, or any health treatment, serve to ameliorate the problem? Will improved social relationships, the reestablishment of feelings of personal

meaningfulness, an increase in sensory or cognitive stimulation, or any other planned intervention make any difference?

4. Is there any mechanical device that can help? Can the problem be helped or corrected by eyeglasses? A hearing aid? An artificial limb?
5. How is the individual coping with the losses, and how can he or she be enabled to cope more effectively? Three people suffering the same hearing loss may respond in three different ways: Person A obtains a hearing aid and begins to learn lip reading; he remains reasonably cheerful. Person B refuses a hearing aid and retreats into a solitary life; he becomes depressed. Person C also rejects a hearing aid, but she manages to find a friendship group that will accept her hearing loss and make the important adjustments themselves.

Although the changes to be described in this chapter are frequently biologically based and are often beyond our present ability to alter effectively, each organism that is affected is an individual with a unique life history, a unique personality constellation, and a unique set of present circumstances. Each alteration, then, has a unique impact on the individual affected.

Often the greatest problems arising out of reduced capacities and lowered effectiveness are their effects on self-concept and social interaction with others. These losses can readily inhibit behavior in such a fashion that overall adjustment is affected. Reduced visual acuity, if extreme and not fully correctable, can make reading difficult or impossible, can reduce mobility by making driving impossible, and can deny the pleasure of watching movies or television. Moreover, each change is a reminder of the aging process that is causing it, and these decrements can be frightening as predictors of things to come.

Fortunately, people are reasonably resilient, and most older persons adapt to such changes by recognizing that the only way to enjoy life is to cope with the changes as effectively as possible, compensate as much as is appropriate, and then go on to other matters. Also, except for those whose losses are premature or extensive, each aging person notes that other age peers are encountering the same difficulties. In a very real sense, this knowledge is supportive; it can lead to a preference for social contacts within the same age group rather than within more vigorous, often less understanding, younger and middle-aged groups.

Age-related changes in the basic process of growing older are the result of interactions between biological and psychosocial occurrences. The kinds of changes to be discussed here are (1) the sensory processes, such as vision and hearing; (2) psychomotor performance, with particular focus on reaction time; and (3) cognitive functions, including learning and thinking.

Before beginning, however, I want to emphasize one point: sensory, psychomotor, and cognitive functioning are all highly interrelated. What affects any one of these capacities will directly or indirectly affect the others. They are all integrated to form the process by which we receive information and respond to it. One way to grasp the continuing dynamic interaction among these capacities is to imagine what a person would be like if any one of them were removed: what remained would no longer be a functioning individual. Further, each of these capacities is greatly affected by both physical and mental health. In fact, the health psychology of aging is becoming an important concern of both health psychologists and gerontologists.

Sensory Processes

A large variety of sensory processes have been observed to show decrement with age, with the decrement tending to accelerate when individuals reach their 60s and thereafter. Since most research on sensory processes has been cross-sectional, we need to be somewhat cautious in interpreting the findings, but there is little reason to believe that more longitudinal research would substantially alter the evidence on patterns of change.

Vision

The eyes perform a variety of tasks in interaction with the perceptual processes occurring in the brain; these interactions produce the visual images that you perceive. You must be able to see near objects and far objects, monochromatic scenes and color scenes, objects in an almost completely dark room, and objects caught in a sudden blaze of strong light.

There is little doubt that a variety of visual capacities diminish in the later years. Although two major studies show somewhat different percentages, the evidence is strong that the proportion of people with 20/20 vision diminishes by 75% between age 60 and age 80, while the proportion whose vision is 20/50 or worse more than triples during the same period (Anderson & Palmore, 1974).

A major cause of visual problems in older persons is the reduced elasticity of the lens, which makes it difficult to see objects near at hand (McFarland, 1968). Thus, older people tend to become farsighted; this fact gives rise to their common complaint, often but not always made facetiously, that telephone books and road maps "must be using smaller print these days." Eyeglasses can normally correct this defect.

Another difficulty of the later years is produced by the reduction with age in the size of the pupil, reducing the amount of light that reaches the retina (Fozard, Wolf, Bell, McFarland, & Podolsky, 1977) and thus limiting the accuracy of vision. Older people are likely to require more illumination for reading and other visual tasks than younger people, although too much illumination can produce glare, which is also an increasing problem for the elderly (Fozard et al., 1977).

The ability of the eye to adjust to changing amounts of light also diminishes with age. Both adapting to the dark and adapting to the light are involved; the older person is less likely to make either adjustment as efficiently as before (McFarland, 1968). Whereas eyeglasses can help problems of distance adjustment, devices to compensate for the loss in ability to adjust to light are not available, and the practical difficulties that arise can be considerable, not only for certain professions (such as aviation) but also for night driving. At night the driver must be able to adapt rapidly to the headlights of an oncoming vehicle without being blinded by the glare and then, with equal rapidity, readapt to being able to see the dark road and surroundings. Decreased ability to make these adjustments is one of the reasons that older persons often avoid driving at night.

Older people also encounter other visual decrements. Their depth perception declines (Bell, Wolf, & Bernholz, 1972); some loss of color perception has been found (Corso, 1971); and peripheral vision shows significant decrement in the later years (McFarland, 1968). Since older people tend to suffer from many kinds of visual decrement at the same time, the task of fitting them with appropriate eyeglasses to correct all the changes becomes increasingly difficult (Fozard et al., 1977).

As must be obvious by now, overall vision becomes less accurate with age, with losses increasing more rapidly beginning in the 50s. By age 65 about half of all persons have a visual acuity of 20/70 or less, some five times the proportion of those who have that degree of visual loss at age 45 (National Center for Health Statistics, cited in Riley et al., 1968).

Reading about all the kinds of age-related decrements can be intimidating unless you return to the questions we asked earlier and deal with each decrement separately, while recognizing that substantial individual differences in reactions do exist. Although all the decrements I described can have a meaningful effect if they are severe enough, many can be corrected or compensated for, whereas others may have only a negligible impact. Wearing eyeglasses can usually correct inadequate visual acuity; learning techniques of driving at night will help compensate for some of the adaptation problems; being careful to move one's head to compensate for reduced peripheral vision can reduce the burden of this change.

Not only older persons themselves but all of us who help shape their environments need to be aware of ways to compensate for these age-related changes. For example, improved design of vehicles and housing will eliminate some sources of difficulty.

So far the discussion has centered on visual decrements that, for the elderly population as a whole, often have no major impact on behavior and functioning. What about severe visual impairment? An interview study conducted by the National Center for Health Statistics in 1963 and 1964 found that the proportion of older persons unable to read newsprint was more than ten times that of all other individuals. Of the 500,000 legally blind persons in the United States, approximately half are over age 65, and more than half of the newly reported cases of blindness come from this large age group (White House Conference on Aging, 1972). The incidence of extensive loss of visual acuity is twice as high among the non-White population as among Whites, with the ratio for absolute blindness greater than 3:1 (U.S. Department of Health, Education and Welfare, 1966).

All in all, blindness and other serious visual impairments affect more than 7% of those between 65 and 74 and 16% of those 75 and over (based on 1957–1958 data reported by the National Center for Health Statistics, cited in Riley et al., 1968). Cataracts and glaucoma are common causes of these visual problems and are often interrelated. The need for these people to develop effective behavior for coping with their deficits is considerably greater than for individuals undergoing the normal changes of aging.

Audition

Changes in hearing resemble those in vision. Although decreases in auditory sensitivity are relatively slight during the early and middle adult years, loss of acuity is more extensive for tones in the higher ranges (Corso, 1971). As with visual acuity, decrements accelerate at later ages.

An obvious result of hearing defects is increased difficulty in understanding speech. Older people frequently ask others to repeat what they say or to speak more loudly or more distinctly. Research has shown that when speech was clear, undistorted, and presented without competing noise, older subjects suffered very little loss in ability to understand. "As the difficulty of the distorted and noise-masked speech became greater, however, very large differences were revealed between the auditory performance of the young subjects and those in their later years" (Bergman, 1971, p. 150). Often the hearing loss distorts only certain frequencies, so that shouting does no good—it merely amplifies the confusion.

Hearing impairments in those over 65 are much more common than visual impairments, reaching 13% of those between 65 and 74 and 26% of those 75 and over (National Center for Health Statistics, cited in Riley et al., 1968). Of an estimated 4.5 million persons with a serious hearing loss, some 55% are over age 65. These findings parallel those on the prevalence of visual disorders.

Although the visual defects of the elderly are generally believed to occur through disease, general deteriorative processes, and, to a lesser extent, accidents, hearing loss is probably more closely linked with environmental variables, such as noise pollution. An investigation of the Mabaan tribespeople in North Africa showed that they suffered much less hearing loss with age, including less loss for the higher frequencies, than did residents of major urban areas (McFarland, 1968). Mabaan tribespeople obviously differ in a variety of ways from residents of the comparison cities used in the study (New York, Dusseldorf, and Cairo), so it is difficult to pinpoint the specific bases for their good hearing; but this study at least helps to emphasize the crucial nature of environmental factors.

Hearing loss, perhaps even more than visual loss, isolates individuals from their social groups. The problems of communicating to someone hard of hearing may be immense, and people suffering hearing defects late in life are much less likely than younger people to learn lip reading or signing. Hearing aids help correct only some of the defects found among the elderly.

Other Sensory Modalities

Other sensory modalities have not been extensively studied, and findings are inconsistent and piecemeal. Studies of smell and taste, for example, are rarely conducted, although these modalities not only affect the enjoyment of food and other experiences but also can be useful in detecting spoiled food and other dangers (Engen, 1977). The results of studies on smell and taste are inconsistent; one authority, for example, proposes that "odor sensitivity seems very stable over age" (Engen, 1977, p. 560), but others propose that sensitivity does diminish (Birren, 1964).

Older people often complain that their food is tasteless or requires heavier seasoning (Corso, 1971), which is an unfortunate situation because many older persons are on low-salt or other diets that preclude the use of desired seasoning—another example of the conflict in which many elderly find themselves. Recent research has shown that older people have more difficulty than younger people in differentiating among foods by either taste (Schiffman, 1977) or smell (Schiffman & Pasternak, 1979), again suggesting that these sensitivities do diminish with age but not eliminating the possibility that smoking or specific health conditions, not aging itself, produced the decrements in acuity.

The confusion and uncertainty in determining the effects of aging on taste and smell are repeated when we review touch, temperature, and pain. One article that reviewed the sparse literature concludes that the majority of available studies do show pain sensitivity diminishing with age, but that this may not be true for all body locations (S.W. Harkins & Warner, 1980). Further confusion is caused by conflicting reports based on clinical observations: although older persons complain about pain more than younger persons, they nonetheless seem to tolerate pain from surgery and other causes better (S.W. Harkins & Warner, 1980).

The problems in studying pain are immense. Not only are people understandably reluctant to offer themselves as research subjects, but response to pain is greatly influenced by expectation, fear, and attitudes. In addition, investigators are often required to accept a person's report of painfulness, although such reports are difficult to interpret.

A few studies on touch and temperature are only suggestive. It appears that sensitivity in the palm of the hand and the sole of the foot diminishes somewhat but that sensitivity in most other parts of the body does not (Kenshalo, 1977). A recent study has also shown that the sensitivity of the finger to pressure diminishes in the later years (Thornbury & Mistretta, 1981). The possibility that temperature sensitivity changes in the later years seems to arise mostly because a small proportion of older people develop health problems that bring this decrement (Kenshalo, 1977).

Changes with age are observed in the vestibular senses. Dizziness, or vertigo, is more commonly found among older people than among other age groups and is one of the major causes of injury and death from falls. As people become older, they are more likely to become dizzy while looking down a staircase and then trip or fall down the stairs. Another common source of falls is misjudging the last step. Deaths from falls among those 65 and over occur more than twice as often as traffic deaths, and the ratio jumps to 4:1 at age 75 (Rodstein, 1964).

Older people have been found to sway back and forth more than younger people, both when their eyes are open and when they are closed. This finding supports the assumption that some deterioration of vestibular function accompanies aging (cited in Szafran & Birren, 1969). Accidental injuries and deaths from falls can be reduced by proper illumination, effective use of colors for top and bottom steps, use of nonskid floor waxes, and care in laying and tacking down rugs and carpeting (Rodstein, 1964).

Dizziness worries older people more than is often recognized. In their study of geriatric health in the United States, Denmark, and England, Shanas and her associates (1968) noted that dizzy spells are much more closely associated by the elderly with self-ratings of poor health than is blindness. This comparison held for all three nations.

Psychomotor Performance

Much of what was said about decrements in sensory capacities can also be said about decrements in psychomotor performance. After surveying the literature, Botwinick (1978) concluded that (1) the reaction time of older persons is consistently found to be slower than the reaction time of younger persons; (2) longer reaction times occur regardless of which sensory modality receives and processes the information (that is, it does not matter whether the individual is reacting to the sight of a dog running in front of the car or to tripping over a curb); and (3) this slowing down with age diminishes the capacity to perform the necessary tasks of life effectively.

What is important to add, however, is that there is relatively little increase in reaction time with age for simple response patterns, those in which one signal produces one response. But when the signals and the responses increase in complexity, older people do find much more difficulty in reacting appropriately than younger people.

Evidence has accumulated to show that longer reaction times are the product of changes in the central nervous system, the result of "loss of cells and age changes in the physiological properties of nerve cells and fibers" (Birren, 1964, p. 111). As we age, we find that driving becomes more difficult, especially driving under complex circumstances, such as in fast-moving freeway traffic or during congested downtown rush hours; we are less capable of performing athletic tasks, such as running, swimming, or boxing (Riley et al., 1968); and some eye/hand-coordination tasks become more difficult—such as work on a factory assembly line, where both speed and accuracy are important.

To some extent these changes are linked to health conditions. Research has shown that even younger persons who suffer from cardiovascular problems or arthritis take longer to respond than age peers who are unaffected (Botwinick & Storandt, 1974). Some of the change is also related to the apparent increase in caution of older persons, who appear to respond less impulsively and therefore less rapidly than younger people. However, neither health nor caution can explain all the differences found among age groups (Botwinick, 1978).

Having given us the negative side, Botwinick (1978) then points out some ameliorating factors: (1) slowing with age is less for tasks that have been learned well through practice; (2) people who are highly motivated to perform a task seem to maintain their capability longer; (3) individual differences are great, and some older people outperform their younger counterparts; and, perhaps most important, (4) the overall impact of this slowing down on the lives and well-being of the elderly is often minimal. Other contributing factors may include personality characteristics leading to caution or enthusiasm. Observations suggest, for instance, that older people display less general enthusiasm than younger people and that this frame of mind may affect speed of performance. Also, older people are probably not as comfortable as younger people in the laboratory setting, where much of this research is conducted, a matter that can influence performance.

The major issue, I feel, is not whether these changes occur—they most certainly do—but why they occur, whether their decremental course can be altered, what implications the changes have for life satisfaction, what coping mechanisms can be most usefully employed, and what efforts others can make to ameliorate the effects of these losses. It is obvious that psychomotor performance cannot be considered in a vacuum but must be interrelated with sensory functioning, cognitive abilities, motivation, personality, and the social setting.

A Practical Application: The Older Driver

The research findings discussed in the previous pages have great applicability both to understanding of the older person and to immediate and highly practical situations. Although implications for work, for leisure and play, and for gardening and home maintenance (which are work for some and play for others) are obvious, I will use the older driver as an integrating example, largely because the tasks involved in driving are familiar to everyone.

According to the previous discussion, older drivers should have a higher rate of accidents than younger drivers. After all, they have greater trouble accommodating visually to varied distances, take longer to adapt to dark and light, suffer from reduced visual acuity and poorer hearing, are more susceptible to dizziness, have slower reaction times, and are more likely to be confused by multiple concurrent stimuli—for example, having to deal simultaneously with rapid traffic flow, freeway on-ramp and off-ramp signs, honking from other cars, and directions given by a passenger. On the other hand, they generally have had many more years of driving experience and tend to be more cautious than younger people in their driving habits.

As part of a test program (Case, Hulbert, & Beers, 1970), seven drivers over 51, with an average age of 65, and three younger drivers (50 and under) drove a specially equipped vehicle in which a variety of measures of their functioning and performance could be obtained. Although the sample in this study is extremely small, some of the results are interesting enough to consider. For example, the mean speed for the younger drivers was slightly—but significant statistically—faster than for the older drivers; the older drivers depressed the brake pedal more often; the older drivers had a significantly slower heart rate than the younger drivers (not an anticipated result); and the older drivers changed their rate of speed more often. These and related findings, by and large, suggest greater caution on the part of older drivers. These investigators concluded that older drivers monitor themselves effectively and accommodate well to their sensory and motor losses and that their judgment remains as good as that of younger drivers. Only when events occur too quickly for them to adjust do older drivers do less well than younger ones.

What about accident rates? It all depends on what you use as the measure. Thus, if your accident rate is based on accidents per 1000 persons within an age group, accident rates for the elderly are low; if the rate is based on accidents per 1000 drivers within an age group, accident rates are moderate; if the rate is based on accidents per miles driven, older drivers have a very high accident rate. With fair consistency, accident rates per mile for ages 70 to 79 equal those of teenagers; but drivers 80 and older have still higher accident rates (Planek, Condon, & Fowler, 1968; Riley et al., 1968). Older drivers are more likely than chance would indicate to end up in accidents through (1) failing to yield, (2) turning improperly, and (3) running red lights; their accident rate from speeding is relatively low, however. When asked what bothers them most in driving, older drivers list lane changing, making left turns, and parking. All of these tasks involve turning, which the data indicate is the second most frequent cause of accidents among the elderly (Planek et al., 1968).

Unlike auto-accident rates, industrial-accident rates show little or no change with age, although the types of accidents do change. Accidents caused by poor judgment appear to decrease with age, whereas accidents caused by sudden events, such as falling or being hit by objects, increase with age (Riley et al., 1968). Both auto and industrial accidents appear to result from slowness in making decisions and acting on them rather than from sensory or motor impairment (Welford, 1977). The data for vehicular and industrial accidents are fairly consistent with each other and with what we know about the functioning of older people.

Given the information we have on older drivers, what kinds of decisions need to be made concerning them? Should older drivers be tested more frequently? Should they be given limited licenses permitting them to drive only at certain hours or in certain kinds of traffic? Should their insurance rates be altered? Should they be kept from driving at all? Should individual terms of freedom to drive be arranged for them, based on each person's accident rate and driving-test scores? (Keep in mind that we seldom do that for younger drivers.)

The significance of being able to drive an automobile is considerable. For the older person who can afford to maintain a car, driving permits shopping, visiting friends, taking a drive in the country, or getting to an appointment. In short, it provides great freedom. Not being able to drive severely limits the options open to older people. They must walk, find adequate public transportation (often not available), take taxis (often too expensive), or depend on family and friends. The loss of a driver's license is also symbolically important: it represents the loss of immediate freedom and the potential loss of future freedoms. It deprives the individual of something that has probably long been taken for granted, and it signifies the loss of one source of independence, mastery of the environment, and social status.

Other Implications

The human significance of loss in sensory and motor capacities, like the significance of any loss, is often far greater than the immediate difficulties that arise from functional changes. For example, people who have enjoyed tennis for many years find that their playing ability begins to diminish. They encounter increasing difficulty in moving rapidly, and they become fatigued more quickly than they used to; they may have trouble following the ball after an opponent's smash or shifting direction quickly when running after an unexpected slice. Aging individuals may begin to play more conservatively and perhaps lose some of their enthusiasm for the sport, which leads to playing less often. These changes thus may result in less enjoyment and less exercise unless a replacement activity is developed. If, in addition, these people must now confront the reality of their own aging process, their losses will be compounded. The friendships and shared camaraderie also cease.

If a person suffers from a decrement in hearing or from an arthritic condition severe enough to make walking or even buttoning clothing difficult, the impact can be even greater. Even though decrements occur only gradually and sometimes not at all, and even though substitute satisfactions are often readily available, we live in an era in which the notion of personal growth is extremely important. The realization that growth in performing certain tasks will no longer occur can be very depressing, especially since it often coincides with other losses, such as the death of friends or the recognition that another promotion will probably never be awarded. Coming to terms with these problems, while still being able to engage in substitute activities and retain a high sense of life satisfaction, is the major demand made on the aging.

Gerontologists try to understand negative aging processes and to learn how to intervene to slow them down or reverse them. For example, one study showed that older women were able to increase their response speed after participating in a training program (Hoyer, Hoyer, Treat, & Baltes, 1978–1979). For the most part, however, older people recognize that losses and gains occur at all ages and that, although losses usually occur more frequently in the later years, they can learn to cope effectively.

Learning, Memory, and Intelligence

When I was in my 20s and very early 30s, I had a distressingly accurate memory for most names and faces. If there were 20 unfamiliar people at a party, I would know the names of at least 15, and perhaps all 20, by the end of the evening, and I would remember at least half of them if we met three months later. I could never comprehend why everyone didn't recall names as I did; I thought they just didn't care. Now, a couple of decades later, I no longer remember the names of people, and I must admit that my recollection for faces isn't very good either. What has happened?

Has something happened in the initial learning process, so that the name, the face, and the association between them no longer get stored in memory? Does something happen in storage, so that the images fade? Does something happen when I want to retrieve the information from storage, so that the name doesn't just fall out almost automatically, as it once did?

Or am I paying less attention? Is it simply less important to me to remember who's who? Or could it be that interference has been established—that I have learned so many names during my lifetime that the old recollections get in the way of new learning? Or, perhaps, that I have so many things on my mind, so many other tasks that draw my energies and effort, that remembering names no longer has a sufficient claim on me?

Another idea is pervasive. If, indeed, my memory for immediate associations is not as good as it used to be, regardless of the reasons, has there been a similar decrement in my long-term or intermediate-term memory? Does this possibility have any implications for other kinds of cognitive processes? For problem solving? For decision making? For dealing with abstract issues? For grasping the significance of world events? For anything from my susceptibility to classical conditioning to my creativity to what I will term, for lack of a better word, my wisdom?

Moreover, why do some older people still have excellent memories (including both long-term and immediate memory)—much better than the memories of those 30 years their junior? Conversely, why are the memories of some younger persons so poor, even though their basic intellectual capacities seem adequate? To what extent do biological factors explain such occurrences? Psychological factors? Social factors?

Research on cognitive changes associated with old age—changes in conditionability, in rote memory, in serial and paired-associate learning, in decision making, in creativity, in remembering and forgetting—is substantial, although the results are difficult to interpret. Cognitive losses are probably not the result of the genetically induced primary aging processes. Rather, they accrue through the diseases and injuries associated with secondary aging processes and, most of all, with the tertiary aging processes of damage to the central nervous system (Cohen & Wu, 1980). However, age changes in the primary aging processes can reduce the ability of the body to resist the impact of secondary and tertiary processes.

Memory

An old war-horse in the stable of geriatric humor has one elderly person commenting to another, "I understand that three things happen when people age: their memory begins to slip . . . and I forget the other two." Like much humor, this quip expresses what some older people actually face. When older people claim that they are having difficulty remembering things, their younger friends and relatives often insist "Your memory is still great—why, I forget lots of things myself, all the time." Although well intended, such comments are not always helpful because they in effect deny the reality for the older person of a very sensitive issue. Fear of memory loss is great, especially since the loss is associated with degenerative diseases that threaten to leave people helpless and confused. And older people may be diagnosed as suffering from dementia or serious deterioration when anxiety, depression, or confusion induced by drugs or medication compounds the problem of slight memory loss (Jarvik, 1980).

Memory, of course, cannot be fully differentiated from learning. You can't remember anything unless you have learned it first; you can't have learned anything unless you remember it. The author of one study concludes that "the decline with age in memory performance is attributable to the decline with age in learning performance" (Moenster, 1972, p. 262). She admits that not all studies support her position but cites several that do.

Although memory can be classified in numerous ways, it is commonly divided into *primary memory* and *secondary memory*. Primary memory involves the fleeting moments when something sensed or experienced is "still at the focus of conscious attention" (Craik, 1977, p. 392). Secondary memory does not necessarily involve the intent to recall at a later time, but the material is nonetheless placed in the storage area for later retrieval. By and large, laboratory studies of primary memory show slight or no decrement with age. However, if there is any kind of interference with the act of memorizing, such as competing stimuli during the memorizing process, evidence of some decrement with age does appear (Bromley, 1974). In secondary memory, recall of the more complex tasks often shows greater losses. For example, the simple task of memorizing a series of numbers in sequence can be done by older respondents almost as well as by younger ones (Parkinson, Lindholm, & Urell, 1980). However, if the numbers are then to be recited backwards or if another task is imposed, such as sorting the numbers into classes, evidence of noticeable decline with age is found (Bromley, 1974).

In discussing possible causes of forgetting, Botwinick (1978) agrees that interference during the process of learning the materials appears to reduce recall and that the effect of such interference is greater for older persons than for younger ones. Since this seems especially true when the older person is attempting to learn two things at the same time, he proposes that focusing on one task at a time may improve learning in the later years. However, even though the learning and memory of older people can be aided through what might be termed information-processing strategies—that is, developing better techniques for learning and remembering information—special training programs have still not been sufficient to enable older people to function at the same level as younger ones (Hartley, Harker, & Walsh, 1980).

These laboratory findings are consistent with the conclusions drawn by those who work with older people. Older people often request that information be presented more slowly, and they frequently seem to prefer dealing with one piece of information at a time. Moreover, interruptions appear to be more disruptive for them than they are for younger persons. However, older people often develop devices for dealing with these changes, and—probably more important—most learning tasks in the real world do not require the kind of memorization used in the laboratory; that is, it is rare that someone needs to memorize a list of words or a series of numbers. When such memorizing is required, it is often in relation to a task, and the experience of the older person can compensate for impaired memorizing ability.

Long-term secondary memory presents even more serious methodological problems. An older person seems to recall events that occurred many years earlier with considerable clarity, but rarely can anyone around confirm the accuracy of such recollections. Also, because of having such long experience, an elderly person's remembrance of certain events and experiences can represent only a small number of recollections out of a vast reservoir of occurrences. Nonetheless, recall of early events is so commonly reported by older persons that we should probably take their claims largely at face value, withholding judgment on how large a proportion of these early experiences has been forgotten and how much inaccuracy does enter the recall of these experiences.

Learning

Familiar stereotypes of older persons suggest that they find learning in general difficult and learning new ideas and techniques virtually impossible. Like many age-related stereotypes, these have been exploded by both research and observations. Older people are highly capable of learning and can also be receptive to new ideas and capable of learning new techniques. Because of biological and, perhaps, psychological changes that sometimes accompany old age, some older people find that their ability to learn has seemed to diminish over the years; other elderly, however, note either no loss of cognitive ability or such minimal decrement that it serves only as a minor nuisance, easily overcome through coping strategies, such as writing all appointments in a datebook or increasing concentration when introduced to a new person.

In spite of the essential cognitive competence of the great majority of older people, formal research conducted in laboratory settings provides evidence that the elderly do not learn as well, on the average, as do younger people. The elderly are at a particular disadvantage when the duration for learning is relatively brief, which brings us back to their longer reaction times. Some of the difficulty experienced by the elderly is attributed to their greater difficulty in using learning techniques, such as visualizing what is to be learned or associating it with something already known. When the elderly received training in how to use these techniques, their learning ability increased substantially (Botwinick, 1978). However, even when speed is not a factor or when older people have been instructed in learning techniques, they still appear to learn less well than younger persons tested under similar conditions (Arenberg & Robertson-Tchabo, 1977).

Another possible explanation of the findings is the tendency of older people to be more cautious, less willing to take risks, which suggests that their fear of failure may be greater than their need to achieve (Eisdorfer, 1969). Health changes provide a further and obvious explanation of loss of learning ability. People of any age suffering from cardiovascular disease perform less well on several measures of cognitive ability than those in basically good health (Hertzog, Schaie, & Gribbin, 1978). Since the elderly are more likely to have such conditions, they are more likely to suffer cognitive decrements.

When the learning task is complex, such as problem solving, rather than a simple association task, older people do not do as well as younger people. It has been suggested that laboratory tasks tend to be abstract and devoid of any intrinsic significance for the learner, whereas older people prefer concrete tasks. This would suggest that motivational differences account for the better performance of the young. Also, since young people often have had more formal education, they might be assumed to be more proficient in learning materials that are abstract or that have no immediate impact on their lives (Botwinick, 1978).

Research on forgetting and remembering in the later years suggests that learning better techniques for acquiring and retrieving information is helpful, although it does not enable the older person to catch up completely with younger people. The results of comparable research on problem solving and concept formation are also optimistic. When given special training in developing information-processing strategies or even the opportunity to develop their own strategies, older people substantially improve their performance (Giambra & Arenberg, 1980).

In evaluating the findings on this topic, we begin by recognizing that an immense variety of studies have shown older people to learn less effectively than younger people. We know many contributory factors, such as caution, fear of failure, lack of familiarity with psychology laboratories, and slower reaction time. What we don't know is the extent to which some of these factors, such as the need of older research participants for more time, occur because of physiological changes within the body, especially the central nervous system, or because of social and personality determinants, such as greater caution (Arenberg & Robertson-Tchabo, 1977).

Intellectual Competence

As we move from the simpler forms of cognitive behavior, such as immediate memory, to the more complex forms, such as intellectual functioning, the evaluation of age-related differences changes from difficult and uncertain to difficult and very uncertain. Not that there is any problem in ascertaining that decrements occur; they most certainly do. Rather, the cogent problem is answering such questions as why they occur, what causes them to occur for some persons and not for others, why they seem to affect certain tasks more drastically than other tasks, and what coping strategies are most useful for compensating.

What is intelligence? Is it ability to succeed in an academic setting? To earn a lot of money? To have insight into what motivates other people? To relate effectively to strangers and friends alike? To know what to do under stress? To hammer a nail in straight? To memorize a page of text? The list could go on indefinitely. Perhaps all these elements are part of general intelligence.

There are several ways to measure intelligence. We can, of course, administer a test of intelligence, but not all intelligence tests give equal emphasis to the same factors. Some are largely measures of verbal skill, whereas others depend more on measuring memory, spatial perception, or arithmetic abilities. It is important to have a good idea of which components of intelligence are being measured; it is particularly important when you are looking into age-related changes in intelligence-test scores.

However, there are other ways to determine intelligence. You might decide that a particular older woman whom you know is wise and that her long experience has given her an ability to achieve her goals, to come to terms with herself and the world, to maintain high life satisfaction, to impart to others her accumulated wisdom and understanding. Her memory may not be too good, especially for recent events; her hand may shake a little when she drives; she may require you to speak a bit more loudly and distinctly than you usually do. But you develop the patience to accommodate to the older woman's needs because you enjoy and can profit from what she offers.

As difficult as it is to measure immediate memory or verbal fluency with accuracy, it is immensely more difficult—perhaps impossible—to measure wisdom. Although people will disagree on the adequacy of the measures of intelligence that are commonly used, they would disagree much more on any measure of wisdom. And, after all, the measures of intelligence that we now use can actually help us in seeing and understanding some of the changes that occur with age, as long as we recognize their limitations.

The results of cross-sectional and longitudinal studies display some similar patterns, but those of the former tend to suggest greater decline and earlier onset of decline (Botwinick, 1977). Though it depends on the particular ability being measured, little if any decline appears before age 60; losses then seem to accelerate around the mid-70s. One study, spanning an eight-year period, found decrement in only a few ability areas (Jarvik, Kallman, & Falek, 1962). After 12 years, when the same respondents were in their mid-80s, more substantial losses in most areas of ability were found (Blum, Fosshage, & Jarvik, 1972).

Patterns of Change

Cognitive research reveals certain patterns of change. Verbal ability declines much less with age than psychomotor performance; tested abilities that require speed or that depend on immediate memory decline more than those that are untimed or that depend on experience. Tests of general information and vocabulary frequently show evidence of increased capacity with age, particularly if the differential levels of the respondents' formal education are controlled. However, speed does appear to be the major factor, to the point that Jarvik and Blum (1971) state that "decline on speeded psychomotor tasks represents a normal concomitant of aging, while decrements in cognitive functioning are pathognomonic of cerebral disease" (p. 205).

Creativity

Creativity has been the topic of considerable writing and research, but very few studies consider older people. One widely cited investigation (Lehman, 1953) determined the age at which well-respected persons in different fields made their major creative contributions. Although the findings varied somewhat from field to field, they left little doubt that creative high points occur in the younger years. Lehman's work has one important methodological flaw, however: most good scientists and artists discover a new approach when they are fairly young and then develop the various ramifications of that approach. If they neglect this subsequent development, the significance of their original work may never be noted, since it is often the accumulation of creative accomplishments, not just one such accomplishment, that signifies a real contribution. When the *total* creative output of each noted scholar, artist, and scientist is considered, it is the 50s and not the 30s or 20s that account for most of these people's richest work. Furthermore, considerable productivity continues well into the 60s, the 70s, and, occasionally, beyond (Dennis, 1966).

The concept of creativity, however, does not need to be limited to artistic and scientific endeavors. In fact, that is a very myopic definition of the term. True creativity, I believe, is the generation of new ideas and new approaches to tasks. An older man who develops a new way of caring for his plants is creative; an older woman who plans an innovative promotional program that doubles attendance at her community's orchestra concerts is being creative also. And innumerable older people use their retirement as an opportunity to investigate new avenues of leisure, including artistic endeavors, creative approaches to earning income, and new possibilities for personal growth.

The Meaning of Cognitive Change for Older People

Eisdorfer (1969) summarizes his own thinking on cognitive change in a helpful fashion:

> nothing . . . should be construed to indicate that there are no truly age-related changes in intellectual and cognitive functioning. Loss of neuronal tissue, change in the metabolic rate of the brain, loss of circulatory capacity, all lead to a level of primary change. The fact remains . . . that we know little about many of these phenomena, and how much they would affect behavior in the absence of other complicating social and psychological variables [p. 247].

When people do find themselves less able to remember events, names of acquaintances, or books they have read, and when they do realize that their problem-solving behavior appears less effective than it was in earlier years, they respond in a variety of ways. One response may be to withdraw from activities or people offering potential stress; another is to become irritable or angry, to insist that what they remember is correct; a third is to increase dependence on family members, friends, or professionals in order to compensate for their own deficits. It is little consolation for these people to learn, for example, that memory decrements occur not so much with age as with cerebrovascular problems, since the changes are equally real in either event. And older people are hardly comforted by learning about cognitive decline, although this matter is of major importance to gerontologists, who can investigate ways to intervene in the course of whatever physical changes are accruing.

Society builds in certain protections against having to confront such losses in its older citizens. No matter how devastating retirement is for some people (see Chapter Six for a fuller discussion), it removes an aging person from competing with younger people whose cognitive capacities are not yet declining. Also, allowance is often made for some forgetfulness and uncertainty on the part of older individuals. Since their forgetfulness may be seen as typical of their age, it does not usually serve as a basis for teasing them or for assuming pathology in them, as would similar behavior in a younger person. However, younger people often stereotype the elderly and presuppose decrements that have not really occurred.

On the whole, of course, any kind of reduction in cognitive competence is likely to reduce the options open to the older person. To the extent that the elderly do become forgetful and are aware of this forgetfulness, they are deeply concerned, often anxious, and sometimes frightened. Some have the fear, not entirely without justification, that their confusion is a sign of more confusion to come; others worry that they are becoming "senile" or "crazy."

Whatever concern they feel about decrements in cognitive capacities, most elderly people recognize that they must cope with this difficulty, and many do so very effectively. Humor is one method of coping; older people themselves constantly joke about memory problems. Another method is the simple expedient of writing things down rather than trusting them to memory. A third approach is exerting extra concentration on matters that need to be recalled. Other strategies used depend on the individual and the situation.

Cautions in Interpreting the Data

Since we respond to older people through those qualities we attribute to them, and since our programming for these people often draws on the same attributions, it is important to avoid stamping the label of ultimate truth on research findings when the researchers themselves view these findings as tentative. This is not an invitation to discard research results but to view them with caution.

Thus, the procedures in both longitudinal and cross-sectional research have their limitations. In the former, for example, there is a tendency for the less competent participants not to return for follow-up testing (Botwinick, 1977). Perhaps they were less healthy at the original testing and became increasingly ill, or perhaps they had some sense of their lower performance and didn't wish to put themselves through a discouraging task again. On the other hand, with cross-sectional research it is difficult, sometimes impossible, to ascertain that the older people and younger people being compared are actually equivalent. Since people from higher socioeconomic groups tend to have longer life expectancies, our research studies may be comparing more privileged older people and less privileged younger people. Conversely, since younger people are more likely to have had more formal education, we might make the reverse assumption. Nor can we safely assume that these factors balance each other out. Another limitation is that older people, having been brought up in an era when behavioral research was not familiar, may be more anxious, confused, or resistant when participating in studies.

More important, it is difficult to measure one process without inadvertently measuring others. If we are trying to measure immediate memory, our results may be confounded by the rapidity with which the information is presented; or, if we attempt to measure ability to learn a simple task, such as learning nonsense syllables, we may end up with data reflecting reaction-time characteristics, perceptual and other sensory limits, and anxiety. The results of one study suggest that older people tire more rapidly in experimental settings than younger people and that learning differences may arise because most such studies take too long (Furry & Baltes, 1973). I would speculate that boredom and lack of motivation, rather than fatigue, might together constitute the intervening variable leading to some age-related differences in research findings.

In the final analysis it seems that we need to shift our focus from "decline or no decline to what aspects of cognitive behavior change and under what set of conditions" (Cohen & Wu, 1980, p. 75).

Another limitation in interpreting age-related test-score changes is *terminal decline.* This term refers to the observation, substantiated by research (Jarvik & Blum, 1971; Riegel & Riegel, 1972), that individuals who show a notable change in any one of a variety of measures of cognitive performance are more likely to die within a few years than are those who show no particular change. This observation suggests that many (but not all) kinds of intellectual decrements may be the result of the same factors that will eventually lead to death; perhaps the significant losses of intellectual abilities are prognostic of death even before medical diagnoses can be made.

Assume, for example, a ten-year longitudinal study of changes in cognitive performance, beginning with people who are 60 years old. When the participants are tested at age 65, there will be a moderate decline in average scores. When they are retested at age 70, some of them will have died or will be very near death. If we eliminate these persons from the sample and then reanalyze the data from the first five years of the study, the decline shown in cognitive performance will be minimal for those remaining in the sample. The implications are clear that physical health, even health-related matters that are not obvious, has a great impact on cognitive functioning.

One final caution. Research on changes with aging has focused primarily on what older people are capable of accomplishing, given their present life situation. Willis and Baltes (1980) propose that we have not yet begun to tap the potential of older persons, providing they can be given maximum motivation, helped to reduce their anxieties in the learning situation, and taught information-processing strategies. These authors thus turn our attention away from a constant comparison of age groups and toward finding out what older people are capable of accomplishing.

Further, ongoing research and programs that reduce illness, improve sanitary conditions, encourage appropriate exercise, and provide better nutrition may have the effect of postponing the time at which significant losses are experienced. The recent substantial reduction in deaths from heart attacks may also mean that the influences of terminal decline and the effects of cardiovascular disease on abilities may not occur until older ages than in the past. These statements, of course, are speculative.

Coping with Aging

The interrelatedness of all human behavior is frequently emphasized by those studying gerontology. We cannot discuss intelligence without questioning the role of memory, the meaning of changes in physical health, the impact of reluctance to take risks, or the importance of earlier schooling. And I could add other topics for the study of intelligence in the elderly: mental illness, feelings of loneliness, simple lack of caring whether they do well on the tests, and failing vision and hearing. (Many persons with a hearing loss either are not fully aware of their problem or choose to pretend they have full acuity; if they don't hear the instructions for tests of learning or intelligence, they fake it.)

Again, let's return to a question I've asked before: assuming that we accept all the decrements described previously (even though the research results conflict somewhat), what difference do the decrements make in the day-to-day behavior of the older individual?

My opinion, which is shared by many, perhaps most, gerontologists, is that the behavior, performance, and life satisfaction of older people are less influenced by the measured decrements uncovered by our research than initial logic suggests. Anticipation is frequently more frightening than actuality, although declines and losses, when extensive, are objectively as well as subjectively important.

In spite of very real problems, many elderly people do appear to cope amazingly effectively with these losses. The following are some of the reasons:

1. These decrements often occur very gradually, and the aging individuals can adapt to slight changes almost without being aware that they are adapting.
2. Other people of their own age are also showing the same signs, and this fact is communicated among them, sometimes openly but often more subtly.
3. Some evidence is available that older people (and, undoubtedly, younger people as well) can adjust to chronic problems and continue to enjoy life, even though the same problem might have appeared overwhelming when it was initially noticed. One study (Shanas, 1962) showed that people who had been afflicted with a chronic health problem rated their health as better than did individuals who were just beginning to confront such difficulties.
4. These decrements and losses are only one aspect of life. If other aspects are satisfying, the importance of the deficits probably lessens. For example, if family relationships remain rich or if effective substitute activities are available, the pain and reduced functioning of an arthritic condition will seem more bearable. (Again, individual differences are important here.)
5. A form of rehearsal for later age roles often occurs. Older people are cognizant of forthcoming decrements, partly because they do notice minor changes when they accumulate sufficiently and partly because they have observed the aging process in other individuals. Many of the elderly, then, have in a way rehearsed what it will be like to be older and thus have anticipated and planned for the discomfort of the actual changes.

In no sense am I suggesting that these physical and mental changes are unimportant. And their importance is made greater by the fact that they are often accompanied by the loss of familiar social roles, the death of close friends and family members, increased social isolation, reduced income, and other difficulties. My major thesis is that the elderly do have personal resources that enable them to continue to function with amazing effectiveness in spite of a variety of decrements and losses, and that those working with the elderly should make a greater effort to help them use residual personal strengths rather than bemoan the losses.

Chapter Three

Physical and Mental Health

Recall the last time you were seriously ill or incapacitated in any way. Your normal functioning was probably restricted; you were lethargic or in pain; you wondered how you were going to take care of your work; you had to miss some social gatherings that you had been looking forward to; perhaps you wondered how long the problem was going to last or whether there would be some long-term or permanent effects; you contemplated the financial cost in medical bills and lost time; you might even have been worried that your condition was life threatening. And your zest for life and your enjoyment of your world were diminished.

For the elderly, health problems produce all these feelings, often intensified by the awareness that they are suffering from a condition that may be with them for the rest of their lives. And in some instances the elderly know that their health problems are a very serious threat to their lives. It's no wonder that health is one of the most serious concerns of the elderly. In one survey of people over age 50, poor health was cited three times more than any other condition as being the worst thing about being elderly (Harris & Associates, 1975).

There are some compensations for poor health. It does offer an apparently justifiable excuse for not doing things you don't want to do in the first place—frequently, if you enjoy being taken care of, someone will take care of you; it allows you to avoid some of the other stresses of life; you do receive attention; and, for some people, it is an unending source of conversation. You may have heard the expression "He enjoys poor health." Some people do enjoy poor health, but the overwhelming majority would gladly trade whatever gains accrue from being sick for the sense of well-being that comes from having good health.

Discussions of health often focus on physical health and disability, but in this chapter I will also discuss mental health. Although there are, of course, valid distinctions between the two concerns, each affects the other so greatly that they need to be viewed as constantly interacting. Poor physical health frequently leads to isolation, significant losses of the ability to perform normal daily tasks, incapacitation, and depression; poor mental health frequently leads to reduced activity, reduced functional ability, confusion, and very likely diminished resistance to physical-health problems.

Maintaining Good Health

"For whatsoever a man soweth, that shall he also reap" (Gal. 6:7). No statement about the health of older persons is more valid than this biblical quotation. What you did yesterday affects your health today, and what you do today will affect your health tomorrow. The health of the elderly is partly a result of their health practices throughout their lives. Nonetheless, it is not necessary to become fatalistic. Health behavior can be altered at virtually any time in the life span and still have some positive effect.

Are the health needs of the elderly different from those of other age groups? As is so often the case, the answer is "yes and no." Proper diet is important at all ages, but the specific nutritional needs of the elderly differ from those of younger people. Exercise is a significant part of health maintenance programs for all ages, but the most appropriate exercise for a 17-year-old is not the same as that for a 70-year-old.

Issues concerning good mental health in the later years require the same kinds of considerations. Stimulation, challenge, and enjoyment are always important, although the activities that produce these qualities of well-being may change with age. Avoidance of too much stress is also a concern, but the amount of stress that is too much and the ways to avoid it may also change. (Avoiding all stress is neither desirable nor possible.)

Older people often experience a variety of stress-causing situations. These include the deaths of those they love, especially spouses; changes in work status because of retirement; moving to new homes, new neighborhoods, or new communities; not knowing how to handle extensive leisure time; coping with such physical handicaps as hearing losses or chronic illnesses; having to live on a reduced income; and coping with reduced futurity and their own eventual deaths. That most older people function so well in the face of these life changes is, I think, remarkable.

Health and mental-health educators are becoming increasingly attuned to the health needs of the elderly, and they reach older people through senior centers, through health-care groups, and through brochures handed out by physicians and others. However, older persons are probably still the least served of any age group by health education.

The basic rules of preventive health care for the elderly will be familiar to you: proper diet, adequate sleep, appropriate exercise, no tobacco, alcohol in moderate amounts or else none, regular health examinations, appropriate dental care, avoidance of unnecessary medications and other drugs, and avoidance of undue stress.

In addition to effective health care, genetic factors also affect your health. There seems little doubt that your heredity predisposes you to certain illnesses that good health practices can influence but cannot totally reverse. For example, heart problems appear to run in families, and a person whose parents both died of coronary disease would be well advised to adhere more carefully than others to a program of proper diet, rest, exercise, and regular health examinations. In the final analysis, of course, illness and eventual death can be postponed, but they cannot be eliminated.

Diet and Nutrition

Overeating can lead to obesity, which is a major preventable cause of health problems and premature death among the elderly. Undereating can lead to being so underweight that health maintenance is difficult, although this is a rare occurrence in countries like the United States and Canada. And improper diet can lead to insufficient nutrition, regardless of the person's weight (Woodruff, 1977). Dental problems that produce loss of teeth and discomfort in eating can also increase nutritional deficits; because eating is no longer pleasurable and may be painful, the individual may not eat enough of the proper foods.

As people grow older, they usually become less active and require fewer calories than at younger ages. However, reduction of calories with age must be carefully evaluated in terms of the needs of the individual. One position states that, because their metabolism slows down, older people expend less energy; but, according to another school of thought, reliable evidence shows that older people expend more energy than younger people in comparable activities, so that more calories are needed (Weg, 1978). Perhaps the issue is activity level rather than age. In any event, it is extremely important to recognize that older people differ from one another at least as much as younger people do and that nutritional needs are also highly individual (Hickey, 1980).

The purpose of eating is not simply adequate nutrition. Eating should be pleasurable, and older people—like people of all ages—should eat foods that they like, as long as their diet is reasonably balanced. Many older people are on special, medically prescribed diets—perhaps fat free or salt free—that are geared to specific health problems. Others take vast amounts of vitamins and other pills or eat seaweed or drink ocean water or combine large amounts of bran with their food. These diets may have value, especially the bran and vitamins if not overdone, but some elderly individuals spend a high proportion of their food budgets on foods or supplements of dubious value.

Food has a very important symbolic meaning to people. Breaking bread is an ancient symbol of welcome and trust. Today certain foods have prestige (for example, white rice may be strongly preferred by older Asian Americans even though brown rice is more nutritious) or rich cultural associations (for example, the soul food of the Black American or the traditional dishes of Jewish or Mexican or Italian families).

Eating is a highly social event, and numerous federal programs have attempted not only to provide nutritious meals for low-income elderly people but to encourage them to use these meals for pleasant social interaction. The eating habits of older people living alone are often erratic. It is not uncommon to find an elderly man or woman, residing in a small apartment, eating directly from a can while standing in front of the kitchen sink. Often no semblance of a balanced diet is followed. Meals are sometimes skipped or eaten at irregular intervals, although these are not necessarily poor practices.

Five small meals a day are usually considered preferable to three large ones (Howell & Loeb, 1969), and undereating is undoubtedly preferable to overeating or even, perhaps, to eating to the point of being moderately full. In experiments with moderately overweight men and women, factors known to cause heart disease were substantially reduced by a program that produced weight loss (Olefsky, Reavan, & Farquhar, 1974).

Sleep and Rest

Most older people learn to pace themselves. They recognize that their strength and endurance are not as great as when they were younger, and they do not schedule the same activity program for themselves as they did earlier in life. As always, individual differences are great, and older people who have remained vigorous much of their lives and who are still healthy can function without added rest. Even those who have led fairly sedentary lives can initiate an exercise program for themselves, probably reducing the rest they need as they develop greater strength.

The sleep patterns of older people often change. Older people seem to take more naps, frequently falling into a light sleep while watching television or reading. And their sleep during the night is more fitful than that of younger people, since they wake up frequently. Insomnia is also common among the elderly, but it is difficult to know whether it is an inevitable accompaniment of aging or whether it develops because of reduced activities or the frequent napping. Many older people take medication to help them sleep, sometimes prescribed by a physician and sometimes bought over the counter. There are, however, potential disadvantages in such a practice, especially when the medication is self-prescribed. The elderly may become over-sedated, use medicines that nullify the effects of other medicines, or purchase ineffective medication.

The age at which sleep patterns change is highly individual and also reflects the amount of enjoyment that older people derive from their daily activities. It is difficult to know whether these changes are the result of psychosocial changes in life circumstances, whether they contribute to apparent cognitive deficits or depression, or whether both or neither of these relationships occurs.

Exercise and Movement

Exercise improves many bodily processes, including respiration, cardiovascular functioning, and digestion. It also seems to make relaxing easier and probably leads to improved sleep patterns. Like eating, exercising should be a combination of pleasure and usefulness. And like eating, an exercise program must meet the needs of the individual older person. The violent movement of calisthenics, such as rapidly jumping up and down and clapping the hands together over the head, obviously is usually inappropriate for older people. Walking, swimming, jogging, or stretching exercises are appropriate for some elderly; others still enjoy tennis or golf; for the very old or those in wheelchairs, exercise is still valuable, although at a much slower pace than for more healthy elderly. Even deep breathing is useful, both to improve lung power and to provide a method for relaxation in the face of stress.

In addition to the usual exercises, two approaches are often valuable. One is yoga exercises, the slow stretching of muscles, with constantly increasing endurance. The other is dance, in which moving in response to music, in either the traditional ballroom and square-dance styles or the more contemporary free form, is both enjoyable and healthy.

Stress and Adaptation

We are subjected to innumerable stresses throughout our lives, and we expend much energy handling these stresses. The situations that cause stress are not all unpleasant. In fact, many of life's greatest successes are highly stressful. These include getting married, having children, getting a promotion, inheriting a lot of money, and traveling in foreign countries. All stress, whether positive or negative, affects the body and may reduce its power to resist disease and to feel relaxed.

The ability to cope with stress is a combination of several factors: the nature of the stress itself, the meaning of that source of stress to the individual, previous experience with that stress and with stress in general, the existence of other stresses, general physical and mental health, resources among family and friends and in the community to help cope with stress, and the psychological make-up of the individual.

As people reach their 60s and 70s, many sources of stress are likely to accumulate at the same time. Thus, an older woman may retire from her job, become a widow, become a grandmother or great-grandmother, and learn that she has diabetes all within a year or so. And, since each source of stress is likely to generate other sources, the overall amount of stress is often greatly increased. The death of her husband and her retirement combine to create a lower income and a difficult financial situation; she finds that she can no longer remain in her home but must move to a less expensive home in a neighborhood where she has no friends; losing her husband and moving to a new home combine to increase her loneliness and isolation; her diabetes threatens her with the loss of vision at a time when she can no longer count on others in her neighborhood to help her get around or shop. Even the birth of a grandchild, which was a basically happy event for her, means that her youngest daughter and son-in-law can no longer spend as much time with her.

It's not my intent to paint a bleak portrait of getting old. Young and middle-aged people often meet with multiple stresses, but not as frequently, and their chances of recuperating and regaining their earlier status are greater. As I've stated often before in this book, what's remarkable is not only that older people survive their stresses and losses, but that they often emerge with good spirits and a zest for life.

Although certain stresses accumulate in old age, others diminish. Older people rarely confront the task of becoming a parent; they have usually left behind the stresses of job-related competition; their relationships with their children have usually stabilized, and the children are no longer fighting aggressively for autonomy; they have learned to accept who they are and what they have been.

Erik Erikson (1963) believes that the major task for the later years is dealing with *ego integrity* versus *despair*. The older person must maintain the wholeness, the adequacy, the meaning of self, in the face of stresses and losses that can readily bring about despair. When faced with their own death—sometimes even encouraged by the pressures of impending death—many older people cope very effectively with the stresses and retain their essential selfhood, their ego integrity.

Another source of stress is the loss of the dream, but I believe this stress also diminishes in the later years. We all have a dream of what we would like to be or do or have as we get older. For many of us, this dream changes with time, and we recognize that we are not going to start our own business, see our daughter finish medical school, retire on a $30,000-a-year income, or have a sophisticated circle of friends all around the world. We adjust to these diminished dreams slowly, but we continue to pursue them in varying degrees. As we reach our 60s, the dreams are either accomplished or compromised or not accomplished. Although we can develop new dreams, they are quite different from the old. Since capturing the dreams is now often impossible, we must deal with the loss, but when that is accomplished, we can cease our striving and get on with the task of living each day as fully as possible. These comments are, of course, highly speculative—you will need to consider them in light of your own experience and knowledge.

Drug Usage

Because older people use so many prescription drugs, we often assume that every older person we meet is taking at least a couple of pills a day. The average person over 65 purchases three times as many prescription drugs as the average person under 65 (Petersen & Whittington, 1977). It is not unusual for an older man or woman to be under the care of three different physicians, each treating a different condition and each prescribing one or more drugs without knowing that their patient is taking several other drugs as well. The mixture of various medications may cancel out the intended benefits of the individual drugs or have unexpected side effects. In fact, more than 5% of hospitalizations of the elderly are for adverse drug effects (Kayne, 1976).

Another drug-related concern is that the body chemistry and physiology of the elderly cause the drugs to move through the system in ways that are different from those in younger persons, so that older people react differently. The eventual effect of these changes is "to decrease tolerance and increase sensitivity to drugs so that older patients require a lower therapeutic dosage of psychoactive drugs . . . and are more prone to side effects and adverse reactions to medications than are younger patients" (Eisdorfer & Stotsky, 1977, p. 726).

The elderly take all kinds of medication for physical and mental problems, including an immense array of tranquilizers. Four of the ten drugs most prescribed for older people are mood enhancers (Petersen & Whittington, 1977). It would seem that some physicians would rather prescribe these pills than spend the time and energy finding out the causes of stress and working to ameliorate them. In a similar vein, many people—regardless of age—would rather take a pill than deal with the bases for depression and anxiety.

Sometimes the elderly patient does not follow the physician's orders for taking drugs in quite the way the physician anticipated. An older person might well say "I have to take one green pill before every meal, one speckled pill three times a day and at least six hours apart, and two red pills when I get up and two more before going to sleep. Then the orange pill whenever the speckled pill makes me nauseous." Not only is such a regimen difficult to remember, but it also assumes that the person eats three meals a day at roughly the usual times and has a sleep pattern approximating the physician's. No wonder one elderly man put all his pills for the week in one bottle and took out four every morning, three at lunchtime, and four every evening, more or less at random.

With so many older people using so many drugs, we might assume that some of them have turned to the illegal drugs, such as marijuana, heroin, and cocaine. The use of marijuana is now so widespread and the drug is so easy to obtain that we can take it for granted that some elderly now use it for pleasure. Also, marijuana use is encouraged for those suffering from glaucoma and diabetes, since it appears to have a salutory medical effect, and for alleviating the nausea accompanying the chemo- and radiation therapies used with cancer patients. And, of course, many people now in their 60s and 70s became either frequent users or addicts earlier in their lives and have continued to use marijuana or other illegal drugs. Data indicate that there are relatively few older drug addicts or methadone-treatment patients, but these figures are expected to increase when today's middle-aged population, whose young-adult years were marked by increasing availability, usage, and acceptance of these drugs, reach their later years (Petersen & Whittington, 1977).

Health Changes in the Later Years

Is your cup half full or half empty? Your views of health in later years may depend on whether you see the world through rose-colored or dark glasses. For example:

—69% of a national sample of noninstitutionalized elderly reported their health as good or excellent compared with that of others their age, but 5% of all older people are in institutions, and 9% of those outside institutions reported poor health;
—more than half of the respondents in a national survey in 1979 stated that they had *no* chronic condition that limited their normal activities;
—only 2% of the noninstitutionalized elderly were confined to their beds, whereas another 2.5% needed help in getting around in their homes;
—older people stay in the hospital about twice as often for about twice as long as younger persons, 82% of this sample had not been hospitalized during the previous year (Brotman, 1981).

It's often said that getting old isn't so bad when you consider the alternative. It's my impression, and that of most others I know who work with older people, that the elderly cope effectively with health problems that appear insurmountable to younger people. About 95% of all persons over age 65 are living in the community, either in their own homes or with family members or friends, and almost 90% are capable of getting around without the help of anyone else. Even these statistics can be misleading because the older people between 65 and 75 are much more likely to be independent than those in their late 70s, and institutionalization does not go up rapidly until the 80s.

A major health concern of older people in the United States is cost. In

1978 the average cost of health care per older person was $2026, compared to $597 for persons under 65, and the gross cost was more than $49 billion. This vast amount of money was paid through both various government programs (63%) and private and personal sources (37%) (Brotman, 1981). Costs are obviously higher today than in 1978, and there is little reason to believe that they will go down. Even given the immense government support through Medicare, Medicaid, and other programs, health costs are a major expense for older persons, frequently a much higher percentage of their incomes than for younger people. Nor can we ignore the immense cost of this health care to the taxpayer. In Canada, where medical care is fully paid for by the government, the cost constitutes a lower proportion of the Gross National Product than in the United States (Simanis & Coleman, 1980).

Physical-Health Conditions

Chronic conditions, those that continue over a lengthy period, are much more common among the elderly than the acute conditions that come and go among younger people. The most common chronic condition is arthritis, reported by 44% of older persons (Brotman, 1981). Because arthritis is not life threatening and perhaps because it is so common, it lacks the drama of heart problems and cancer, and therefore it does not gain much public attention. However, it causes tremendous suffering and incapacitation for millions of people, including many in their early and middle years.

According to 1979 data (Brotman, 1981), next to arthritis, hypertension (39%), hearing impairment (28%), heart conditions (27%), and visual impairments and arteriosclerosis (12% each) are the most commonly reported chronic conditions of older persons. Obviously, the reports of vision impairment are underestimates, since far more than one older person in five wear eyeglasses. However, many visual problems are easily corrected and may not be considered impairments by many people.

Arthritis and poor vision and hearing, among the most common of all chronic health conditions, are not life threatening. As Table 3-1 indicates, heart conditions, cancer, and strokes cause most deaths among the elderly. Nearly 75% of persons over age 65 die of one of these three conditions, with 44% dying from heart disease alone.

Not all groups of elderly suffer equally from the various diseases. In one survey 20% of the older White respondents said that poor health is a very serious problem for them, whereas 35% of the Black respondents made the same statement. These figures are a continuation of the ratio for younger Whites and Blacks; 18% of the Black respondents between 19 and 64 stated that they have very serious health problems, compared to 9% of the Whites (Harris & Associates, 1975). Other minority groups, such as Hispanics and Native Americans, also have more severe health problems than Whites at all ages, including old age.

Other chronic health problems, often ignored by people working with

Table 3-1. Causes of death among the elderly.

Cause of Death	*Age 65 and Over*	*Age 65–74*	*Age 75–84*	*Age 85 and Over*
Heart diseases	44.0%	41.4%	44.5%	47.7%
Malignant neoplasms (for example, cancer)	18.0	25.1	17.0	9.3
Cerebrovascular diseases (for example, stroke)	12.8	9.0	13.8	16.7
Influenza and pneumonia	3.8	2.2	3.9	6.2
Diabetes	2.0	2.2	2.1	1.4
Accidents	1.9	2.0	1.8	2.0
Bronchitis, emphysema, and asthma	1.4	1.9	1.4	0.7
Cirrhosis of the liver	0.7	1.4	0.4	0.1
Infections of the kidneys	0.5	0.4	0.5	0.4
All others	12.5	13.7	12.4	10.9

Based on 1976 data from the National Center for Health Statistics, *Vital Statistics of the United States: Mortality*. Washington, D.C.: U.S. Public Health Service, 1976.

the elderly, include foot problems and dental problems. As many as half of all persons over 65 have lost all their teeth. Although improved dental care is reducing the severity of that problem and improved bridges and plates reduce its significance, the fact remains that dental problems are important in the later years. Not only do older people face frequent trips to the dentist's office for expensive and painful work, but the entire process of eating is affected for some. And people with missing teeth or inadequate bridgework or plates are often reluctant to participate socially.

Foot problems often lead to pain or discomfort, to rapid fatigue, and to reduced ability to stand for extended periods or to walk. One of the exercises encouraged by the SAGE Program (see Chapter Seven) is foot massage to improve circulation in the feet and to reduce the effects of strain and fatigue.

Organic cognitive disorders

One well-accepted and highly distressing fact is that people are increasingly likely to be affected by organic cognitive disorders as they become older. These disorders include the conditions commonly referred to as *senile dementia* (often mistakenly called *senility*), leading to extreme forgetfulness, confusion, and, in a relatively few but dramatic instances, a virtual vegetative state. Complete agreement on what term best describes this form of impairment has not been reached. *Dementia* is now widely used, but so are *organic brain syndrome*, *chronic brain syndrome*, and *brain failure*. A British investigator is reported to have found "severe dementias" in between 1% and 7% of older people, depending on the definition of the term and the basis for diagnosis (Eisdorfer & Cohen, 1978).

The definition of *dementia* is in behavioral terms, although the causes are defined as physiological. Therefore, an elderly person is diagnosed as suffering from dementia when his or her thinking or memory has deteriorated to the point that the loss seriously interferes with social and occupational performance (Jarvik, 1980). The symptoms of dementia include impaired memory, diminished abstract-thinking capacity, reduced judgment, low impulse control, and personality change, though not all symptoms are found in all persons diagnosed as suffering from dementia (Jarvik, 1980). At present, some dementia cannot be treated, but some victims of organic brain syndrome improve when their medication is changed, suggesting that the initial diagnosis may have been wrong. In addition, people who suffer from it can be helped in some ways to handle their lives more effectively.

However, diagnosis of dementia is complex and often uncertain. Organic brain change and actual behavior do not always correspond closely. Some people whose autopsies show extensive brain damage displayed no meaningful behavior change, whereas others whose autopsies show little actual brain damage had many symptoms of dementia (Simon, 1971).

Further complicating the diagnosis of dementia is the possibility that the symptoms being observed are caused by other factors that are amenable to treatment: acute (as opposed to chronic) confusion, heavy drinking, excessive medication, malnourishment, depression, and psychological or social stress (Jarvik, 1980). These are all treatable conditions, and the symptoms can be reduced or eliminated. Therefore, it is extremely important that we not simply label a confused, forgetful older person as senile and then ignore the potential for his or her response to treatment. The diagnosis of senility can too easily be a self-fulfilling prophecy, since it implies that nothing can be done, and people so labeled may then be placed in a physical or social environment that offers no stimulation or treatment possibilities.

One organic cognitive disorder that has recently received a great deal of attention is Alzheimer's disease, a type of presenile dementia. The symptoms are memory loss, reduced attention span, and eventual loss of "orientation as to time, place, and person" (Eisdorfer & Cohen, 1978, p. 13). This disease is a progressive one, becoming steadily worse over time, and some elderly victims began to display symptoms in their 50s or even late 40s (see the following case history). Because Alzheimer's disease victims are aware of their confusion and forgetfulness, they may become depressed and anxious (Eisdorfer & Cohen, 1978).

Alzheimer's Disease: A Case History

A good friend of mine, a woman then in her middle 50s, asked me to evaluate her increasing forgetfulness. She was a highly successful executive and an amateur artist, and I told her that my own forgetfulness was nearly as bad as hers, and I was ten years younger.

But I erred greatly. She later sought a diagnosis from a neurologist, then from another neurologist, both of whom told her what I had: that nothing was wrong and that she had to "expect those things at your age." Finally a neuropsychologist found definite indications of Alzheimer's disease. In the meantime my friend had noted increasing confusion and forgetfulness, and she was becoming very anxious and severely depressed. Having married late in life, she had two teenage sons, and her husband had recently retired due to severe arthritis, so she was deeply concerned about what their fate would be if her condition continued to worsen. She was able to accept death, although she hardly welcomed it, but the thought of extensive deterioration put her in an understandable state of panic.

About three years later she left the management-consulting firm she had helped organize and took a position as an administrator with the local school system, where her symptoms would be less noticeable and she could enroll in an excellent health-care plan. She became less sociable and outgoing, and her sexual interests, which apparently had always been strong, diminished considerably, although I never knew how much of this decrease was due to her depression and how much to her disease.

By the time she was 61, her episodes of forgetfulness were frequent, and the changes had led to tension in her marriage. Her husband was torn by his love for her and his fear that he would spend years caring for a confused and deteriorating woman when he himself was having serious health problems. He was also embarrassed by his wife's confusion and forgetfulness when they were out with other people, and she was made even more anxious by his embarrassment.

There is no known cure for my friend's Alzheimer's disease, but this does not mean that she and her husband need to wait passively for her to deteriorate further and eventually die. I encouraged them to go for family therapy, with their now young-adult sons, in the hope that such treatment would diminish the depression and anxiety that accompanied the disorder. I don't know whether they did seek psychotherapy, and I also don't know many psychotherapists who have had any experience or training in working with families facing these problems.

My friend's situation is familiar to those who work with older people, but very few resources are available for helping either the victim or the victim's family. It is important to note that, even though nothing can be done about the organic symptoms of the disease, a great deal can be done through counseling and psychotherapy to help the family face what is likely to come. Yet such services are very difficult to find.

Another source of organic cognitive disorder is cerebrovascular brain syndrome, caused by strokes or other insults to the cerebrovascular system. This syndrome is difficult to differentiate from Alzheimer's disease on the basis of behavioral symptoms, although the diagnosis becomes clear on autopsy (Eisdorfer & Cohen, 1978).

Not all organic cognitive disorders are irreversible. Acute brain syndromes can sometimes be treated. Therefore, it is extremely important that an accurate differential diagnosis be made (Eisdorfer & Cohen, 1978). Nor do all cognitively disoriented people deteriorate steadily. A study of elderly mentally impaired women showed that more than one-third remained stable over a two-year period and that a handful actually improved. The women whose condition remained stable were less impaired medically and cognitively at the beginning of the study than were those who declined in capacity (Kleban, Lawton, Brody, & Moss, 1976). Here is more evidence that we should not give up on older people with cognitive impairments.

Mental-Health Conditions

The interrelationship between good mental health and good physical health is well known. It's much easier to feel good about yourself and the world when you are free from pain, discomfort, disability, and worries about the future. Conversely, when you are feeling good about yourself and the world, your body seems to function better, you seem more resistant to illness, and you are probably better able to deal with physical-health problems that do happen.

But, like physical disorders, mental-health problems do occur, and they probably occur with greater frequency in the later years. There are several ways to categorize these, each of them valid and each taking us in a somewhat different direction. They are:

1. *Affective and cognitive.* The term *affective* refers to *feelings* or *mood*; *cognitive* refers to *thinking* or *knowing*. Although serious depressive disorders are found more frequently among younger people, the *symptoms* of depression occur much more often among the elderly (Gurland, 1976) and constitute the most common mental-health problem of the later years (Epstein, 1976).
2. *Chronic and acute.* These terms were defined earlier. Chronic affective conditions among the elderly are frequently found in persons with a long history of depression; more familiar are acute episodes of deep depression but with some chronic symptoms that are distressing but not incapacitating (Gurland, 1976).
3. *Functional and organic.* Functional disorders develop from environmental stresses and reactions to the many losses that occur in the later years. Organic disorders arise from changes in the biochemistry or physiology of the individual, such as the loss of neurons or other degenerative conditions that affect the brain.
4. *Reversible and irreversible.* These categories are often viewed as closely related to functional and organic, although this is not inevitably the case. Presumably, every condition is reversible if we only knew enough about the environment or the brain to know how to reverse it. Many organic conditions continue to advance because we don't know how to intervene; this is especially true for cognitive disorders. Functional disorders, since they often stem from environmental and interpersonal stresses and losses, are presumably reversible if we can intervene to alter the stress-producing situations.

   However, some individuals suffering from manic symptoms, with presumed underlying depression, and some suffering from depressive symptoms have been helped by medication. The former have been treated with the drug lithium, which, in spite of potential side effects with improper dosage, has been fairly successful; the latter have been given a variety of antidepressants, but research on the effectiveness of these treatment programs is inconclusive, with some studies reporting success and others not (Schaie & Schaie, 1977).

Functional disorders. Functional disorders in later life are just as diverse as they are among younger persons; the diagnoses include schizophrenic disorder, paranoid disorder, and affective disorder which includes bipolarity (periods of manic elation and depression) and depression. Some people with these disorders develop them late in life, whereas others have a history of hospitalization for or at least manifestation of the symptoms. One authority in the field has estimated that about 15% of the older people in the United States suffer from "significant, substantial, or at least moderate psychopathology" (Pfeiffer, 1977, p. 652).

Although some people first exhibit these symptoms in their later years, others who had been diagnosed as suffering from functional disorders seem to burn out: their more obvious symptoms disappear, although their lengthy period of hospitalization may leave them unable to function adequately in the community. Nonetheless, about half of those hospitalized who are between 65 and 75, and nearly 40% of those 75 and older, were diagnosed as having functional psychosis (1963 data, from Simon, 1971). Considering the multiple losses that the elderly suffer—friends and family, functional performance, social roles—it is not surprising that many are emotionally disturbed. The real emotional-disturbance rate among the elderly may be higher than the official rate, since many people will tolerate behavior in an older person that would send them rushing to the authorities if the same behavior occurred in a younger person.

There is no doubt that depression is the most common functional disorder among the elderly. The familiar symptoms of depression include reduced self-esteem, a negative view of the future, great sadness, and a diminished involvement with people and activities. The physical symptoms accompanying depression include decreased appetite, weight loss, fatigue, and constipation. These are core symptoms—other symptoms displayed with less regularity include agitation, weeping, and great tension and anxiety (Pfeiffer, 1977).

Two basic kinds of depression have been described. The first is similar to psychotic depressive disorder, and the symptoms include guilt, self-deprecation, and some form of bodily complaints. The second is more truly a neurotic depression that occurs in response to external sources of stress, such as illness or social or financial losses. The symptoms often include "apathy, inertia, withdrawal into solitude, and quiet self-deprecation" (Epstein, 1976, p. 280).

Depression in the later years frequently comes and goes. It is reversible through medication or psychosocial intervention. The possibility of eliminating all neurotic-depression symptoms in an elderly patient is slight, but the chances of producing an immediate improvement are good (Epstein, 1976).

Sometimes depression becomes so great that the older person's cognitive abilities seem to have been impaired, and a diagnosis of organic brain damage is made. In other instances the individual suffers from organic brain damage and is also depressed, resulting in a lower level of cognitive functioning than would have otherwise occurred. A problem for the diagnostician is to determine whether the symptoms observed in a particular older person are irreversible and organic or whether they are potentially reversible or at least ameliorable to some extent.

It is easy to make errors in diagnosing a depressed older person. Such individuals may be seen as suffering from anxiety neurosis, a physical disorder, or organic brain syndrome (Gurland, 1976). Since an accurate diagnosis is extremely difficult to make, it may be wise to treat the older person as though his or her condition can be reversed through a medical or drug program, through psychotherapy or counseling, or through improving the individual's social situation and relationships with others. The specific program requires knowledge of the specific medical, psychological, and social situation the person faces, and a team effort is advisable.

Not all affective disorders among the elderly are depressive. Manic behavior occurs in a small proportion, exhibited as undue elation, extreme optimism, feelings of powerfulness, rapid speech, and hyperactivity. Use of the drug lithium has done a great deal to reduce manic states among all age groups (Pfeiffer, 1977).

Inevitably, some elderly people are paranoid, and others display the symptoms of schizophrenia. The former become very suspicious of others, and the condition is found most frequently among elderly persons suffering from visual, auditory, or cognitive deficits; apparently, their reduced ability to process information from the world around them leaves them victims of their own fears (Pfeiffer, 1977). Elderly paranoiacs are often amenable to treatment, whereas elderly schizophrenics are so frequently younger schizophrenics grown old in mental institutions that they may resist treatment because they have become so accustomed to their institutional surroundings. Symptoms of schizophrenia include delusions, hallucinations, and inappropriate affective responses.

Suicide and suicide attempts. When depression is intense, when the future appears hopeless, and when the older person feels helpless, suicide may be seen as an appropriate alternative. Suicide rates tend to go up with age, so that they are highest among the elderly, but when the figures are categorized by sex and race, a somewhat surprising finding emerges: suicide rates for White women drop after the middle years, whereas rates for both male and female non-Whites, most of whom are Black, also go down in the later years (U.S. Public Health Service, 1974). Rates for White men increase steadily throughout the life span.

Another statistical shift in suicide rates with age is the ratio of attempted suicides to those ending in death. Among younger people, attempts are much more numerous than deaths; in the later years a much higher proportion of attempts do result in death. In a study of suicides in Hawaii, it was evident that men, older people in general, and those of Asian ancestry were more likely to die from their attempts than women, younger people in general, and those of Hawaiian or Caucasian ancestry (Kalish, 1968). Other studies have supported these findings (see Pfeiffer, 1977).

Suicide attempts are often seen as a cry for help, usually when all other avenues to relief that the individual can see are closed off, and the individual feels a sense of helplessness and hopelessness. Suicide can also be viewed as an action meant to have an impact on the survivors, perhaps a kind of punishment for being neglectful. Undoubtedly, however, some people commit suicide simply because they want to die. I believe that older people who attempt or commit suicide are less likely than younger people to be calling for help or to be attempting to punish or otherwise affect their survivors. So many of their suicide attempts lead to death because death is in fact what they want (Kalish, 1968; Pfeiffer, 1977). Their depression feels so painful and their hopes for the future seem so futile that death is the only alternative they see.

Older people are much less likely than younger people to get in touch with a suicide-prevention center when they feel depressed. The Los Angeles SPC reported that only 2.6% of its calls were from people over age 60, which was about one-fifth of the statistically expected incidence of calls from that age group. "The elderly persons who call the SPC are lonely, distressed, often hurting physically, and frequently angry at feeling either deserted or abandoned" (Farberow & Moriwaki, 1975, p. 336). Many of these older callers had a history of problem drinking, and a number of men described difficulties in obtaining sexual satisfaction, either because their sexual partners were refusing their requests or because death or abandonment had left them partnerless (Farberow & Moriwaki, 1975).

Alcoholism. Moderate use of alcohol appears to have life-enhancing qualities, but extreme use reduces life expectancy (Woodruff, 1977). Alcoholism, the compulsive use of alcohol, certainly diminishes life expectancy and is a mental-health problem of considerable magnitude, even though problem drinking, estimated as affecting between 2% and 10% of older persons (Schuckit, 1977), seems to be found less often among the elderly than among younger age groups (Mishara & Kastenbaum, 1980). There are several possible explanations for this finding, but two seem most likely: either problem drinkers reduce their drinking in their later years, or problem drinkers die before they reach their later years. Perhaps both factors play a role.

By far the greatest number of elderly alcoholics have had a long history of drinking problems, whereas those who began drinking heavily in their later years often did so following either retirement or the death of someone close, most often a spouse. It has been speculated that poor health has also led to problem drinking, but, although the relationship is certainly logical, the evidence for it is not strong (Mishara & Kastenbaum, 1980).

Caring for Health Problems

The physical and mental problems of the elderly are like those of other age groups, except that they occur much more frequently, last longer, are more likely to be chronic and irreversible, and are more often life threatening. All this would suggest that health-care facilities would be heavily geared up to provide services for the elderly. Whether this is true seems to be in the eye of the beholder. There are, of course, a vast number of nursing homes and other facilities; physicians have developed the newly recognized specialty of geriatric medicine, and medical schools are setting up programs to educate these specialists; and educational opportunities for nurses, aides, physicians, health educators, and others have greatly increased. On the other side of the ledger, I would certainly say that the health-care needs of the elderly are far from being adequately met, in terms of either quantity or quality, by the existing facilities and staffing.

The mental-health field is well behind that of physical health. Community mental-health centers, although required by law to provide services for older persons, have probably remained less responsive to their needs than to the needs of other age groups. As mental hospitals are being emptied of their patients, many confused or depressed elderly are being returned to their communities, where they are either placed in long-term care facilities, which usually have no one skilled in mental-health care, or permitted to live in the community without adequate support services.

Physical-health and mental-health professionals are known to prefer working with young or middle-aged people, perhaps because they themselves are young or middle-aged, perhaps because they feel that older people are going to die soon and their efforts will be wasted (the allocation of professional resources presents a fascinating ethical problem), perhaps because they don't know what to do, perhaps because encounters with older people remind them too clearly of their own aging process.

Whatever the reasons, the results are the same: the physical and mental problems of older people are not given proper attention. Often the elderly or their family members are told "You have to expect those things at that age," which sometimes means "Don't bother me anymore." When the vague term *senility* or *chronic brain syndrome* is used as a diagnostic category, the implication is often that nothing can be done to influence the course of the disorder. If a specific disease can be diagnosed, labeling it somehow provides a kind of medical respectability for the condition, and researchers can begin to understand the biochemical or psychosocial conditions under which the disorder operates (Eisdorfer, 1978).

Institutional Care

Few matters pertaining to the elderly have caused greater unhappiness than institutional care. Not only have the facilities providing the care come under frequent attack for their inadequacies—both social and physical—but the cost of institutional care is immense, and Medicare and Medicaid payments often fall far short of covering the expense. Although only 5% of the elderly are in a long-term care institution at any one time, some 20% to 25% or more spend some time in such a facility (Kastenbaum & Candy, 1973).

When we think of an institution for the elderly, we are likely to have an image of a nursing home, sometimes called a convalescent-care facility. These institutions care for those elderly people who need considerable attention, either because of physical problems or because of mental confusion. Some nursing-home residents are highly debilitated; they may sit and stare all day long at a television set without really knowing what they see; they can be incontinent, unable to feed themselves, or apparently unaware of where they are or even who they are.

Although very few elderly people ever reach this stage, and although the condition of some who seem to have declined to that stage could be improved through proper psychosocial treatment, many lay people conjure up exactly this image when they think of "the old folks." This misperception is not expressed by only the nonelderly. Often an 80-year-old will be heard referring to "the old people," meaning people in nursing homes. Such an image of aging and of institutions has been one of the factors causing people to wish to have as little contact as possible with the elderly.

Another geriatric institution is the home for the aged, or the board-and-care home. These are geared for people who require some help or supervision but who can basically care for themselves. The residents can normally bathe and feed themselves and are unlikely to be very confused. These facilities emphasize social services rather than health-care services. Social interactions are more frequent, and activity programs are often planned.

A third category, established more recently, is that of the intermediate-care facility, which tries to fill the gap often left between the nursing home and the home for the aged.

In practice, however, divisions among these three levels of care are not so clear as they are in theory. An elderly person may end up in a particular home—one that may be inappropriate—because it is run by his or her church, because a physician had heard it gave better care than the more appropriate facility, because of expense, or because no appropriate facility is located nearby.

Relatively few long-term care facilities have attempted to provide intellectual or sensory stimulation for their patients. This lack is particularly true of nursing homes, in part because the cost of running a nursing home is so high that additional staff are taken on only with great reluctance, and in part because the responsiveness of many of the patients is so minimal that only the most persevering worker will continue to try to elicit their reactions. Unfortunately, the less staff members interact with the patients, the more they do things for the patients instead of taking the extra time to help the patients do things for themselves, the more—in short—they give up on the patients, the more the patients sink into despondency and turn their thoughts and feelings inward.

Most nursing-home staff members have had no training in the field before coming to the home, receive little or no in-service training, and are very poorly paid. Relatively few of them enjoy the tasks they are required to perform, and many are not particularly attracted to working with people as confused and sick as nursing-home patients often are.

Administrators are frequently so involved with the immediate and highly demanding problems of day-to-day functioning that they have little time to consider staff training and little energy to encourage the necessary programs and social interactions that might help their patients. Lacking cognitive or sensory stimulation, those patients who are already ill and confused become more so. Yet to place full blame on the owners and administrators is to overlook the fact that minimal amounts of money are provided for nursing-home care, even with the support of Medicare and Medicaid, and the fact that maximum demands are made on the time and energy of administrators. (One administrator referred to himself and his colleagues as the "human-garbage collectors," not because he felt that way about his patients but because he felt that society in general regarded him in that fashion.)

Making matters worse is the sad fact that a life must end in the depersonalized atmosphere of an institution, away from the friends and family and community among whom that life was lived. The truth is well known both to the elderly who enter these institutions and to all others: for most, it is a final stopping place before their death. One retired economics professor, who entered a nursing home shortly before his 93rd birthday, wrote to me:

> There are very few of the kind of people that I'd like to associate with here in the hospital. The men are old and decrepit. The women are similar. Only one or two that are out of the ordinary in looks. I miss my neighbors of the past. But since it cannot be helped I must put up with it. The food and service are excellent. My son and wife are about four minutes away from me. This is not an ordinary hospital. People come and stay until they die. I undoubtedly am in that class.

Another institution for the elderly is the state psychiatric hospital, although the trend has been for these hospitals to return their patients to the community or, often, to send them to long-term care facilities, which are—in turn—often reluctant to accept any mental patients whose symptoms might upset the other patients or be especially troublesome to the staff.

Although institutional care often reduces the individual's potential for mastering the environment and developing personal strengths, it sometimes provides the best available alternative. In evaluating the appropriateness of institutionalization, not only the elderly person but others in the family need to be considered. In some instances, when proper programs are available, institutional treatment can change behavior in a positive fashion; but nursing homes unfortunately do not often have social-therapy programs and are not reimbursed by Medicare or Medicaid when they do put such programs into effect (Gottesman, Quarterman, & Cohn, 1973).

Another Approach to Health Care

The health of older people is not static. They get better; they get worse; they change in other ways. The services needed for a slightly confused 80-year-old man change when he is found to have a serious heart condition; a 73-year-old woman who has just suffered a major stroke needs a different kind of care once her speech and walking ability are sufficiently improved. Most institutions were initially developed to care for one level of health problems, but new programs are increasingly being developed that permit an older person to remain in the same facility as he or she improves or worsens.

Specialists in aging often talk about a "continuum of care." This means that one facility or several facilities working together can provide competent care for an elderly person at various stages of physical and mental health. Thus, if an elderly man enters an institution just after being released from a hospital following a stroke, he can remain there and receive proper treatment and care as he recovers; conversely, if his condition worsens, he can still remain there. When a continuum of care is lacking, the elderly person must either be moved from facility to facility or accept a program that is geared for people who are either healthier or sicker than he.

For example, a large facility might have 30 two-story buildings housing well elderly in their own apartments. Other buildings on the grounds might be a small hospital for a dozen patients and a nursing home with 40 beds. The facility might also be linked with a hospice, an institution providing outpatient and sometimes inpatient care for people who are terminally ill, even though the hospice is, say, 4 miles away.

In addition, there might be a day health center on the grounds. The day health concept is fairly recent. Although the exact nature of a day health center varies with the specific facility, its primary role is to provide health and numerous other kinds of programs for older persons who are not fully capable of caring for themselves but who do not require 24-hour custodial care. Perhaps they live with family members who work during the day; perhaps they live with another elderly relative who is no longer capable of providing all the necessary care; perhaps they are marginally self-sustaining.

The day health program usually arranges for transportation for the elderly to and from the facility, a variety of health services while they are there, and numerous other services, including physical therapy, recreation, a hot lunch, and other programs that I will discuss in Chapter Seven. It's not unusual for a day health program to include the services of a barber and a beautician, a chiropodist (foot doctor), a nutritionist to counsel family members on appropriate diets, and even a laundry arrangement and a bath for older people who cannot easily tend to these personal necessities in their present living arrangement.

The day health center is neither a senior center, which is for the well elderly, nor a nursing home. It provides needed services in a setting that permits people to remain in their own homes and communities, where they can retain as many of their previous life patterns, friendships, and so forth as possible.

Most day health centers are either independent or attached to a hospital or nursing home. However, a few are a part of multipurpose geriatric-care centers, which offer a number of health, social, and housing programs for older persons, usually at one physical site, that are integrated to provide an effective continuum of care.

Psychotherapy and Counseling

The usefulness of psychotherapy for older persons has been debated for a long time. Freud appears to have believed that people as young as 50 years old were already too old to profit from therapy because they cannot change. My beliefs and observations and those of most gerontologists run counter to Freud's (see, for example, Kastenbaum, 1964; Oberleder, 1966). Perhaps the lengthy and expensive form of psychoanalytic therapy is inappropriate in all but a few instances, but there are many other forms of psychotherapy and counseling that have seemed to work (Kastenbaum, 1978; Richards & Thorpe, 1978).

The barriers to psychotherapy with the elderly are several, and they often loom large. First, most older people have low incomes, and they are reluctant to spend their limited money for therapy. Second, community mental-health centers, for the most part, have not encouraged older people to seek their therapeutic services. Third, the popularity of psychotherapy began when today's elderly were already well into their middle years, and many are very suspicious of psychology and psychiatry, perhaps seeing therapy as being only for "crazy people" and certainly not seeing it as appropriate for themselves. This situation, of course, is likely to change as today's middle-aged and late-middle-aged people become elderly. And, finally, there is what Kastenbaum (1964) has termed "the reluctant therapist," a person who wishes to spend his or her time and effort on people with whom there is a longer payoff in terms of futurity and whose experiences are more easily understood. Added to this problem is the lack of training and experience that psychotherapists have had with the elderly, since specific training in the clinical psychology and clinical psychiatry of the elderly is just beginning. Another problem that has been suggested is that many psychotherapists have not fully solved relationships with their own parents, so that relating therapeutically to older people brings up some of their own unresolved problems. Further, working with older people may distress psychotherapists, since it forces them to examine their own aging process and their own finitude (Kastenbaum, 1964).

One discussion of psychotherapy for older persons with organic cognitive impairments has pointed out that the therapist often needs to establish limited goals, such as the elimination of specific undesirable behavior or the improvement of social participation (Eisdorfer, Cohen, & Preston, 1978). This may also be true for older persons who are not cognitively impaired but who desire therapy to help them handle the immediate and pressing disturbances of depression and anxiety that arise from their present situation.

Older people are not all alike, as I have been emphasizing, and the kinds of psychotherapy appropriate for them differ greatly. Some individuals will find the traditional 50-minute-hour most useful; others, including those in institutional settings, may respond best to 10- or 15-minute informal therapy sessions or to such kinds of personal help as advice on taxes or the name of a good optometrist. In between is a wide variety of possibilities, including group psychotherapy or counseling and family or couples therapy. Successful instances of each of these have been described in the literature (see, for example, Herr & Weakland, 1979; J. A. Peterson, 1973; Wolff, 1963).

One extensive review of the literature lists several psychotherapeutic techniques that have been found useful at various times:

1. Using a directive approach, including direct suggestions for changes.
2. Involving the client in a life-review process, including an extensive life history and reminiscing, in order to put her or his life in perspective and to understand better the positive and satisfying aspects of the past.
3. Referring clients to appropriate agencies that can help with needs affecting mental health and well-being, such as housing, financial problems, and loneliness.
4. Providing reinterpretations and alternative explanations for behavior and occurrences that the older person might view as inadequacies, together with reassurance.
5. Helping the older person express strong feelings, such as anger and guilt.
6. Permitting the client to retain some ways of handling the environment that might initially seem psychologically harmful but, on further examination, appear to have served the client effectively as a buffer against some of the distresses of aging [adapted from Knight, 1978–1979].

After reviewing 75 books and articles, the same author concluded that the "evidence that is presently available suggests a more optimistic view of therapy with the aged community resident than is generally accepted" (Knight, 1978–1979, p. 232).

My own observations here, as virtually everywhere in working with older people, suggest that the elderly can be approached in ways similar to those used with other age groups, while allowing for the specific changes that occur in the later years—such as reduced life expectancy, physical handicaps, and financial and health problems—*to the extent that these occur for the particular individual* being considered. In other words, psychotherapy with a healthy, moderately well-off 65-year-old woman would be very much like psychotherapy with a 35-year-old woman of comparable health, income, family status, and so forth. It is important that we avoid looking at aging as a global issue when we are concerned with individual treatment and that we consider the unique qualities of the individual, only one of which is chronological age and its meaning to that person.

The Meaning of Death and the Process of Dying

The meaning of death is a highly significant issue to all of us all the time; the process of dying affects primarily those persons who are dying, those who are close to them, and those who are working in relevant settings. Both the meaning of death and the process of dying are of particular concern to older people. Both matters are certainly mental-health issues, and the process of dying is simultaneously a physical-health issue as well.

Death can come at any age, but today, more than at any other time in history, death is predicted by age: death is seen only rarely among young people, occasionally among the middle-aged, and frequently among the elderly. Awareness of death, including one's own, does not occur suddenly in old age, although the full impact of the significance of death can be felt in a dramatic moment at any age and is often felt during the later years.

To a young woman getting ready to enter college, graduation seems endless years away. Although she may make a few plans for the years after she graduates, and although she fully recognizes that the time will come when she will no longer be in college, it is difficult for her to plan for this eventuality. As she enters her senior year, and with increasing frequency as the year slips by, she begins to think in terms of how many days, weeks, months, exams, term papers, or classes remain. She no longer speaks of having been in college for three and a half years but of how much time she still has left.

My metaphor must be obvious, except that the enormity and inevitability of dying place it in a category by itself. People often assume that death is more frightening for the elderly than for the young, perhaps because of its imminence. Research evidence, however, indicates just the opposite. Although both statistics and observations indicate that older people think about death more frequently than younger people, considerable evidence has accumulated that they fear death less than younger persons do (Kalish & Reynolds, 1976).

Some people contend that the elderly do not actually fear death less than younger people, but that they are simply denying their fear. However, I believe that there are several explanations for the data and that we do not need to assume that older people are using denial more than persons of other age groups. First, older people recognize that they have relatively little futurity. The deaths of age peers and younger people and the awareness that their lives are coming to a close make them think more about death, and, being forced to think about death, they work through some of their fears and anxieties. Second, in many instances neither their future nor their present is as attractive as that of younger persons. Third, most elderly are aware that general life expectancy is about 70 years, and if they have lived beyond that age, they feel they have received what they were entitled to receive. Fourth, they have coped with innumerable losses already, so that coping with the losses that come with death is more closely related to previous experiences and is more effectively accomplished (Kalish, 1981).

During an interview, one 86-year-old man commented, "When you're as old as me . . . you'll learn that time devours you; it eats you right up." Toward the end of the same interview, he said "I'm doing nothing all the time, nothing. That's the worst punishment a man can have—nothing to do" (Kastenbaum, 1966, p. 332). The dilemma of the elderly is that the weeks, months, and years zoom by at an accelerating pace, with only death at the end, while at the same time the minutes and hours can drag by when filled with nothing.

As time and their future become briefer, many elderly begin to reminisce, to review their lives. This life review can be extremely helpful in enabling older people to see their lives as an integrated whole rather than as a series of episodes, to reflect upon their accomplishments, and to deal with feelings of nostalgia and regret (Butler, 1963). Some older people begin to write their life histories, often at great length, with the dual motive of leaving something of themselves behind for their children and grandchildren and of seeing their entire past spread out before them.

The "trajectory" of dying is an expression proposed by two sociologists to describe the nature of the downhill path from normal health to death (Glaser & Strauss, 1968). For a cancer patient, the trajectory would move slowly and irregularly down; for a person suffering from a series of heart attacks, the trajectory would resemble a series of downward steps of different sizes; for a suicide, the trajectory would look like one large step. The way in which individuals die is much more than the outcome of the way they lived. It also reflects their terminal condition, the kinds of care they receive, the degree to which they are sedated, the pain and discomfort they suffer, and the human relationships that surround them.

A well-known psychiatrist has suggested that five stages mark the normal and appropriate pathway to death, at least for those whose trajectory permits the time and the necessary awareness. These stages are (1) denial and isolation, (2) anger, (3) bargaining (attempts to postpone death), (4) depression, and (5) acceptance (Kübler-Ross, 1969). Not every person goes through each stage in this sequence, and people may move back and forth between stages or may even be in two stages simultaneously. In the last stage the dying come to accept impending death; they have made peace with themselves and with others and are ready to die. In many ways they are almost completely disengaged from everyone and everything except very close family members (perhaps only their spouses and children or even only their spouses), one or two friends, and the hospital staff, who, during the last days, are vitally important people (Kübler-Ross, 1969).

Although these stages have received considerable attention, there are serious questions about their general applicability. Many people who are experienced in working with the dying have proposed other stages or have expressed doubt that any one sequence of stages can be designated at all (R. Schulz & Aderman, 1974). Further, there is the danger that so many older people are familiar with these stages that they may see themselves as failures if they do not move through them as anticipated, while so many health-care professionals are familiar with the stages that they may inadvertently pressure dying people to die according to the stages (Kalish, 1981).

Many issues concerning death and dying are especially meaningful for the elderly. Whether a dying patient should be informed of the prognosis has been heatedly debated, although most people say that they themselves would wish to know and admit that most dying people do know when they are dying, even if they are not directly informed (Kalish & Reynolds, 1976). Another important question is how long to use what the medical profession terms heroic methods to keep patients alive, especially when there is good evidence that extensive brain damage has already occurred. Closely related is the suggestion that people be permitted to dictate, while still healthy and alert, what should be done for them when and if they are in great pain or have suffered extensive brain damage—in other words, that they have the option to choose death through what is called a living will.

Physicians, family members, and others, usually well meaning, may suggest to a terminally ill older person that he or she become resigned. When a dying person is given a counsel of resignation, he or she is really being given a plea, perhaps even a demand, to die peacefully and not place pressure on the physician to intercede (Weisman, 1972). The elderly simply do not elicit the same reactions during their terminal stages that children do. "The terminally aged may be as helpless as a child, but they seldom arouse tenderness" (Weisman, 1972, p. 144).

Although it is very difficult for those who are not old to understand what a dying elderly person must face, a noted psychiatrist has listed seven questions that each person can try to answer in order to come a little closer to feeling what the elderly feel as they confront death:

1. If you faced death in the near future, what would matter most?
2. If you were very old, what would your most crucial problems be? How would you go about solving them?
3. If death were inevitable, what circumstances would make it acceptable?
4. If you were very old, how might you live most effectively and with least damage to your ideals and standards?
5. What can anyone do to prepare for his own death, or for that of someone very close?
6. What conditions and events might make you feel that you were better off dead? When would you take steps to die?
7. In old age, everyone must rely upon others. When this point arrives, what kind of people would you like to deal with? [Weisman, 1972, p. 157]

A Last Caution and Some Last Thoughts

There are distinct hazards in viewing physicians, mental-health professionals, and other service providers as villains. First, this viewpoint tends to place the responsibility for insufficient service on these individuals and their institutions, thus absolving the rest of us from our own responsibilities. Second, it ignores the fact that these persons are also human, subject to human errors and frailties, and permits the rest of us to maintain a dangerous position of moral superiority. Third, it draws attention away from the complex of factors that leads to inadequate care, including the unwillingness of older persons to seek service.

Rather than condemning people and programs presently serving the health and other needs of older persons, those of us concerned with the well-being of the elderly may need to consider how to produce change. Advocacy, community education, outreach programs, and personal contacts are among the possibilities. There will be some additional discussion of these alternatives in Chapter Seven.

Reading about the physical and mental health of older people is a lesson proving that the more you know, the more you know how much you don't know. New research findings, new treatment programs, new understanding of health and illness, all continue to pour forth. Each new finding, program, or understanding serves as a spotlight to light up vast areas of ignorance.

I have no doubt that the next two decades will bring significant new additions to our knowledge of the health of the elderly and that new and better treatment programs will be developed. I also have no doubt that the physical and mental health of the elderly will require just as much attention, just as much new research, and just as many innovative treatment programs at the end of this century as it does now.

Chapter Four

The Older Individual: Personality and Role

What were you like ten years ago? What are you like today? What took place during those ten years that changed you from what you were to what you are? What accounts for these changes? To answer these questions is to gain some insights into the impact of aging on self-concept, personality, and roles.

To grasp what happened during the last ten years, you must examine more than one dimension of your past existence. You obviously have had ten years of experiences—pleasant and unpleasant, exciting and boring, warming and embittering, ego building and ego destroying. These experiences have helped to mold the person you were ten years ago into the person you are today.

But these experiences affected an already formed organism. You are a human being who not only is acted on but acts, a person who is not a helpless pawn of fate but has some degree of power in shaping your own existence. Therefore, you might examine your past ten years of experiences, as they acted on you and you reacted to them, in terms of your personality.

Moreover, the biological component of this organism that is you has also been changing. You don't look or act the way you did ten years ago: your weight, hair color, stamina, hand grip, sleep pattern, body contour, and physical health—any one or several of these—may have changed notably in ten years.

And society reacts to you differently. Your various positions and statuses have been in the process of change. For instance, it may be that you are no longer a student but an employed person, no longer single but married and a parent, no longer financially dependent on older people but living on your own resources, no longer the child of two healthy parents but the emotional support of your widowed mother. Others expect different behavior from you as a result of your new positions in society, and you probably expect it from yourself.

Furthermore, the world has changed. Scandals and wars, peace treaties and political upsets, and successful and unsuccessful attempts to establish new political forms have all occurred during the past ten years. New forms of familial and community living have been tried; some have failed and others have endured, although frequently in altered form. The technology, advertising, ecology, and health care of today are not those of ten years ago.

Not just the world at large but your own personal world is considerably changed. You probably are not living in the same residence you were living in ten years ago; you have lost touch with some of your closest friends of a decade ago; people you know have married or divorced, have embarked on careers and changed careers, have had serious accidents or have attempted suicide, have won contests and been on television. And all these changes of the past decade have interacted with one another and your self-concept—with what you think and feel about yourself—to make you what you are today.

The same constellation of forces leads to age-related changes at any point in the life cycle, but the specific elements of these changes differ according to the time in life at which they occur. To understand individuals at 60 or 70 or 90, we also need to look at their views of themselves, at their changes in social positions and roles, at their self-concepts and personalities as these relate to the biogenic changes they are undergoing, and at the situational changes arising in the world at large and in their own personal worlds.

The Changing Self-Concept

The self-concept is the individual's image of himself or herself; it reflects actual experiences and the ways these experiences are interpreted. To a large extent the self-concept is a reflection of the way others react to the individual, but some people, as they grow older, are better able to see themselves in positive ways, even when they reach an age that is frequently viewed by others in a deprecatory fashion.

Two of the most important components of the self-concept are *self-esteem,* the extent to which a person's self-perceptions are positive or negative, and *body image,* the individual's concept of his or her body and related health concerns. Each of these is influenced by the aging process, and each, in turn, affects the psychosocial aspects of the aging process.

Self-Esteem

Given the stresses and losses that come with increasing age, given the lack of respect shown the elderly, given their diminishing physical capacities and sometimes their diminishing cognitive capacities, it is only common sense to believe that people's self-esteem should drop, perhaps drastically, as they enter their later years. Except that this common-sense conclusion is not borne out by the research data. When common sense and research data clash, we have three options: (1) to accept common sense, (2) to accept the data, or (3) to reconcile the conflict.

Some studies show that self-esteem increases with age (Gurin, Veroff, & Feld, 1960), some show reduced self-esteem (Kogan & Wallach, 1961), and some show no change. In trying to make better sense of these data, a pair of Texas researchers (Kaplan & Pokorny, 1970) looked at the interaction among chronological age and other variables as they jointly affect self-esteem. They found several factors that helped explain previous inconsistent results (although their study hardly exhausted all the potential explanatory factors). First, for people who had not had any recent disruptive life experiences, age was positively related to self-esteem; for people who had encountered such experiences (such as a business loss, a death in the family, the loss of a job), no age-related increase in self-esteem was found. Second, for people who felt they were living at about the same standard of living that they had anticipated earlier, self-esteem was higher among those 60 and older; for people whose standard of living was lower than they had anticipated, self-esteem for the 60-plus age group was lower; and even among those whose standard of living was better than they had anticipated, the self-esteem of older respondents was slightly lower. Third, having had a childhood fear of being left alone also proved significant; among respondents not recalling such a fear, the older group had higher self-esteem, and just the reverse was true for those admitting to considerable childhood fears.

Each of these findings makes sense. If the older people have a reasonably stable recent history, an anticipated standard of living, and no strong fears of being left alone, their self-esteem rises with age. Conversely, when disruptive forces occur, when the standard of living is well below the level of aspiration, and when fears of being isolated and alone are strong, the older person is more vulnerable. This study suggests the need for future work in probing additional characteristics.

Another approach to the same problem was taken by Riley and her associates (1968) in their extensive review of the gerontological literature. They juxtaposed a number of findings from various studies on self-esteem as a function of age. Compared to younger people, older individuals were (1) less likely to admit to shortcomings, (2) less likely to consider themselves in good health, (3) less concerned about their weight, (4) (among those still working) equally likely to view their job performance as adequate, (5) almost as likely to view their intelligence as being as good as others', (6) more likely to consider themselves as having positive moral values, and (7) somewhat more likely to feel adequate in their marriage or as parents.

In the early 1970s a national polling organization interviewed a carefully selected sample of more than 4200 persons, nearly 2800 of them 65 years of age or older. Among the many questions asked were several concerning self-esteem. From Table 4-1 you can see that the self-esteem of older persons did not differ much from that of the nonelderly except in matters related to physical and sexual activity and wisdom (Harris & Associates, 1975). When income was controlled, the differences diminished even more.

In the final analysis, then, it appears that we cannot judge the self-esteem of one age group in comparison to another on a global basis but must look at the individual components of self-esteem and self-concept. Some aspects of self-esteem appear to rise in the later years; others become lower.

Body Image

Physical appearance is important to most people, and except for the occasional person whose face is judged "interesting," the physical appearance of an older person is not usually seen as attractive and certainly not as sexually attractive. Older people often make comments such as "When I look in the mirror, I see the face of an old person. It isn't me—I have the spirit of a young person." Or "I am a prisoner of my body. It's not really me with arthritis, with sagging breasts and loose skin—it's someone else."

Again, the research findings do not confirm the hypothesis that older people are more concerned about their appearance than younger people. One study showed just the opposite (Maddox, 1963), and the results of a more recent investigation indicated that "a person's bodily worries and discomforts are not related to age *per se,* but reflect special life circum-

Table 4-1. Self-esteem of elderly and nonelderly persons.

Personal Quality	*Self-Perceptions of Persons 18–64* (n=*1457*)	*Self-Perceptions of Persons 65 and Over* (n=*2797*)
Very friendly and warm	63%	72%
Very wise from experience	54	69
Very bright and alert	73	68
Very open-minded and adaptable	67	63
Very good at getting things done	60	55
Very physically active	65	48
Very sexually active	47	11

Reprinted from *The Myth and Reality of Aging in America,* a study prepared by Louis Harris and Associates, Inc. for The National Council on the Aging, Inc., Washington, D.C. © 1975.

stances" (Plutchik, Weiner, & Conte, 1971). Table 4-1, however, does show that older people do perceive themselves as less physically and sexually active than younger people perceive themselves. We don't know whether those perceptions are reflected in a general sense of lowered self-worth.

The concept of body image is not restricted to physical appearance. It also incorporates the individual's perceptions of his or her physical strength, ability to move around, general health and vigor, physical pain, sexuality, and other characteristics. Sensory-awareness training, as well as dance and movement therapies, can improve body image and thereby improve both health and self-esteem.

Explanations and Implications

Although helpful for understanding the changing self-concept of older people, the existing research is far from completely satisfying. To return to my earlier statement that "people's self-esteem should drop, perhaps drastically, as they enter their later years": why does research have to complicate and obscure the obvious?

One explanation lies in the research methodologies themselves. Perhaps the investigators are asking the wrong questions; perhaps elderly research participants are atypical older people having unusually high life satisfaction and morale; or perhaps older respondents distort their answers, either because they feel defensive or because they lack accurate insight.

Another possibility is that older people are comparing themselves with their own age group rather than with the entire age spectrum. They may not be considering their life situation in relation to what it once was or to what they would like to be but, instead, in relation to some of the difficulties they see their age mates encountering.

Another probable factor is the misinterpretation others often give to what the elderly say. Many people—professionals, adult children of the elderly, concerned observers—begin with the premise that self-esteem in the elderly is low. When these views are confirmed by the research or by the claims of the elderly themselves, the confirmation is accepted at face value. However, when older people deny that their self-esteem is low or that their self-concept is poor, these observers assume that the denial must arise from defensiveness or from some form of conscious or unconscious distortion of their true feelings. Therefore, what the elderly say about themselves often makes little difference, since interpretation precedes observation.

An alternative approach to this issue is to assume that the elderly are indeed denying their own feelings of lower self-esteem, but that such denial is an appropriate and effective mechanism for adaptation at this point in their lives. Defense mechanisms perform an important function in permitting people, at any age, to maintain an adequate self-concept. Defense mechanisms can also promote difficulties. But we really have no sound information on their adaptive function for this age cohort and this context.

Another form of bias deserves more attention than it receives. Many people work with the elderly in settings in which they regularly encounter troubled older people. (Those who are physically well, socially and emotionally stable, and financially secure do not normally come to the attention of agencies and institutions.) Therefore, the professional social or medical or recreational geriatrician, who is a major molder of public opinion, interacts largely with those elderly people whose situations suggest that their self-esteem is below average for their age group.

All these factors undoubtedly carry some weight in explaining the discrepancy between research findings and common sense, but I feel that the comments in the previous paragraph on what could be dubbed the squeaky-wheel effect ("the squeaky wheel gets the grease") are insufficiently recognized by both professionals and nonprofessionals who work with the elderly. If so, it is not that the research is in error, but that the perceptions of the public are unduly affected by well-publicized atypical examples.

Personality Changes and Aging

One definition of personality is *the changing and interacting organization of characteristic qualities, seen as a whole, that leads people to behave as they do and that makes them different from one another.* These qualities include, but are not limited to, needs and motives, methods of adjusting, temperament and mood, potential for growth and accomplishment, and abilities.

Although each individual, regardless of age, is unique and can be fully understood only in terms of this uniqueness, we often describe people in terms of salient personality characteristics or qualities, even while recognizing the inevitable oversimplification that results. Some of the adjectives applied to the elderly are *cautious, rigid, wise, patient, irritable,* and *forgetful.*

Do these adjectives accurately describe personality changes that accompany old age? Although behavioral scientists have traditionally emphasized change processes that occur during infancy and childhood and have often ignored, or even denied, the possibility of meaningful change during the adult years, observers and theorists alike have recently come to view personality development as a lifelong process. The question that arises is whether the changes that occur when people enter their 60s are in any way predictable. In other words, is there any discernible change in personality that is likely to take place in older people in general or in any identifiable group of older people—such as women, grandfathers, Filipinos, Jews, introverts, college graduates, rural dwellers . . . ?

And if such predictions can be made with at least modest accuracy, what underlies the age-related changes? Are the changes inevitable, or almost inevitable, for all older persons who reach a particular age or who have a particular health condition or economic status? Are the changes most likely to occur only to the elderly in the Western world, or in the United States, or in the American middle class? Can the changes be readily altered by planned interventions that are presently within our power to carry out if we allocate the personal and financial resources?

Furthermore, we may wish to differentiate between changes in personality that derive from the interpersonal and psychological aspects of aging and those that result from changing health or from retirement. For example, that the elderly are more lonely than the nonelderly may reflect the greater likelihood that older persons will be living alone. Similarly, that older people think more about their bodies is probably a direct outcome of their being more likely to have a chronic disease or to be uncomfortable or in pain. Determining which causal factors are attributable to aging itself and which arise from events that accompany aging is not always possible; but we could attempt to compare young and old retirees, or young and old with chronic diseases. Although methodological difficulties are considerable, such studies would at least shed more light on this confusing issue.

The Research Findings

Probably the most consistent research finding on the relationship between aging and personality is that personality characteristics remain basically the same over the years (Botwinick, 1978; Ward, 1979a). This statement does not mean that older people do not change. Rather, it means that the personality qualities that exist in early and middle adulthood *tend* to exist when the person reaches the 60s and 70s.

One representative study, unusual in that it focused on rural elderly, followed people over a 19-year period (Britton & Britton, 1972). At its inception this study included almost all the elderly living in the designated area. However, attrition through illness, death, and relocation left a very small number of persons for the final analysis. The investigators found that some participants were better adjusted at the end of the study than they were at the beginning and that others seemed to be less well adjusted at the end of the 19-year period; however, the investigators found no differences between the two groups that would help to *predict* which elderly people will improve personal adjustment as they age. Given the competence of the initial planning and the thoroughness with which the study was conducted, this lack of distinguishable group patterns demonstrates the complexity of predicting personality characteristics in late adulthood and old age.

Another longitudinal study, which followed young adults for 40 years, did find some personality changes, but many of these could be accounted for by the changes in life situations of the aging participants. For example, women who went to work in their later adult years changed in ways that can be understood in terms of increased autonomy, a greater diversity of experiences, and access to a variety of kinds of people unlike those they had known before (Maas & Kuypers, 1974). This fact indicates that, when we state that personality does not change in the later years, we mean only that, although no overall pattern of change has consistently been found among the elderly, individuals *can* change in accordance with their ongoing experiences. The implication, I believe, is that old age does not shut off access to opportunities for personal growth and change.

Although the most significant research findings point to a basic continuity in personality across the adult years, this does not mean that *no* general changes have been found. Neugarten (1977) proposes that only one change occurs with reasonable consistency: increase in introversion. Introverted older people focus more on their inner lives than on the external environment; rather than try to change the world around them, they are concerned with themselves and their inner worlds. Neugarten's proposition is certainly consistent with the familiar observation that younger people work diligently to change the world and to move up the ladder of success, whereas older people accept the world as it is (even though they may not like it) and are less aggressive and less competitive than younger people.

Other indications of introversion in older people are that they often need to be with other people less and they often find satisfaction from reminiscence, fantasy, dreams, and meditation more than younger people. To the observer this pattern may indicate withdrawal, and the disengagement theorists may have been describing the results of increased introversion when they claimed that adjustment to late adulthood is improved by the pulling back from each other of the older individual and those in his or her social milieu (Cumming & Henry, 1961).

Other research findings support the observation that older people tend to turn inward "with a diminished intensity of energy and affect" (Botwinick, 1978, p. 82). The authors of an earlier review of the literature also concluded that sociability diminishes with age (Chown & Heron, 1965). According to still other studies, older people become increasingly cautious and less impulsive (Botwinick, 1978; Riley et al., 1968); they are more rigid and less flexible (Riley et al., 1968; Schaie & Strother, 1968); and they see the world as more complex and dangerous (Neugarten, 1968). Reduced sociability, increased caution, less impulsiveness, greater rigidity, increased perception of danger—all of these, it would seem, can combine to form the introverted personality, a person who is reluctant to try to have an impact on the external environment.

Further confirmation of the introversion/withdrawal proposition comes from an anthropologically oriented psychologist who investigated several different cultures, including the Navajo people, Mayans in Mexico, and an Arab community in Israel. In each society, as men became older, they tended to move from active mastery to passive mastery to magical mastery (Gutmann, 1969, 1974). Active mastery is, in effect, working toward autonomy, competence, and control, depending on one's own physical strength and aggressive verbal persuasiveness; passive mastery requires that the individual change to fit the demands of those in control; magical mastery depends on the use of ritual and magic to influence the physical and social environments, and people who used magical mastery often confused their personal wishes with real actions.

As you examine the kinds of behavior just described, you may see them as adding up to a kind of hopelessness. Perhaps older people withdraw and move into a richer inner life because it seems hopeless, given their reduced physical strength and energy and a rapidly diminishing futurity, to attempt to produce change directly. Hopelessness, of course, would give rise to depression, and this too is seen frequently among the elderly (Botwinick, 1978), although their depression is often masked by attempts at denial and further obscured by the tendency of many people to ignore the complaints of the elderly (Goldfarb, 1967).

One more set of research findings complicates an already complex subject: as they age, women often change in ways contrary to the ways men change. Cross-cultural research shows that women in both the United States and other cultures shift to more domineering, more active behavior, whereas men seek to become more passive, more nurturing, and more involved in developing personal relationships (Gutmann, 1975).

Do these changes, assuming that future research confirms their existence, result from inevitable occurrences in the later years, such as the loss of loved ones and the awareness of one's own proximity to death? Or are they caused by diminished feelings of meaningfulness and loss of status through retirement and reduced income? Or both sets of factors? Or something else altogether? The answer is important if we are to combat the hopelessness and depression. Although we don't know the answers, we do know one approach to avoid: don't tell older people "Stop worrying—you'll be around a long time"—or any other statement that says to them that their fears are absurd. What that tells them is that you don't see or understand their world and that you are unwilling to become involved in their concerns.

If you have found the sometimes contradictory or ambiguous statements in this chapter irritating and frustrating, gerontologists share your feelings. When we discuss personality changes in the later years, we must try to sail a narrow course between the Scylla of grandiose, all-encompassing statements with little supportive research and the Charybdis of overly cautious statements based only on finely detailed, compulsively executed studies of highly limited segments of behavior.

One point, however, is very clear—at least to me. The tendency of older people to become increasingly introverted stems from two sets of causes, as indicated in Table 4-1. One set is essentially the stresses of later years, and introversion results from hopelessness and depression; the other is essentially the recognition of the richness of the inner world and of the reduced need to respond to social demands for success and participation. I believe that too many people—gerontologists and geriatricians among them—react with distress to this moving into an inner life and that they pressure older people to remain elderly versions of middle-aged people. Rather than aiding the elderly, they may actually be interfering with the positive consequences of a natural and significant process. The difficulty, of course, is determining how to reduce the stressful aspects of later life that lead to introversion through depression and hopelessness while encouraging the enriching aspects of healthy reminiscing and spiritual well-being.

Successful Aging

Success is in the eye of the beholder, and individual differences are as great in the perception of successful aging as in the perception of being a successful parent or salesperson or politician. Four possible definitions of successful aging have been suggested:

1. *A way of life that is socially desirable for this age group.* This definition assumes that society in general knows what is best for older people. For example, if the weight of social pressure directs older people to be submissive, uncomplaining, accommodating, cheerful, and active in social organizations, these characteristics become the criteria for successful aging. The views of the elderly themselves, although reflected in this definition, are not paramount.
2. *Maintenance of middle-age activities.* This definition assumes that the more older people function and behave as they did when they were younger—the more they are like a middle-aged person—the more successfully they are aging. This line of thought is ageism at its worst, but it is implicitly (although rarely explicitly) accepted by many professionals and nonprofessionals. (Intriguingly enough, we often respond to young people on the same basis; that is, the more they resemble middle-aged adults in their behavior, demeanor, and values, the "better" they are.)
3. *A feeling of satisfaction with one's present status and activities.* This definition presupposes that older people's feelings of success primarily reflect how active they are and whether their health status, financial status, and so forth are adequate.
4. *A feeling of happiness and satisfaction with one's life.* This definition "assumes that a person who is aging successfully feels satisfaction with his present and his past life" (Havighurst, 1961, p. 10). To measure life satisfaction, five components were defined and five relevant rating scales developed by one group of investigators (Neugarten, Havighurst, & Tobin, 1961). The components selected were (1) zest versus apathy (enthusiasm and ego involvement versus listlessness and boredom, whether alone or in interaction with others); (2) resolution and fortitude (willingness to accept personal responsibility for one's own life versus either blaming oneself overmuch or placing blame on others); (3) relationships between desired goals and achieved goals (extent to which aspirations were accomplished during one's past lifetime and are being realized at present); (4) self-concept; and (5) mood tone (happiness, optimism, and spon-

> taneity versus sadness, loneliness, and bitterness). These components should be of more than passing concern because they have formed the basis for a great deal of research and speculation in the field of aging.

Any definition of successful aging actually turns out to be, at least in part, evidence of the values of the person offering the definition. For example, one highly active older woman decided that there was no excuse for any retired person's not making contributions of time and effort to the community, and she explicitly defined successful aging as the extent of this contribution.

Successful Aging and Life Satisfaction

Recent research on changes in life satisfaction across the life span has produced some interesting results. In one major study 14 "domains," or areas, of life satisfaction were developed, as well as an overall life-satisfaction score and a measure of subjective happiness. On the whole, younger persons claimed greater happiness but less overall life-domain satisfaction than older people. Life-domain satisfaction was about average for persons 55–64 years of age, then rose substantially for the next decade before falling back slightly for people 75 years old and older. Happiness, in contrast, was moderately high for those 55–64 years old, fell to below average for the next decade, and then fell steeply among those over 75 to the lowest of any age group (Campbell, Converse, & Rodgers, 1976).

When we look at the individual domains, the life-satisfaction data begin to make more sense. Satisfaction in nine domains, such as leisure activities, neighborhood, community, and life in the United States, rises fairly steadily with age from the 20s through the 60s, then drops slightly thereafter. Satisfaction with family rises in the 50s and remains above average; marital satisfaction begins to rise in the 50s and moves rapidly upward. Only satisfaction with health is high in the early years and moves steadily and rapidly downward thereafter (Campbell et al., 1976).

One might question the preceding data on the basis of older people's wishing to present themselves with undue optimism, but that would not explain the drop in self-ratings of happiness. (Of course, these interviews were conducted in the early 1970s—responses might differ today.) It seems as though, except for health, older people *on the whole*, and especially those under 75, are not particularly dissatisfied with most of their life domains. It is not lack of friends, poor family relationships, inadequate income, or housing problems that they find especially distressing. Rather, it is apparently other factors, including health and—perhaps—reduced futurity, lack of meaningfulness, and losses in functional capacity, that produce their unhappiness.

The authors of an earlier study used lengthy interviews to examine sources of high morale or life satisfaction among a group of 65 elderly people in San Francisco, half of whom lived in the community and half in longer-term care facilities of some sort. These researchers developed six general themes, from the information shown in Table 4-2, that serve as the basis for high morale, life satisfaction, or self-perceived successful aging: (1) sufficient autonomy to permit continued integrity of the self; (2) agreeable relationships with other people, some of whom are willing to provide help when needed without losing respect for the aging; (3) a reasonable amount of personal comfort in body and mind and in one's physical environment; (4) stimulation of the mind and imagination in ways that do not overtax physical strength; (5) sufficient mobility to permit variety in one's surroundings; and (6) some form of intense involvement with life, partly in order to escape preoccupation with death (Clark & Anderson, 1967).

One particularly cogent issue regarding successful aging still remains unresolved and, indeed, virtually unexplored. People commonly assume that those who have led satisfying lives find it easier to grow old. They believe that these older people feel fulfilled, that they do not see themselves as cheated, and that they are able to reminisce satisfactorily. Moreover, they may well retain more resources—personal, spiritual, social, physical, financial—than do those whose young and middle years were less satisfying. Nonetheless, another kind of logic can be applied. For a highly energetic and active person, for someone who is productive and involved, the losses

Table 4-2. Sources of high and low morale for 65 elderly San Francisco residents.

Sources of High Morale	*Percentage Reporting This Factor*
Entertainments and diversions	69%
Socializing	57
Productive activity	54
Physical comfort (other than health)	52
Financial security	46
Mobility and movement	40
Health, stamina, survival	20
Sources of Low Morale	*Percentage Reporting This Factor*
Dependency (financial or physical)	60%
Physical discomfort or sensory loss	57
Loneliness, bereavement, loss of nurturance	50
Boredom, inactivity, immobility, confinement	38
Mental discomfort or loss	18
Loss of prestige or respect	12
Fear of dying	10

From Clark, M., & Anderson, B. C. *Culture and Aging*, 1967. Courtesy of Charles C Thomas, Publisher, Springfield, Illinois.

that aging sometimes brings can be even more destructive than for a person with more limited aspirations.

I once met an older man who was embarrassed to be seen in a bathing suit. Was his difficulty partly created by his remembrance of how good he once looked in a bathing suit? Is the person who never looked appealing better off when age begins to change his or her appearance? Similar questions can be posed when we consider the high achiever. The difference in accomplishments between work and retirement is slight for the low achiever, but the high achiever is removed from a major source of satisfaction when prevented from working. Are earlier successes detrimental to later feelings of success in aging? Or does the memory of earlier success compensate for current awareness that potential future achievement is limited?

These as yet unanswered questions lead us to another concern: can we provide any kind of planned intervention, educational or experiential, that will increase the likelihood of successful aging? These possibilities will be discussed in Chapter Seven.

Disengagement

"I'd rather live a full life and die when I'm 40 then live until I'm 70 and watch the fullness of my life slowly dribble away." This and similar statements have been made by any number of 20- and 30-year-olds (although by very few 39-year-olds). Being fully involved and absorbed in life is often viewed as one criterion of successful *living* (see the earlier "zest versus apathy"), but the picture grows hazy when we try to judge successful *aging*.

"At successive ages, people become more preoccupied with the inner life than with events in the external environment. . . . There is also less willingness to deal with wide ranges of stimuli or with complicated and challenging situations" (Neugarten, 1972, p. 10). At the same time that the individual is withdrawing from society, society tends to withdraw from the individual. This process of mutual withdrawal in the later years has been termed *disengagement*; it results in reduced social roles, social relationships, and feelings of meaningfulness in the elderly (Cumming & Henry, 1961).

Two kinds of disengagement have been described: (1) social disengagement, which refers to reducing the number and duration of social interactions, and (2) psychological disengagement, which refers to reducing the extent of one's emotional commitment to or involvement with these relationships and with what is going on in the world in general (Havighurst, Neugarten, & Tobin, 1968). Although they are related, these two forms of disengagement are not identical. Some people have many social interactions but experience minimal personal involvement in them. Others have very few social contacts but may maintain a strong commitment to these few.

When the concept of disengagement was initially applied to the elderly, it was not only proposed as a descriptive theory of what occurs but also posited as an inevitable, natural occurrence (rather than one imposed by other individuals or by social institutions and forces), and it was thought to be a positive, adaptive approach to successful aging (Cumming & Henry, 1961).

There is "convincing evidence of decline in both social and psychological engagement with increasing age. Disengagement seems to us to be a useful term by which to describe these processes of change" (Havighurst et al., 1968, p. 171). Pressures on the older person and his or her social milieu to disengage from each other come from three related, but far from identical, quarters:

1. The social structure undergoes change. This process is evident when family roles, work roles, power sources, and so forth change to place pressure on older people to restructure their lives. Their responses are likely to be in the direction of both social and psychological disengagement.
2. Signals come from within the body. "The aches and pains, the reduced energy level, the sporadic forgetfulness, the added nuisance of some chronic illness that must be coped with, all these turn the individual into himself and persuade those in his community to withdraw from him" (Kalish, 1972, p. 87).
3. With an increasing awareness that their future is limited and that death is not only inevitable but no longer far distant, older persons may be more likely to attend to themselves and to whatever is extremely important to them, simultaneously pushing away whatever is not extremely important. The ultimate example of this behavior has been observed in the terminally ill patients who exclude from their bedside all but the two or three persons closest to them (Kübler-Ross, 1969).

But to establish that disengagement occurs is not the same as to establish that disengagement is a natural or inevitable process, and most certainly it is not the same as to claim that disengagement is a positive aid in successful aging. When disengagement does occur, it does *not* inevitably lead to successful aging. One study of 250 older people (Maddox, 1963) showed that their morale was directly related to their level of activity. Furthermore, increased activity levels over time were predictive of increased morale, and decreased activity levels were predictive of decreased morale.

The majority of both popular and professional opinions supports the idea that not only are involvement and activity helpful in successful aging but they also may even help in maintaining survival itself. Nonetheless, one of the best studies on this matter (Havighurst et al., 1968) supports both the activity theory of optimal aging and the disengagement theory, ending with the statement that neither theory is sufficient to account for all the changes that occur. The researchers postulate two concurrent forces within the lives of the older person, one pressing for withdrawal and enjoyment of a more leisurely way of life, the other requiring activity in order to retain a sense of self-worth. And they also remind us that even those elderly people who disengage from role activities are not likely to disengage from the social values they have internalized over the decades. In the final analysis, disengagement is an inadequate response for some; for others, it is adaptive; and, for still others, it is merely the continuation of previously established behavior patterns.

Patterns of Successful Aging

As research on disengagement continues, it becomes increasingly obvious that neither the disengagement theory nor the activity theory is sufficient to define successful accommodation to aging. Following a different approach, Bühler (1961) describes four accommodation patterns, two successful and two much less successful. Older people may (1) wish to rest and relax, content that they have completed their necessary life work; (2) want to remain active and do so; (3) lack the strength, ability, or determination to continue their work (even though they are not fully satisfied with their accomplishments), but feel forced to accept their limitations and resign themselves, often unhappily, to their situations; or (4) feel frustrated and guilt-ridden, having led lives that they now find meaningless.

To these four patterns, I would like to add another: (5) people may, regardless of the degree of previous satisfaction they experienced, find in their later years some meaningful activities or relationships that compensate for whatever changes old age has required of them. One such person, a retired economics professor who was in his 90s when I first met him, had spent more than 20 years engrossed in raising chrysanthemums, developing hybrids, and establishing an organization for others who shared his love for these flowers. When a series of strokes forced him into a convalescent-care facility, he continued to work in the institution's garden, regretting only that his 40 or 50 hours of involvement per week had to be diminished.

If you refer to the five criteria for life satisfaction just listed, you will note the relationship between the patterns Bühler (1961) considers most successful in aging (the first two) and Havighurst and his associates' (1968) notion that zest and relationship between desired and achieved goals are two major components of high morale.

Two other studies shed light on successful patterns of aging. Although both were restricted to relatively small numbers of participants, both sets of investigators spent a great deal of time with each subject. One project grouped people in five categories based on their adjustment to aging: (1) the mature type, (2) the rocking-chair type, (3) the armored type (those who depend on an elaborate set of defenses to ward off the anxieties of the aging process), (4) the angry type, and (5) the self-haters (Reichard, Livson, & Petersen, 1962). The terms are essentially self-explanatory.

In many instances the person's mode of adapting to old age was a direct outgrowth of a long-term adjustment pattern. For example, the rocking-chair type "welcomed the chance provided by old age and retirement to take it easy. Society grants, in old age, permission to indulge needs for passivity and dependence that it does not grant young people. Thus they were free to be more truly themselves" (Reichard et al., 1962, p. 130). This passage suggests that one kind of lifestyle is more adaptive for people's retirement than for their earlier years.

An inevitable hazard in such research is that the investigator, or other concerned persons who are primarily young or middle-aged (or, even, unusually active and engaged older persons), will define successful aging according to how *they* believe they will want to live when they are old. If not properly aware of this tendency, gerontologists and geriatricians may not perceive that many rocking-chair types have made a very adequate adjustment to aging. Many nonelderly people who are well aware of the difficulties the elderly experience in accepting the values and behavior of younger people are themselves unable to grasp what it would be like to be old. They fail to perceive that the elderly, even if they had been highly engaged in earlier years, might wish to withdraw or disengage to some extent. Similarly, highly active people of any age often have little sympathy and absolutely no empathy for people who prefer to avoid active involvement.

In the second project Neugarten, Havighurst, and Tobin (1968) went a step further. They not only categorized personality types but related these types to role activities and life satisfaction. Working with 59 men and women in their 70s, they found that those termed *integrated* all had high life satisfaction, regardless of the extent of their role activity. The "armored/defended" elderly had high life-satisfaction levels if they were active, but two of the four people with low activity levels lacked high satisfaction. Among the "passive/dependent" and the "unintegrated," high activity levels were rare, and medium and low life satisfaction were common. These investigators concluded that "in normal men and women, there is no sharp discontinuity of personality with age, but instead an increasing consistency. Those characteristics that have been central to the personality seem to become even more clearly delineated, and those values the individual has been cherishing become even more salient" (p. 177).

Clearly, the relative roles that disengagement and activity play in the later years (and, very likely, throughout the life span) are only beginning to come into focus. The importance of these roles makes this area a fruitful and necessary one for continued investigation, through both formal research and careful clinical observation. Neugarten (1972) offers an appropriate concluding statement:

> There is no single pattern by which people grow old, and . . . older persons, like younger ones, will choose the combinations of activities that offer them

> the most ego-involvement and that are the most consonant with their long-established value patterns and self-concepts. Aging is not a leveler of individual differences except, perhaps, at the very end of life [p. 13].

Adult Socialization and Roles

First, two definitions: (1) "Socialization encompasses the group of processes that result in the development of the individual into a social being capable of participating in society. Socialization is learning that either directly or indirectly affects the individual's ability to function socially" (Atchley, 1980, pp. 69–70). (2) A role is the *behavior expected of an individual who occupies a particular position in the social scheme.* Such positions in society include age, leadership, vocation, and innumerable others.

Your initial socialization into the adult role and into the role of an older person began when you were very young and you became aware of what is expected of adults and of older adults. As you grew older, your perceptions of these roles underwent change, based on your observations of how adults behave and what is expected of them. Socialization, however, does not end when childhood ends. *Adult socialization* refers to the continued socialization during the adult years, the internalizing of new values and forms of behavior consistent with the changing positions and roles of the adult years (Rosow, 1965). The perception a child has of the role of an older person often changes when the child views the later years from the position of an adult. Thus, the expectations each of us has regarding the role of the elderly change as we become older and our own life situation changes.

In this regard, you might ask yourself how you believe you will act, feel, and think when you are an older person. How do you expect to behave when you are 65 or 80? How do you feel an older person is supposed to act, think, and feel? Differently from a middle-aged person or an adolescent?

One line in a musical comedy song describes a Jenny who lets her skirts down and puts her hair up. As a young woman now, instead of a child, her role calls for longer skirts and pinned-up hair. What do older women do about their dress and their hair in our society, and to what extent is style of dress and hair determined by convenience, by response to society's expectations, and by the overriding preference of the older people themselves?

The Roles of Older People

The role of the older person in our society is sometimes described as a "roleless role" because there are no expected ways of behaving (Burgess, 1950). However, I don't believe this is the case. In fact, I see two things occurring: (1) in some ways the expectations for persons who have recently reached retirement age are continuous with the expectations for people in their 40s or 50s; and (2) in other ways the expectations for older persons are discontinuous and do change abruptly—for example, being retired, a grandparent or great-grandparent, or a Medicare recipient is quite different from being a worker, a parent, or a group-insurance recipient.

In some cultures the roles of older men and women are carefully delineated. In rural Japan the elderly who are in adequate health are traditionally expected to have technical knowledge of weather and soil conditions and to contribute to the family by repairing tools, sewing, doing light housework, and looking after the children so the parents can tend to the farm (Kiefer, 1974). They are taken care of by their oldest son and his wife, who are frequently subservient to the older couple. An older person in the rural United States or in rural Canada may also contribute in some of these ways, but the expectations will be fewer and less specific.

This has not always been the case. Some 30 years ago the elderly in one typical rural community studied had been socialized to be active in the church; spend much time with age peers; develop a special interest, such as gardening, or a hobby involved with collecting things; be deeply concerned about grandchildren or great-grandchildren; retain contact with their grown children while maintaining considerable autonomy; and avoid financial dependence as long as possible (Havighurst & Albrecht, 1953). The situation today is not always different, but now these values must compete with more contemporary options: to be politically active, to receive religious sustenance through televised sermons in order to avoid dealing with urban transportation problems, to watch television rather than be actively involved, to attend a senior center rather than gossiping at the store, gas station, or church.

Role expectations for the elderly seem to be becoming more flexible. True, some people still appear to assume that older people *should* retire, *should* be asexual, *should* be cautious, *should* dress sedately, or *should* prefer quiet activities to more lively ones. But the rigid role prescriptions of the earlier part of this century seem to have diminished.

Age-role behavior has never been totally fixed—there has always been some flexibility, especially in societies like ours that reflect so many cultural patterns brought by people from Europe, Asia, and Africa. Given the diversity of lifestyles in the United States and Canada, an older person who found the role expectations of the mainstream unpalatable could frequently find a group of people who would respect his or her preferences.

Table 4-3 shows some of the age-related functions believed to be age-appropriate by one group of respondents some 20 years ago. You are likely to have different ideas, although you may still expect people to "act their age." Older people who deviate from your expectations in a positive fashion—a 70-year-old woman who camps out and takes long hikes—may please you with their acting outside the boundaries of your anticipated age role. More often, however, a deviation is seen as negative. A 60-year-old widower who prefers the company of 20-year-olds to that of his own age group may elicit snickers and jokes. What are your feelings about the age ranges that most people in the study summarized in Table 4-3 designated as appropriate or expected?

Although some of the restricting role expectations for older persons may be diminishing, there are losses along with the gains. There is the claim that young people don't respect their elders "the way they used to." However, if my impressions are correct, this comment is heard much less frequently now than 20 years ago. Perhaps the position of the elderly is afforded greater respect; perhaps the great presumed respect for the elderly is now buried too deep in the past to be recalled by many still living. Or perhaps this great respect was more a part of the tradition of the "old country" (Italy, Ireland, Greece, Japan, Poland, Hungary) than of the United States or Canada. Simić (1978) reports an elderly man in Yugoslavia as saying "When we were young we strived to please our elders, and now we must please the young. When are we to live?" (p. 78). The powerful hold of the elderly Japanese has also been broken in both Japan and the United States (Kiefer, 1974). You might contemplate ways in which this change has benefited the Japanese and ways in which it has been detrimental to their well-being.

Role Differences in Age Cohorts

People who are over 65 years old today experience their roles as older people in ways that differ from how they will be experienced by those who are 45 or 25 years old today. And, in turn, those who became 65 in 1960 or 1935 had still different experiences. One reason is simply the proportion of people in the population who are over 65; the increasing numbers and percentages offer older persons more potential age-peer companionship. Another reason is inflation: when you are living on a modest, largely fixed income, an inflationary economy produces frustration and anxiety not known to people in more financially stable times.

Not only do today's elderly face circumstances that differ from those of their predecessors and, undoubtedly, from those of their successors, but they bring their own unique characteristics to the situation. If you were 65 or over in 1935, the chances were slim that you had ever been divorced, that you had a college degree, or that you had ever been in an airplane; the chances were much greater than today that you had arrived in the country as an immigrant, that English was a second language for you, and that you had lived much of your life in poverty. You probably also experienced your children's moving up the socioeconomic ladder, whereas the chances were that you weren't eligible for the forthcoming Social Security program, that you had never even conceived of what would later be called Medicare, and that you wanted to work as long as you could because you had no money and the Great Depression had wiped out what little savings you had previously accumulated.

This is a very different picture from that faced by the newly elderly today. To carry the picture along, compare two men, each 65, but one born

Table 4-3. Consensus in a middle-class, middle-aged sample of 50 men and 43 women regarding various age-related characteristics.

	Age Range Designated as Appropriate or Expected	*Percentage Who Concurred*	
		Men	*Women*
Best age for a man to marry	20–25	80%	90%
Best age for a woman to marry	19–24	85	90
When most people should become grandparents	45–50	84	79
Best age for most people to finish school and go to work	20–22	86	82
When most men should be settled on a career	24–26	74	64
When most men hold their "top" jobs	45–50	71	58
When most people should be ready to retire	60–65	83	86
A young man	18–22	84	83
A middle-aged man	40–50	86	75
An old man	65–75	75	57
A young woman	18–24	89	88
A middle-aged woman	40–50	87	77
An old woman	60–75	83	87
When a man has the most responsibilities	35–50	79	75
When a man accomplishes most	40–50	82	71
The prime of life for a man	35–50	86	80
When a woman has the most responsibilities	25–40	93	91
When a woman accomplishes most	30–45	94	92
A good-looking woman	20–35	92	82

From Neugarten, B. L., Moore, J. W., & Lowe, J. C. Age norms, age constraints, and age socialization. *American Journal of Sociology*, 1965, *70*, 710–717. © 1965 by the University of Chicago Press. Reprinted by permission.

in 1898 and the other in 1918. How did each experience war? How old was each during World War I, World War II, the Korean and Vietnamese Wars? When in their lives did the depression of the early 1930s come along, and how might have its effects differed? What kind of world did each face at the age of 18? Of 35?

Then repeat the exercise for women. How might the changing roles of women in our society affect women becoming 65 in 1963 differently from those for whom 1983 marks the 65th birthday? How might life be different for women who won't be 65 until the year 2003? It obviously matters a great deal whether you experienced the power of the women's movement when you were in your middle 70s, your middle 50s, or your middle 30s.

Neither age nor age cohort is the only factor that determines when someone faces a particular role. We have grandparents at 37, retirees at 38 (after 20 years in the military, for example), people who face their own death following a chronic disease at any age. When a person experiences life under conditions that resemble those associated with older people, that person frequently thinks and behaves much like an older person who lives under the same conditions. I vividly recall having a temporary hearing loss when I was 25 years old. I had so much difficulty being with my friends that I decided to isolate myself until I could visit my physician. The difference, of course, was that my condition was remediable, whereas the hearing defects of most elderly are not. It was not that I "felt" old, but that I behaved in much the same way that older people with similar disabilities behave.

Group Identification

Ask people to tell you who they are in a series of phrases. They will probably respond by citing sex, education or vocation, ethnicity, national origin, religion, community, and, eventually, age. The designation of old or elderly is often not highly salient for people who would normally be thus defined. Anyone who has worked in a senior center or some other program or facility for the elderly has heard the comment "I don't want to be around all those old people"—even though the speaker is chronologically older than most of those he or she is referring to. Many people in their 60s and 70s refer to themselves as middle-aged.

Being socialized to the age role of "senior citizen" is often perceived as a step down in status and power. The behavior, values, and performance levels expected for this role can easily have negative valence, and this age group is the only one from which there is no escape. There are younger people who comment that they would rather die young than live to be old.

In recent years more and more older people appear to identify as a member of a group defined by age. Are the elderly, then, a minority group? My own reaction is that they are not. They certainly don't share a distinctive and separate culture. On the one hand, membership in the group is almost universal; on the other hand, the group encompasses only one part of the life cycle (G. F. Streib, 1965). But the major issue is the extent of identification the elderly have with other elderly people as part of a "collective consciousness" (G. F. Streib, 1965, p. 46). It is probable that political consciousness of age-group membership has been raised by organizations such as the Gray Panthers and the National Council of Senior Citizens, but *active* membership does not seem high enough in these and other groups to turn an aggregate of individuals into a self-aware group.

The Role of the Older Woman

An inevitable danger in a book like this is to discuss older people in general and ignore the differences between groups and among individuals within groups. Such differences are apparent, for example, between the circumstances faced by older women and those faced by older men. And even here there is the danger of ignoring differences on another level if we combine women who were physicians with those who spent their working lives as department-store clerks, or women who worked all their adult lives with women who never worked, or women who have many attentive children and grandchildren with women who are childless, and so on.

The interest in older women came late in both the women's movement and in the surge of interest in aging; as late as 1972, an article could appear accusing the women's movement of ignoring the elderly (Lewis & Butler, 1972). More recently, the older woman has been the subject of a substantial number of articles, academic publications, and conferences, with much emphasis on the double jeopardy of older women in comparison to older men (that is, women are in jeopardy because they are old and because they are women) (M. M. Seltzer, 1979).

Are older women truly worse off than older men? After all, they do live longer and remain in better health; they do adapt to change more readily; and they are emotionally better prepared for old age (M. M. Seltzer, 1979). One author has chronicled the other side of the story:

1. More than half of older women are not presently married; the great majority of these are widows. Therefore, older women are forced into the company of other older women, whether they wish to be or not, because of the lack of men and the unlikelihood of the existence of extended families.
2. Older women are much more likely than older men to live alone, and this at an age when transportation may be a problem and when fears for personal security reduce mobility.
3. Older women must live on a considerably lower income than men, whether the comparison is made between working women and working men or nonworking women and nonworking men (Miller, 1978).

These are the practical problems of life, those faced by all older people and particularly by older women. Older women also appear to be more depressed than older men (M. M. Seltzer, 1979) and to have lower self-esteem (Turner, 1979). Even the women's movement has not had a uniformly positive effect on older women. On the one hand, many older women have supported the women's movement from the beginning, and others have come to support it over the years; the growth of opportunities for women was applauded by many women in their later years. On the other hand, some older women have expressed bitterness that the opportunities created by the women's movement are too late to help them. They now see themselves as having spent a lifetime deprived of equality, whereas younger women are offered wonderful opportunities. What proportion of women feel this anger is not known—it may be many, or it may be only a small percentage—but what one recently widowed 66-year-old said probably represents what others have felt: "Thank God I'll never have to take orders from a man again."

Do the disadvantages of older women begin in the later years, or are they merely continuations of a lifetime of being "one down"? In many instances it seems obvious that the disadvantages of women follow them throughout their lives.

Last Comments

When I first began to teach psychology, a professor on the verge of retirement told me his two basic principles of human behavior: people are alike, and people are different. These principles certainly apply to older people. In many ways they are very much as they were when they were younger; they also differ in other ways. Similarly, in many ways they are like younger people, especially those with similar backgrounds; in other ways they differ.

I was once told of a man, a specialist in recreation, who had recently begun working with older people after 15 years of working with adolescents. He knew that the elderly need exercise and movement, just as much as and perhaps more than younger people; he was warm, cordial, and concerned. What he did not take into account are the differences in reaction time and the diminished capacity for violent movement of the elderly. Therefore, he put the participants in his exercise class through such rapid calisthenics that the elderly who were not in excellent condition could not keep up with him. Nor did he bother learning what kinds of exercises are especially relevant for people with arthritis, for people who have been smoking for 50 years, or for people who are embarrassed about their bodies. When attendance dropped to near zero, he concluded that older people don't want to exercise, and he canceled the course. We are all alike. We are all different.

In considering self-concept, personality, and roles in older people, we need to be aware of the changes that inevitably come with age, the changes that our society imposes on older persons, the era in which older people were initially socialized into various beliefs and values, and the immediate situations in which they find themselves.

Chapter Five

Relating to Others

Myths die hard. People seem to struggle to hold onto the notions that children are asexual beings, that individuals who threaten suicide will never make a serious attempt, and that dying persons will fall apart if they are informed of their prognosis. Add another to the list: older people are usually lonely, lack friends and confidants, and are alienated from their children.

The data consistently indicate just the opposite. When asked what they believed were "very serious" problems for "most people over 65," 61% of the younger and 56% of the older respondents cited loneliness as second only to low income. However, when the respondents were asked about "very serious" problems "for you personally," the numbers dropped dramatically: only 12% of the older persons indicated loneliness as a serious personal problem; low income, poor health, and fear of crime were all more important. Further, 7% of the nonelderly described loneliness as a very serious personal problem (Harris & Associates, 1975). Apparently, loneliness is a significant problem for quite a few people, regardless of age, but it affects only a fraction of the number it is believed to affect.

Table 5-1 provides one kind of picture of the family and friendship contacts of older persons. It does not, of course, say anything about the quality of those contacts; perhaps they are brief or unpleasant. Nor does it prove that older people cannot be lonely, since loneliness is a subjective feeling, and it is possible to have many social relationships and still be lonely or, conversely, to have few or no contacts and not feel lonely at all. Finally, the table does not provide information about contacts with casual friends and neighbors or, for that matter, with spouses.

Family relationships and friendships diminish as the elderly move into their late 70s and beyond. Health limitations and mobility problems restrict the ability of the older person to be with close friends or family, and the illnesses or deaths of age peers further reduce opportunities for social contacts. Harris and Associates (1975) devised a scale of social and family

Table 5-1. Contacts of younger and older persons with friends and family.

Contact		Last Seen				
		Within Last Day or So (or Living with)	*Within Last Week or So*	*A Month Ago*	*2–3 Months Ago*	*Longer Than That*
Close friends						
18–64	97%*	64%	30%	3%	1%	2%
65 and over	94%	60	31	5	2	2
Children						
18–64	73%	87	8	2	1	2
65 and over	81%	55	26	8	3	8
Brothers and sisters						
18–64	91%	31	31	12	6	20
65 and over	79%	22	22	15	10	31
Parents						
18–64	70%	48	24	9	5	14
65 and over	4%	32	23	8	11	26
Grandchildren						
65 and over	75%	46	28	10	5	11
Grandparents						
18–64	30%	24	10	18	8	30

*The percentage of respondents in this age group who had such relationships.

Reprinted from *The Myth and Reality of Aging in America*, a study prepared by Louis Harris and Associates, Inc. for The National Council on the Aging, Inc., Washington, D.C. © 1975.

involvement and administered it to both elderly and nonelderly adults. The two groups fared virtually identically, but of particular interest was the finding that involvement scores dropped steadily between the ages of 18 and 65, jumped up during the late 60s, dropped slightly during the 70s, and then fell sharply during the 80s. Presumably, those who have just retired enjoy a surge of social contacts that diminishes only slightly in their 70s. It isn't until the very late years that contacts with family members and friends become painfully few.

Older people actually have many family roles: parent, spouse, aunt or uncle, cousin, brother or sister, and, not infrequently, the child of living parents. Of course, older people are likely to be grandparents or great-grandparents; even five-generation families are not unknown. They also have many kinds of friendship roles, ranging from casual acquaintances or organization colleagues to very close friends and confidants.

One role that relatively few older people have, however, is that of part of a three-generation household. Such households have never been an everyday occurrence. Multigenerational families in the same household appear to be neither less nor more common today than they were a century ago (Beresford & Rivlin, 1969), amounting to about 8% of all U.S. families (Troll, Miller, & Atchley, 1979).

Husbands and Wives

The marital relationship is one of the most important—perhaps the most important—relationships experienced in the adult years. Satisfaction with marriage reaches its low in middle age and rises thereafter (Atchley & Miller, 1980), with the elderly expressing greater marital satisfaction than any other age group (Campbell, Converse, & Rodgers, 1976).

The marital relationship is just as dynamic and just as changeable in the later years as it is during any other period of life. One source describes changes from preretirement through late retirement. When the couple are between 55 and 65, most husbands and wives still live together, and most men and almost half of the women are working. Although only 70% of all women are married at this age, 87% of the preretirement men are (Brotman, 1981). Children have usually left the home, and earnings are fairly high with two incomes. Husbands and wives experience greater closeness and companionship and give strongly positive descriptions of each other (Lowenthal, Thurnher, & Chiriboga, 1975).

During the 65–74 decade, the death rate for men increases rapidly; 81% of the men are still married, but only 49% of the women are, and very few of either group are still employed (Brotman, 1981). The role of the husband shifts from that of provider to that of helper, and the role of the wife demands that she provide a greater amount of love and understanding than before (Troll, 1971). Now the husband spends much more of his time at home. Marital relationships that were sustained largely because the wife and husband were busy and could avoid encountering each other may become stressful. As one woman expressed it, "I married him for better or for worse, but not for lunch."

In the late retirement stage, husband and wife are over 75, and 69% of the men but only 22% of the women still have spouses (Brotman, 1981), and some of these represent remarriages. Health becomes a much greater source of concern, and wives become more dominant in the marital relationship than at any other age, undoubtedly in part as a function of the diminished health of the husband (Troll et al., 1979).

Overall, the picture of marriage in the later years is a very positive one, disturbed primarily by health problems and by the eventual death of one spouse, usually the husband. However, a large proportion of the people discussed so far have been married 30, 40, even 50 or more years. Given the present high divorce rate of young and middle-aged people, the future picture may differ, since increasing numbers of marriages of older persons will have been for briefer periods. In addition, these people will be involved with children and grandchildren not related by blood to or brought up by both partners.

When Marriages Fail

In spite of the basically favorable picture of marriage in the later years, there are about 5000 to 6000 divorces involving people over 65 each year, and the divorce rate for people who have been married 25 years or more has risen in keeping with increases in the overall divorce rate. It is no longer unusual to hear a 68-year-old woman talk about having wanted a divorce for 20 years but needing that long a time to gain the courage.

But the divorce rate for older people is not a complete measure of unhappy marriages. For every late-life divorce there are countless unhappy marriages, often with a long history of unhappiness. The new awareness of the importance of psychological services for couples and families has had almost no effect on providing such services to older persons whose marriages are inadequate.

Sometimes a marriage that has held up reasonably well first runs into trouble in the later years. These difficulties represent "an attempt to manipulate and master the social environment, in order to decrease feelings of helplessness and fear at a time when certain essential needs are not being met" (Goldfarb, 1968, p. 117). Older people who have long received support from each other may find that, due to illness, increased dependency, or other factors, available support is no longer adequate. These marital stresses are often amenable to psychological treatment, even when they emerge in a marriage that has been less than adequate for a long time, but older people rarely seek professional help, and the professional helper is even more rarely capable of knowing how to help them.

Remarriage

Although divorce is still relatively uncommon among older people, remarriage is a familiar occurrence. In 1978 more than 57,000 persons over age 65 married, only 5% of these marrying for the first time, whereas 75% had been widows or widowers. Nearly two-thirds of older persons who marry are men (Brotman, 1981; Treas & VanHilst, 1976). Since men tend to marry younger women, since women tend to live longer than men, and since men in general are more likely to remarry, many more older men marry than older women. In fact, the ratio is roughly 6:1 (Troll et al., 1979).

According to one intensive study of 100 retirement marriages, companionship is the most important basis for remarriage late in life. The author believes that meaning and purpose in life can be enhanced by a good marital relationship and that these are often lacking for older people who live alone. Also identified as an important reason for remarriage was sexual satisfaction, which the author defined as embracing more than intercourse and as including many kinds of physical touching and emotional responsiveness. Financial and health reasons for remarriage were also cited (McKain, 1968).

A major impediment to remarriage is that women realize they are likely to be healthier than men their own age and are expected to marry men some years their senior. They may pull back rather than spend their future caring for an ill husband with whom they have not had the years to develop the intensity of commitment they had in their earlier marriage. Another barrier is adult children who don't wish their parent to remarry. The children may be concerned about inheritance; they may not understand their parent's need for companionship and a sexual relationship; they may be so attached to the memory of their deceased parent that the idea of the surviving parent's entering into another marriage is virtually blasphemous.

Widows and Widowers

In 1979 more than half of all women over 65 were widows. This proportion goes up to 70% among women 75 years of age and older (Brotman, 1981). There are six times as many widows as widowers among those aged 65 to 75 and nearly five times as many among those over 75 (Metropolitan Life Insurance Co., 1977). The sex differences undoubtedly result from three factors: women live longer than men, women marry men older than themselves, and more widowers remarry than widows (Bequaert, 1976). These are the same reasons found for the higher remarriage rate of men that was described earlier.

The most serious form of loss of family role occurs through the death of a family member, especially a spouse. "The cultural evolution that has made marriage an integral part of our social organization has done little to ensure that the functions that it performs will be adequately carried out after its dissolution" (Parkes, 1972, p. 8). As a result, the surviving widow or widower suffers not only the grief arising from the loss but also the deprivation that comes with the spouse's absence. Loneliness, lack of someone with whom to share affection and work tasks, and loss of sexual satisfactions are some of the deprivations that accompany the death of a spouse (Parkes, 1972). It is possible to find substitute relationships that alleviate the sense of deprivation without reducing the sense of loss and grief. Conversely, some survivors may never experience grief—and may even be somewhat pleased that an encumbering unhappy relationship has ceased—but may still feel deprived by the absence of the not-especially-loved dead person.

Stigmatization, as well as loss and deprivation, is often felt by a surviving spouse. The role expectations of an elderly unmarried person are quite different from those of an elderly married person or from those of a younger unmarried person. Friendship patterns change; adult children begin to talk of combining households (or at least they worry about it); the elderly person's motivation to cook good meals, to retain good grooming practices, and to keep a neat house may diminish. While the widow or widower often disengages, at least temporarily, from the social milieu, people in the environment seem to disengage from him or her even more, as though the widow or widower were stigmatized. Companionship, except with others of the same status, is often difficult to find. "People . . . previously friendly and approachable become embarrassed and strained" in the bereaved person's presence (Parkes, 1972, p. 8).

Older widows do not appear to share the significant increase in incidence of physical illness that younger widows undergo shortly after their bereavement. This fact may be partially explained by the phenomenon termed *rehearsal for widowhood.* This syndrome can begin in the middle or even in the younger years. The woman begins to anticipate what her life will be like when and if she is later widowed. In this way she can work through some of the emotional problems of widowhood before the actual occurrence. Elderly women, of course, have lived through the deaths of many others and have probably rehearsed extensively for widowhood. (Men undoubtedly experience a comparable phenomenon, but I believe that their rehearsal for widowerhood occurs less frequently and with less intensity.)

Widows tend to socialize with other women; some of them are previous friends who are still married, but many of them are also widows. Obviously, some widows maintain friendships with both members of a couple, but there is a strong tendency for couples to participate socially with other couples. In one study 38% of the widows stated that they had a less active social life than before the death of their husbands, but 43% claimed to have perceived no change, and 12% even had a more extensive social life (Lopata, 1973).

Bereavement requires that the elderly survivor abandon old assumptions about the world and begin to live with new ones. This transition can be difficult, and the survivor often feels the deceased person to be "still very close" or thinks of the dead "as though he were still alive and with me." Visiting with the dead in dreams, sensing the person's presence, or experiencing, seeing, hearing, or touching the dead is not uncommon (Parkes, 1970).

Whereas the older widow has a wide potential group of other widows to whom she can reach out for companionship, the older widower has relatively few male friends, although he is likely to feel somewhat compensated for this lack by the many widows available for social—and often sexual—relationships. The bereavement of the surviving husband can also be more disruptive than that of the surviving wife, because it requires him to undertake household tasks for which his previous experience and self-image probably did not prepare him and because he may have greater difficulty in establishing intimate relationships (Berardo, 1970).

Whether men or women lose more through the death of a spouse may, in the long run, be a ridiculous question. That both are deprived is evident. Each has lost someone important, even if the relationship was far from ideal. During the relationship a network of close associations and shared experiences developed over a period—often a lengthy period—of time. Prior to the marriage was a courtship period, when this association began and received initial testing; mourning is like the courtship period in reverse, as the widow or widower begins reducing emotional involvement in the relationship with the dead spouse (Marris, 1975). Often, perhaps usually, some sense of attachment, of connectedness, continues indefinitely.

Those Who Never Married

Only about 5% of older people have never married (Troll et al., 1979), and these people seem to adjust quite adequately to being single. Although they admit to being isolated, for the most part they have always been isolated from others, and they don't seem more lonely or unhappy than when they were younger or than other older people; in fact, by avoiding some of the wrenching losses suffered by married people through the death of a spouse, they find a significant advantage to their single status (Gubrium, 1975). Many, of course, are not isolated in the true sense of the term. They have numerous friends and family members, and they often live with a brother or sister (Shanas, 1979).

One study indicated that never-married younger persons (under age 50) were somewhat less happy than their married age cohorts but found their lives more exciting. Among those over 50, however, the never-married respondents no longer saw life as more exciting. In retirement the never married seemed more troubled, perhaps because family relationships were not available to compensate for the losses of work roles and relationships. Differences between the never-married older people and those who are married might alter when today's younger, better-educated never-married people become older. Since never-married older people with limited education appear to be the least happy, as the present group is replaced by never-married older persons with greater formal education, the outlook for this group may become more favorable (Ward, 1979b).

Parenthood, Grandparenthood, and Great-grandparenthood

Slightly more than 80% of older people have living children; some 75% have living grandchildren (Harris & Associates, 1975); 40% (the percentage is higher for those in their late 70s and beyond) have living great-grandchildren (Ward, 1979a); and a very small proportion have living great-great-grandchildren. About 4% of persons over 65 have living parents. In the later years, especially as age peers die and work-related friendships diminish, the elderly often find that these relationships grow in significance.

Parenthood

According to much of what you read in newspapers and magazines, older people are frequently isolated from their adult children. The implication is that these children show no gratitude to the parents who nurtured them. Similarly, many older people are popularly supposed to suffer from the empty-nest syndrome, which results from the children's leaving home.

Research findings and the views of most gerontologists suggest just the opposite in both instances. In the early and middle years of parenthood, the mother and father provide emotional, social, and financial support for their children. When the children finally leave home, which usually occurs when the parents are middle-aged, not elderly, the parents enjoy their freedom from responsibility and are able to become closer to each other and to participate in activities that interest them (E. B. Harkins, 1978). Conversely, when the mother and father become elderly, their middle-aged children normally provide various kinds of support for them and, with less frequency, for other older family members.

Further, older people and their children have frequent contact with each other. In one study, more than half of all older people outside institutions had seen at least one child "within the last day or so" (Harris & Associates, 1975); another study indicated an even higher proportion (Shanas, Townsend, Wedderburn, Friis, Milhoj, & Stehouwer, 1968). If you add telephone contact, the proportion becomes higher still. In the study by Harris and Associates, only slightly more than 10% of those elderly who had children had not seen any of them for two months or more.

Sex differences do appear in these intergenerational relationships. Married daughters seem to maintain closer ties with their parents than do married sons, and greater conflict may occur between daughters and their mothers-in-law, perhaps resulting from their competition for the role of providing emotional support for the man (Sussman, 1965). There is an overall tendency for a middle-aged couple to be closer to the wife's family than to the husband's (Troll, 1971). An intriguing question arises: how will the increasing tendency toward egalitarian sex roles, and the increasing number of women who work outside the home, influence such relationships?

Of course, the quality of the interaction between adult child and elderly parent is at least as important to life satisfaction for the parent as the frequency of contact between them (Rosow, 1967). In fact, numerous studies have shown that "neither frequency of interaction with one particular child nor total contact with all children had any significant impact on morale" (Lee, 1979, p. 353). The author of this quotation hastened to emphasize that frequent contact may provide the older person with a greater sense of security or with other valuable advantages, but a simple count of how often an older person sees his or her children does not relate to morale or life satisfaction. Obviously, the quality of the contacts is more difficult to investigate; we can't count it, as we can count the number of contacts, and we sometimes must be skeptical about what people tell us, since they may be motivated to make the situation appear either better or worse than it actually is.

The results of other investigations add support to the notion that adult children visit and, when necessary, care for their elderly parents (Shanas, 1977; Sussman, 1965). The services each generation offers the other are a function of income, health, family relationships, needs, and family status. For example, grandparents are more likely to provide baby-sitting help and to give money and valuable gifts when their grandchildren are young, when they themselves are healthy, and when finances are not a major problem. Help during periods of illness is often exchanged; presumably, the elderly receive more and give less as they age. And each generation often helps the other in times of crisis, such as financial reversals or divorce. In general, parents and their adult children maintain an active exchange of money, gifts, help, and advice.

An analysis of three adult generations within the same family showed that the grandparents received more support than they gave in terms of economic help, emotional gratification, care in times of illness, and help with household management. At the same time they gave more help with child care than they received, not an especially startling finding (Hill, 1965). However, Troll (1971) suggests that social-class differences in these support patterns may be important: the middle-class elderly tend to give help to their children until much later in the children's lives, whereas the working-class elderly are more likely to receive help from their children. Middle-class parents are also more likely to give their children money, whereas working-class parents are more likely to give them services.

Relatively few older people live in the home of one of their children—one estimate is only about 4% (reported in Howell, 1980). A somewhat larger proportion of elderly are heads of households that include one or more of their children, which means that the children are living in the parent's household, not the opposite, as is often assumed. When an older person does live in the household of his or her child, the reason is usually financial stress, poor health, or the death of one of the parents, leaving the other without adequate support. And such older people are likely to live with an unmarried child, usually a daughter, rather than with a married child (Troll et al., 1979).

In our society both the older person and the adult children usually prefer maintaining separate households for as long as possible. Older people have had many decades of autonomous living, and they are not likely to want to give up their privacy and freedom by living with their children.

Family responsibility in the United States, and probably in Canada as well, is perceived as essentially serial rather than reciprocal; that is, each generation is seen as primarily responsible for the support of the succeeding generation. Parents, during the years when they are most capable, are expected to care for their children, but when the parents become less capable and the children more so, the children—now adults—are expected to attend to their own children first and to their parents second.

The term *role reversal* has been used to describe the circumstance in which adult children take care of their elderly parents in ways that resemble the care parents normally provide for their young children. The roles have reversed, with the children now being parents to their parents. This notion has produced considerable controversy, however, and Blenkner (1965) has urged the use of the term *filial maturity* to signify that adult children should be capable of permitting their parents to depend on them. The roles, therefore, are not seen as reversed; instead, changing roles are seen as a natural outcome of the increasing maturity of adult children and their acceptance of what is appropriately expected of them.

When parents become very old or when their health deteriorates seriously or when their cognitive competence diminishes markedly, the stresses on the parent/child relationship mount. Adult children often do not understand the significance of these changes, especially cognitive changes, in their parents. To make matters worse, the possibility of institutionalization emerges, which adds still more stress to the lives of all concerned. Handling cognitive losses and experiencing the need to care for their parents in ways they perceived as confining were the two major sources of stress found in one investigation (Robinson & Thurnher, 1979).

Many older persons state—and most, I'm certain, are sincere when they do—that they do not wish to be a burden on their children. Their statement is consistent with the national value of retaining one's independence. I have sometimes asked these older people—or middle-aged people, when they make the same statement—to consider why they were so willing to accept their children as burdens for so many years but are not willing to be the recipients of equivalent support. In spite of the prevailing value of serial responsibility, and in spite of the innumerable well-documented stories of children who refuse to provide financial or emotional support to elderly parents, many gerontologists—myself included—believe that the elderly are not nearly so maltreated by their children as is often supposed.

Neither should we jump too quickly to the conclusion that children are simply ungrateful if they do not offer their parents proper care. In many cases, for example, there may have been a long history of estrangement between parent and child. Since our society does not invoke severe sanctions against children who ignore their parents, support of the elderly tends to be based on either feelings of love and affection or a sense of obligation and duty—or both. The middle-aged child is often caught between feelings of obligation to his or her own children, spouse, and work and feelings of obligation to his or her parents. Elderly parents themselves frequently insist that a grandchild attend college even when it means a loss of financial support from their children.

Another factor to consider in discussing the relationship between elderly parents and their adult children is that a middle-aged couple today is much more likely to have one or more parents to be concerned with, whereas in times past relatively few people lived long enough to become dependent in their old age. But selfless as well as selfish adult children do exist: the problem is too often seen only from the viewpoint of one generation or the other. Relationships between the generations are obviously a complex matter, not helped at all by making villains of the elderly (for being difficult to relate to) or of the adult children (for being ungrateful).

Grandparenthood and Great-grandparenthood

One family role that has received virtually no attention until recently is the role of grandparent. This neglect seems especially odd in that more and more people now live to be grandparents or even great-grandparents. Furthermore, "more grandchildren have an association with a grandparent now than . . . in 1900" (Nimkoff, 1961, p. 735). This statement is true both because of increased longevity and because many residents of the United States at the turn of the century had left elderly parents behind in Europe or elsewhere, and their children simply never saw their grandparents.

But there are deeper reasons that we should be concerned with understanding the grandparent role. Being a grandparent may take on special meaning to the elderly as other areas of role performance become closed to them. Furthermore, grandparents can have satisfying contacts with grandchildren that involve a minimum of obligation and responsibility, so that both can be freer and less guarded in the relationship than parents and children can be. Interactions between grandparents and grandchildren include (1) both brief and extended visits, (2) exchange of gifts, (3) exchange of letters and other communications, and (4) exchange of experience; the grandparents can follow the growth, development, and adventures of the young, and the children can share the wisdom and experience of the elderly (Smith, 1965).

In a recent study of grandparenthood, interviews were conducted with 286 grandparents—nearly three-fourths of them women—to probe the meaning to them of being grandparents. They ranged in age from 40 to 90, in education from second grade through postgraduate degrees, and in annual income from less than $3000 to more than $250,000. The author found that five dimensions of grandparenthood emerged from her work, each with its own expectations, satisfactions, and disappointments:

1. *Centrality.* For some, grandparenthood was central to their lives. Being a grandparent meant (a) making the activities and feelings of being a grandparent central in their lives, while other feelings and activities diminished in importance; (b) viewing grandparenthood as a central element in their personal identity; and (c) seeing their personal meaning in life as revolving around grandparenthood.
2. *Valued elder.* Other grandparents saw themselves in terms of the wise, esteemed older person. This view included (a) being a resource person for their grandchildren and (b) being concerned about how their grandchildren regard them now and later, when the grandchildren are older.
3. *Immortality through the clan.* These grandparents saw their significance as related to using their grandchildren as a source of personal immortality and of family immortality.
4. *Reinvolvement with one's own past.* Some grandparents found themselves reliving their own earlier experiences and recalling their own grandparents.
5. *Spoiler.* The last group consisted of grandparents who were lenient, often to the point of indulgence, with their grandchildren, somewhat like the stereotype of what grandparents should be like.

All the grandparents seemed to view themselves in all five ways at one time or another, but one dimension seemed to predominate for each individual. The predominant dimension did appear to change over time, and the specific associations and meanings of these dimensions were not the same for grandmothers as they were for grandfathers.

Grandparenthood, according to this study, is more important than is usually assumed. Many grandparents used these relationships to work through earlier concerns in their lives that had not been adequately resolved, thus improving their psychological well-being. And the grandparent role and relationships enabled many of these persons to compensate for other losses that they were encountering.

One especially significant finding of the study was that the experience of being a grandparent was strongly influenced by the relationships that the individual had had two generations earlier as a grandchild. Interestingly enough, grandfathers, but not grandmothers, who lacked contact with their own grandparents were most likely to emphasize the spoiler dimension (Kivnick, 1980).

Throughout the discussion of grandparent/grandchild relationships, it is important to keep two matters in mind. First, the relationship changes over time: when the grandparent is 51 and the grandchild is 7, they may be very close and visit places together, and the grandchild may greatly enjoy spending a night or a month with the grandparents. When the grandparent is 61 and the grandchild is 17, or the grandparent is 71 and the grandchild is 27, the relationship is obviously dramatically different.

The second matter is the relative ages of grandparent and grandchild at any point in the relationship. The relationship between a 43-year-old grandparent and a 3-year-old grandchild is going to differ from that between a 53-year-old grandparent and a 3-year-old grandchild or that between a 63-year-old grandparent and a 23-year-old grandchild. Changes in grandparent work schedule, time availability, and health are all significant, but undoubtedly more significant are the changing needs, wants, and interests of the grandchild. Grandparents, according to one study, are more able to enjoy being with grandchildren who are quite young than with those who are in late childhood or adolescence (Kahana & Coe, 1969).

Other influences on the meaning of being a grandparent are the personalities of grandparent and grandchild and the frequency and quality of interactions between them. The geographical distance between them, the ways in which the parents structure the child's time and availability, and the adequacy of income and transportation are all major determinants (Neugarten & Weinstein, 1964).

Grandparents serve another kind of function, one not often considered even by those most intimately involved. Young children observe the ways in which their parents relate to their grandparents. Although no research has been done (to my knowledge) in this area, it would be interesting to learn whether the reaction of adult children to their elderly parents is in any way reflected when those adult children become elderly and their children must work out ways of relating to them.

Sometimes an affinity is noted between grandchildren in their teens or early 20s and their grandparents. Perhaps each can relate to the other without the tensions that exist between parent and child. Their closeness might be due in part to the circumstances that the young and the old share. Both are (1) age groups adjacent to the age group that dominates society, but neither has much power or much influence on the decision makers; (2) constantly reminded that they are viewed as nonproductive (at least the retired elderly and the not-yet-working young), and both see themselves as taking from society without putting anything back in, although the potential of the young to be productive in the future is denied the old; (3) seen as having a life filled with leisure—education and retirement are seen as pleasure, not as work or boredom; (4) viewed as living with their time relatively unstructured—the time structure that does exist for them is not perceived by the middle-aged; (5) thought to be inadequately educated—the young are not yet educated by experience, and the old often lack formal education; and (6) often poor and therefore vulnerable and therefore weak.

When one group of young adults was asked about their grandparents, their responses clearly indicated that they did not view their older relatives as either old-fashioned or out of touch. Most of them enjoyed visits, but neither they nor their grandparents did a lot of specific things for each other; both young and old seemed to expect primarily emotional support and love from each other rather than financial support or advice, although the latter were also mentioned. Perhaps most significant, 92% of these young adults agreed that "a child would miss much if there were no grandparents when he was growing up" (Robertson, 1976, p. 138). One young college student exemplified the results of this study when she reminded her father that her grandmother was elderly and might not live much longer, and that both she and her father needed to take every opportunity to enjoy her company.

Studies of great-grandparents are virtually nonexistent, so we have little information about the kinds of relationships between these people and their great-grandchildren. Do they feel close to each other? Do they have a sense of connectedness? We really don't know.

Before leaving the topic of grandparenthood, I want to comment briefly on the role of grandparents whose children are divorced and, perhaps, remarried. Given the increase in divorce today, large numbers of grandparents find themselves in this situation. After the divorce, if their child has custody of the grandchildren, they may find themselves providing much more extensive support than they had while the adult child was married; this support includes both money and services. Conversely, if their child does not have custody, they may suddenly realize that their access to their grandchildren has suddenly diminished, although many divorced ex-children-in-law recognize the potential significance to their children of grandparents and do not permit their anger with their ex-spouse to interfere with the grandparent/grandchild relationship (Kalish & Visher, 1981).

When the child remarries, the grandparent role again changes. Once again there is a second parent, although often not someone with the same feelings of closeness to the child. Grandparents can improve the chances for success of the second marriage, or they can interfere through forming an alliance with their grandchildren against the new spouse (Kalish & Visher, 1981).

The importance of grandparents can easily be underestimated; it can also be overestimated. Individual differences in grandparent/grandchild relationships are immense, varying as a function of sex, health, distance from each other, other roles and activities, personality, the age of each, and numerous other factors.

Other Family Members

Husbands, wives, children, grandchildren, and great-grandchildren do not exhaust the possible family relationships of older people. There are still brothers and sisters, aunts and uncles, cousins, nieces and nephews, and others, although none of these has received much attention in the literature. Perhaps there is good reason. In our society at least, a sister or a cousin or a nephew might well be extremely important in the life of a particular older individual, but such people do not appear to be important as a class.

Visits with brothers and sisters, for example, occur most frequently for older persons who have never been married or had children, but—as with having contact with adult children—research has not turned up any relationship between morale and frequency of contact with siblings (Lee & Ihinger-Tallman, 1980). When asked whether they were close enough to someone to talk about things that really bothered them, 13% of older persons did list a brother or sister, more than twice as many women doing so as men (presumably because more men had wives to confide in than women had husbands) (Harris & Associates, 1975). This is virtually the same percentage indicated by nonelderly persons, so siblings apparently do not become more important as confidants with age. Thus, it isn't that having a brother or sister has no meaning for older people, but that the relationship cannot compare with that with a spouse, friends, children, or even grandchildren. In fact, nearly two-thirds of older people who had living siblings felt close or very close to at least one brother or sister, while only 5% did not feel close to any (Cicirelli, 1980).

Morale does appear to be better when older people are more active and more involved, so that we might at least speculate that the more family members the older person can draw on, the greater the opportunity to be engaged and active and, therefore, to have high life satisfaction. Whether relationships with any particular class of relative lead to higher morale, however, is not known.

The relationship of older people to still-living parents deserves at least brief comment. As indicated earlier, some 4% of persons over age 65 have at least one living parent. Among those in late middle age, this figure is much higher. Thus, as some older people look toward retirement and try to cope with their own age-related concerns, they are also responsible for parents who are well into their 80s or 90s and who are frequently making demands for time, attention, energy, and money.

Friends and Neighbors

Almost all older people have close friends—some 94%, according to one study, compared to 97% of the nonelderly (Harris & Associates, 1975). By definition, all older people have neighbors, although either physical or social distance from these neighbors may be great enough that they are, to use Cantor's (1979) expression, not "functional"—that is, not people with whom the individual interacts in any meaningful fashion.

Since friends, unlike relatives, are people who select each other, they tend to have qualities that are similar or that complement each other. Although friendships come and go, many older people have developed lasting friendships that not infrequently date back to early adulthood or even to childhood. These friendships tend to be with people who are viewed as social equals and who have similar occupational backgrounds and similar interests (Hess, 1972).

Close friendships can develop only over time (Atchley, 1980), although we have all had the experience of meeting someone and liking that person immediately. But even these relationships require time and testing, with very rare exceptions, before the friendship can provide shared intimacy. One difficulty faced by older people who leave the community in which they have lived—to be closer to their children or to enjoy a better climate or to live where there is more to do—is to begin the task of developing new friendships. It's not at all unusual for an older couple or individual to select a specific community because old friends have already relocated there. Thus, we find a colony of people from the northern suburbs of Chicago living near one another in a Florida retirement community, whereas people from west Los Angeles gravitate to a community an hour's drive to the south.

For older people who do not relocate, most close friends live nearby. A study of the elderly in the inner city of New York City found that nearly three-fourths of functional friends lived either in the same building or within walking distance; fewer than 2% were outside the metropolitan area (Cantor, 1979). And the older the person is, the less likely he or she is to have close friends living some distance away, especially if health or financial limitations restrict mobility (Cantor, 1979).

Involvement in social activities with friends is consistently related to morale and life satisfaction (Larson, 1978), although, as I discussed earlier, this does not appear to be the case for either adult children or siblings.

Cause and effect, of course, are difficult to determine: we can't be certain whether being with friends increases life satisfaction or whether people who have generally high life satisfaction are more capable of participating in activities and developing friendships. Perhaps both occur. In any event, researchers studying the ability of elderly people to cope with social and emotional stresses have discovered that the availability of a close friend or confidant often differentiated those who were coping effectively from those who were not (Lowenthal & Haven, 1968).

Older people frequently develop what is termed an informal support network involving family members, friends, and neighbors. This informal network is in contrast to the formal support network of social agencies, health organizations, and other official support services. Although the formal support is often more evident, there is little doubt that most people, certainly most older people, receive their major support from their informal network. We can tabulate fairly easily the number of times older people seek help from the formal network, but we have much less knowledge about the informal network. Older people are most likely to look to their family members for informal support—emotional, practical, financial—but friends and neighbors also provide a great deal of such support. And the latter are more frequently used when the older person does not have a child or other close relative readily available (Cantor, 1979).

Friendships Within and Across Generations

A frequent source of disagreement among gerontologists and others concerned with the elderly is whether older persons prefer friendships with others roughly their own age or whether they will gain more satisfaction from having friends whose ages are spread fairly evenly across the entire age distribution. I tend to agree with Rosow (1967), who states that "there is an effective social barrier between the generations which propinquity and contact apparently do not dispel" (p. 34). Even when young and old live near each other and have contact with each other, friendships do not often emerge. I do not say that they never emerge or that no older person prefers social interactions with young people. You can ask yourself what proportion of your available leisure time you would wish to spend with people 10 years younger than yourself (if you are under 30) or 15 years younger (if you are over 30).

Perhaps older people feel most comfortable with their age peers because they feel excluded and unwanted in groups of younger people; or perhaps they feel more at home with people who have shared their life spans, memories, and—probably most important—period of early socialization. They share recollections of the same ballplayers, movie actors, automobiles, and politicians; they remember dancing the same dances, using the same slang, fighting in the same wars, wearing the same clothing styles.

People who share common racial, linguistic, religious, or national backgrounds often cluster together; age is simply one more basis for such clustering.

It has been pointed out that what we often describe as the generation gap is actually a combination of three factors: (1) the parent generation is older, has different roles and responsibilities, and has developed values and ideas through greater experience; (2) the age-cohort effect suggests that the parent generation was socialized during a different period of history and, therefore, has developed values and attitudes reflecting their own history; and (3) parents and their children continue to work on their unique family interactions, such as the desire of the younger generation to gain autonomy, which places more tension on their relationship (Bengtson & Cutler, 1976).

Two major studies confirm that older people do very well when they live close to many others in their own generation. One, a study of older apartment dwellers in Cleveland, showed that older people who lived in buildings in which 50% or more of the households had at least one resident over 65 had more friends than those living in buildings with few elderly people (Rosow, 1967).

The second study drew from a national sample of older people living in public housing. Those living in age-segregated facilities had higher morale, were more satisfied with their housing, were more active, and got around more in their neighborhood; in fact, 83% preferred living in an environment limited to people 62 and over (Teaff, Lawton, Nahemow, & Carlson, 1978).

None of this data is to be interpreted as suggesting that the elderly *should not* spend more time with younger people; such occurrences are certainly to be applauded. However, people do appear to prefer spending much or most of their time with others of their own age group, and relationships within generations appear to develop more easily and naturally than relationships between distant generations, except perhaps for relationships within a family, where a strong feeling of connection is already likely to exist.

To the extent to which preference for age peers results from feeling victimized by prejudice and discrimination on the part of the young, program planners may wish to contemplate ways to intervene. To the extent to which this preference reflects a sincere desire to remain with one's reference group, program planners should probably avoid interfering. The problem is to determinc the relative impact of each of these pressures. Most gerontologists prefer the idea of providing the elderly with as many options as possible and then permitting each individual to make his or her own decision.

Simply counting the number of friends a person claims to have or the number of visits made to neighbors is not a sufficient measure of effective social integration in the community. Such social integration is based on three dimensions: values, formal and informal group memberships, and social roles. "People are tied into their society essentially through their beliefs, the groups that they belong to, and the positions that they occupy" (Rosow, 1967, p. 9).

Two Issues in Relating to Others: Independence and Sexuality

When you were a child or an adolescent, two of the major concerns in your life were likely to be gaining independence and handling your sexual feelings and drives. Independence and sexuality do not cease to be concerns when you are 21 or 35 or even 62 or 75. Although the specific nature of the related problems does change over the years, the broader issues remain important throughout life.

Independence and Dependence

One of the recurring themes in the writings of gerontologists is dependency. Independence and mastery of oneself and one's environment are basic values to most Americans. To be dependent is to be weak and vulnerable, to have to give up a certain amount of power over one's own life, to be unable to make certain important decisions, and to be in what is commonly called a one-down position.

The concept of dependency as applied to the elderly is really a grouping of separate concepts. For example, we can consider dependency in terms of an interpersonal relationship in which one person gives and another receives. Or dependency can be related to a quality or condition of the individual, implying that some incapacity in the individual produces the need for help. A blind person, for instance, depends upon others, even though he or she may not have any dependency relationships. Or dependency can be approached as a relatively enduring personality characteristic. Finally, dependency can be seen as residing in individual acts rather than in relationships, a given condition, or the personality (Kalish, 1969).

Older people (or, indeed, persons of any age) often attempt to manipulate someone perceived as stronger than themselves with the aim of obtaining a protector who will relieve tension and anxiety, offer satisfactions, and aid in coping with an environment that is seen as threatening (Goldfarb, 1969b). When such a person is found, or when these needs are satisfied in some fashion, stress is reduced, and feelings of anxiety subside. One psychiatrist reduced the number of telephone calls and visits to a hospital clinic from elderly people with dubious medical complaints simply by being available when they wanted him, regardless of whether they had any real medical problem. Once the elderly people found that a stronger person was available to give them help when they really needed it, they no longer felt that they had to express their dependency needs through constant clinic visits (Lipsitt, 1969).

Four kinds of normal dependency in aging have been listed.

1. Economic dependency occurs when the older person is no longer a wage earner but must depend on some combination of retirement and Social Security payments, welfare, and family gifts.
2. Physical dependency arises when the person's biological functioning deteriorates and no longer permits the performance of necessary tasks such as walking, shopping, visiting others, or preparing food.
3. Mental dependency parallels physical dependency; it occurs when deterioration or change in the central nervous system produces marked defects in memory, orientation, comprehension, or judgment.
4. Social dependency arises with the loss of meaningful others in the elderly person's life. It produces a reduced awareness of the larger society, reduced individual power, and limitations on social roles [Blenkner, 1969].

Although elderly individuals will often work out a solution to dependency needs by themselves or within their families, society at large is sometimes required to help with one or more of the needs (Blenkner, 1969). And, since help with one kind of dependency tends to alleviate problems with the other kinds of dependency, such outside help can have a salutary effect. For example, helping a person meet physical needs may enable him or her to feel less anxious, to regain former cognitive-performance levels, and to interact with others and cope with social-dependency needs.

Many of the elderly deeply resent their own dependency. They would rather retain mastery over their environment than to have to call on others for help. Ironically, their resentment of their condition can cause them to complain, to worry, and then—for fear of losing their necessary relationships with others—to become yet more dependent.

Not all cultures place so much emphasis on independence, although this value is found in varying degrees in major Western cultures. The Igbo in Africa, for example, are quite different:

> The Igbo elder is no more productive in his advanced years, but he can demand care as a publicly acknowledged right without any sense of guilt, ego damage, or loss of face. Whoever fails to give such care is subject to public scorn and ridicule, cut off not only from the spiritual benefits of the ancestors but also from the material benefits of the system [Shelton, 1969, p. 104].

Sexual Relationships

Sexual activity exists at virtually all ages. The intensity of the physiological drive may change, the potential for intercourse may change, and the methods of sexual expression may change, but sexual activity itself continues throughout the life span.

There is no doubt that the frequency of sexual activity drops in the later years. One cross-sectional study of people ranging from their late 40s to their late 60s showed a significant drop in the frequency of sexual intercourse for both men and women. Of the younger men in this study, 95% claimed to have intercourse at least once a week; of the younger women, the figure was 60%. Comparable figures for those in their late 60s were 28% and 11% (Pfeiffer, Verwoerdt, & Davis, 1972). Although increasing limitations due to health may explain some of this change, even healthy older adults appear to be less sexually active than younger adults (Elias & Elias, 1977).

Obviously, diminution does not mean cessation. Active participation in sexual activity has been reported by adults well into their 70s and 80s. In fact, in a longitudinal study, between 20% and 25% of the men and a small percentage of the women were found to have an increasing incidence of sexual interest and activity as they became older (Pfeiffer, 1969).

The reasons for reduction of sexual activity with age are numerous. Some older people, of course, have health problems that reduce their sexual desires and/or capacities; others have never cared for sex in the first place and use old age as an excuse to avoid sexual behavior; and our culture has, at least in the past, created an image of older people as lacking sexual desire and responsiveness, which must have influenced many of today's elderly. Perhaps more important, numerous older people do not have ready access to a sexual partner. With the death of a spouse, especially after a lengthy marriage, the surviving spouse has difficulty finding an acceptable person for sex; this is especially true for widows, who not only are likely to be more selective than men in accepting a sexual partner but also face a world in which there are few available male age peers. In addition, of course, both widows and widowers may have personal values that preclude sex outside marriage.

Many older people who are not presently married see their own bodies as not being sexually desirable to the opposite sex—and many do not find other older people exciting sex partners. Simone de Beauvoir (1973), once the mistress of the famous author and philosopher Jean-Paul Sartre, described an attempt to go out on the street and pick up a younger man for a sexual encounter. No man would respond to the sexual signals of an elderly woman. Even older married people, although engaging in decidedly more sexual activity than those not presently married, may have become bored with the same sexual partner after so many years but find it unacceptable to seek sex outside the marriage.

Although the common assumption has been that people in general disapprove of sex among older people, recent data question this view. Residents of a Southern city, mostly between 25 and 55 years of age, rejected the statements that older persons are not interested in sex (76%) and that they are unable to have intercourse (70%). The respondents were much more accepting of extramarital affairs among older than among younger persons and were slightly more accepting of older couples' living together than of younger couples' doing so (Roff & Klemmack, 1979).

It is not appropriate, however, to define intercourse as the only measure of sexuality. A healthy sexual relationship can be expressed in a variety of ways, including touching, holding, massaging, and sexual play that does not necessarily include intercourse. If the definition of sexuality is broadened to include these approaches, older people have the potential for many different kinds of sexual behavior.

An alternative form of sexual behavior at all ages is homosexuality. The familiar stereotype of homosexual relationships between elderly males is negative, but one extensive study of older gay men in the Los Angeles area indicated that more than 80% of the gay men over 65 were sexually satisfied, a considerably higher percentage than for those 50–65, even though most were not involved in a long-term gay relationship (Kelly, 1977).

From time to time, I have heard people suggest that the elderly who have difficulty finding adequate heterosexual relationships should develop homosexual relationships. This statement has been made with particular reference to older women. Nonetheless, it still seems likely that an elderly woman or man who preferred heterosexual relationships for an entire lifetime would find the change to homosexuality very difficult. Long-term care facilities for the elderly would appear to offer a setting for homosexual relationships, since people spend all their time in close proximity to one another, and roommates would have ample opportunity to become sexually involved with each other. However, I have not found any information on how often or under what circumstances this occurs.

A Concluding Comment

Relationships—with family, friends, neighbors, or sexual partners—are the source of many of life's most exciting, pleasurable, and satisfying moments. They are also the source of many of life's most frustrating, upsetting, and restricting moments. Individual differences in the desire for relationships with others are great, but all people, even loners, depend on some relationships. The elderly, now with more available time and less available money, find relationships with others extremely valuable. At the same time, when health becomes less adequate and age peers become ill and die in increasing numbers, older people find it more and more difficult to establish and retain healthy friendships and family relationships. Nevertheless, many elderly people maintain rich relationships with family members, friends, and more casual acquaintances throughout their lives.

Chapter Six

Practical Issues: Money, Retirement, and the Living Environment

Money, work, leisure, housing, and transportation are matters that concern us throughout our adult lives. They are matters of no less concern when we enter our later years, and in some ways they become of greater concern. Both the changes within our bodies and the changes produced by the society around us are reminders that our world is no longer what it was when we were 29 or 49, and this is certainly true in considering finances, work, leisure, housing, and transportation.

Income and Outgo

With a few exceptions, people have less money to live on in their later years than they had earlier in their lives. For most people, retirement causes a drop in income of 50–65%, and, on the whole, older people have about half the income of the nonelderly (Brotman, 1981). In 1979, one out of nine persons of all ages (including children) lived in households below the poverty line, while one out of seven older persons did so (Brotman, 1981). Older women living alone or as the head of a household and older minority-group members were especially likely to be among the poor. Although the percentage of elderly poor dropped from 30% in 1959 to 19% in 1972 and to 15% in 1979, this decline did not represent a sudden surge in income; rather, it meant that a substantial number of elderly changed in status from poor to near-poor.

The expenses of older people are also less, since some expenses are work related, but these reduced expenses seldom compensate for reduced income; in fact, the major reduction in expenses comes some years before retirement, when the last of the children becomes financially independent

(J. H. Schulz, 1980). And expenses are not always low among the elderly, since taxes continue to rise, and health costs for the elderly can become astronomical when private insurance and Medicare cease to be sufficient—and this is a common occurrence. In 1976 Medicare covered only 71% of the hospital costs and 55% of the physician costs of its beneficiaries (not all elderly are beneficiaries), meaning that substantial amounts had to come out of the individual's pocket or through other programs. This is especially true for long-term care, for which Medicare pays only a very small proportion of the national bill. All public programs combined covered 67% of the health-care expenses of the elderly in 1977 (Iglehart, 1978).

Not all older people are poor or near-poor. In 1979 more than 1.8 million older families had incomes of more than $20,000, and more than 1.1 million older individuals had incomes of more than $10,000. Further, when the head of the household was fully employed, the mean family income for older families was more than $29,000 (Brotman, 1981). The implications are obvious: a modest proportion of older people—perhaps about one in six—live quite well; a much larger proportion live in or near poverty.*

When older people themselves are asked how they feel about their finances, their responses are easy to interpret. A 1969 study in the Detroit area indicated that 57% of retired people felt their present finances to be inadequate (D. A. Peterson, 1972). An extensive national study shortly afterward showed that more than one-third of the respondents had trouble paying housing costs, and more than one-half stated that they did not have enough money "to make ends meet" (Institute for Interdisciplinary Studies, 1971). In a more recent survey 15% of the older respondents said that not having enough money to live on was a "very serious" problem, and another 25% said that it was a "somewhat serious" problem. Only fear of crime and poor health ranked higher (Harris & Associates, 1975).

Sources of Income

The largest proportion (39%) of elderly people's money comes from Social Security, with another 13% from private or government pension plans; 23% comes from earnings; 18% comes from assets, such as bank interest or rentals; the remaining 7% comes from a variety of sources (J. H. Schulz, 1980). Obviously, these earnings are not evenly distributed; those

*The economic status of the elderly in Canada differs considerably from that in the United States. In Canada more than half of those 65 years of age and older receive so little money that some 70% or more of their incomes is required for such necessities as food, shelter, and clothing. However, the health insurance provided in Canada for all persons means that older people cannot be impoverished by a health catastrophe, which can and does happen in the United States. In general, it is difficult to make definitive statements or comparisons about the economics of aging in Canada because relevant research data are extremely limited. See Marshall (1980) for a review of the available information.

who work and those who have assets would be expected to have a much higher income than those who are living only on Social Security.

Some 90% of retired persons are drawing Social Security (Atchley, 1980); for about 30% of these individuals, Social Security is the only form of income (ERA, 1980). About 40% of older couples and 16% of older individuals have some earnings; about half of the elderly have income from assets, although the amount is small, with a median of less than $900 a year (ERA, 1980).

Social Security payments have increased steadily over the years; they are well over ten times as high today as when they were first distributed in 1940. However, inflation has taken a significant toll, so the increase in *real* income is about two and a half times the 1940 payments (J. H. Schulz, 1980). The amount that we pay into Social Security has also increased greatly over the same period, and part of that increase is due to the extension of benefits. Originally only a retirement program, Social Security now includes health insurance (Medicare), disability payments, and survivor benefits, as well as a small amount for burial.

Sources of Outgo

The expenditures of older people also differ from those of the nonelderly. (See Table 6-1.) Averages, of course, can be misleading. The higher a person's income, the lower the percentage that must be allocated for food and other necessities and the more that is available for personal care and recreation. The Bureau of Labor Statistics has developed three levels of budget for older couples: high, intermediate, and low. In 1979 the low budget was $116 a week, above the poverty level but certainly not providing much in the way of luxuries, and the incomes of more than 18% of older couples fell below this amount. The incomes of an additional 18% fell below the intermediate budget of $165 a week, and 62% of older couples received the high budget of $244 a week or less (Brotman, 1981). The budget in Table 6-1 is based on an average income, which is close to the intermediate budget.

Notice that the elderly spend a much higher percentage of their budget than the nonelderly for gifts and contributions and health care and a moderately higher percentage for food and housing. However, since their overall income is much lower than the nonelderly's, their food budget is under two-thirds of what the nonelderly pay, and even their housing budget is only 60%.

Some Psychological Stresses

Money is a major source of stress at all ages. It causes countless arguments between husbands and wives and is the basis for many divorces; it produces anger between siblings; it leads to strikes and lockouts, to seeking

Table 6-1. Expenditures of older people (1972–1973).

Category	*Percentage of All Expenditures*		*Ratio of*	*Percentage of Expenditures by Older Persons Based on*
	(A) Under 65	*(B) 65 and Over*	*(B):(A)*	*Amount Spent by Those Under 65*
Food	18.2	21.4	118	63%
Alcoholic beverages	0.9	0.6	67	35
Tobacco products	1.4	1.1	79	41
Housing	26.0	28.9	111	60
House furnishings and equipment	4.4	3.2	73	40
Clothing	7.3	5.4	74	39
Transportation, excluding trips	17.9	12.8	72	38
Health care (out of pocket)	4.8	8.3	173	94
Personal care	1.0	1.5	150	78
Recreation, education, trips	7.1	6.2	87	47
Insurance and pensions	8.7	3.3	38	20
Gifts and contributions	4.1	9.1	222	120

Adapted from *Every Ninth American*, by H. B. Brotman. Draft prepared for "Development in Aging, 1980" for the Special Committee on Aging, U.S. Senate, 1981.

new jobs and to disruptive behavior on present jobs. But in the later years many people who have never truly suffered from limited income face poverty or near-poverty for the first time.

Younger people having limited financial means can always hope for future improvement; older people have no such hope for themselves. The low income associated with old age comes at the same time that other resources diminish. A younger person can walk to save bus fare, but the older person may have difficulty in walking; the younger person can borrow money against future prospects, but the elderly have few future prospects of added income; the younger person can get a part-time job, but work often is not available for the older person.

Not only does the lack of money represent a limited potential for purchasing goods and services, but some people in our society look upon poverty as either the fault of the individual or, in a few instances, fate or the will of God. Therefore, according to some, those who are poor deserve to be poor, and many of the elderly themselves were brought up to accept this view. Poverty in old age thus can be destructive of feelings of adequacy and self-esteem in many ways.

Work and Retirement

The transition from work to retirement is one of the major changes occurring in the later years. Although retirement has been primarily a concern for men, increasing numbers of women have entered the labor force during the past decade. Work—and therefore retirement—will be a vital consideration for women as well in the future.

It is easy to become trapped in the present, to assume that what exists today has always existed. However, retirement is a new institution. Up until a few decades ago, the rich could retire, but other people had to work until poor health, physical handicaps, or inability to find a job forced them out of the labor pool. In 1900, 68% of American men 65 years of age and older were working, whereas by 1960 the proportion had been halved to 32% (Riley & Foner 1968). As of the end of 1979, only 20% of men over 65 were still employed; by the age of 70, probably not more than 10% continue to work. Nearly 8.5% of women over 65 were working in 1979 (Brotman, 1981), a statistic that has not changed greatly over the past years.

Older Workers

The job performance of workers in their late 50s through mid-70s seems to be as good as, and often better than, that of younger workers. Attendance records are better (although when absences do occur, they tend to be for a longer period), and industrial accidents are less frequent. Many older workers have shifted from jobs that require great strength or rapid movement to other kinds of positions, and recent technological advances have reduced the number of jobs that require great strength or speed, which also operates to the benefit of older workers. Given that the less capable older workers tend not to stay at their jobs and that the workers who do remain appear competent, much of the worry over the performance of older workers is unnecessary. The general consensus is that relatively few older workers will wish to remain at their jobs unless economic conditions cause them to worry about the adequacy of their pensions (Singer, 1978).

Dimensions of Retirement

Retirement means different things to different people. On the negative side of the ledger, it means reduced income; the need to adapt to an altered role, no longer that of someone who is gainfully employed but of someone who *was* gainfully employed; the loss of informal social contacts; the loss of one basis for personal identification and sense of meaningfulness. On the positive side, retirement means increased freedom and the opening up of innumerable options, including the opportunity to pursue intriguing projects or to travel or to move to a more desirable community or to an area with a better climate.

I'd like to look more carefully at the meanings of retirement, with special consideration of finances, physical health, interpersonal relationships, ability and power, meaningfulness, and the work itself.

Finances. In spite of the numerous discussions of the importance of feeling meaningful, of having job-related status, and of liking the social relationships work provides, the one thing that retirees report they miss the most is still money. In one study nearly half of those retired cited money as the most serious retirement-related loss (Shanas, Townsend, Wedderburn, Friis, Milhoj, & Stehouwer, 1968).

The economics of the later years was discussed earlier. However, much of the fear and anxiety of retirement results from knowing that future income will be considerably less than present income. In some cases—government work, teaching, police and fire work—retirement incomes are often substantial and can be drawn early. In other cases, especially among the self-employed and persons working for small businesses, pensions are limited, and income after retirement is minimal.

Physical health. According to the folklore of aging, retirement causes major emotional problems and frequently leads to increased physical-health difficulties. Everyone has at least one tale to tell about a friend or acquaintance who was in excellent health until retirement, but then quickly became morose and depressed, then ill, and soon died (or at least died psychologically).

I'm certain that many of these examples are valid, but the overall evidence indicates just the opposite. A review of research on the health of recent retirees found many more reports of improved health than of health declines (Eisdorfer, 1972). A recent study of several thousand rubber-tire workers showed that age at retirement did not have any effect on subsequent health; the only factor that predicted which workers died soon after retirement was their health prior to retirement (Haynes, McMichael, & Tyroler, 1978). Since certain jobs are physically or emotionally strenuous, some reports of improved health following retirement undoubtedly reflect the opportunity to leave the rigorous demands and stresses behind.

Interpersonal relationships. Social relationships on the job have been considered one of the most important factors in job satisfaction and, for the same reasons, one of the major losses suffered in retiring. Although this is undoubtedly still the case in many communities and in many work organizations, in North American society as a whole, work associations may be losing some of their outside-of-work influence. Nonetheless, one-sixth of the respondents in one study reported that their greatest loss in leaving work was contact with their friends (Shanas et al., 1968).

As retirement approaches, the worker finds that other employees are beginning to plan for his or her successor and to function as though he or she were already absent; in other words, those in the work milieu have begun to disengage. If she has an administrative or supervisory position, others are already vying for the job; if he is a teacher, the principal no longer appoints him to committees, and other teachers no longer include him in their plans for future programs.

Returning to visit the business or factory or organization after retirement can also be disappointing. After the first visit, which often meets with an enthusiastic reception, the visitor may find that the other employees have new topics of conversation, new subjects for gossip, new work roles, and new staff alliances. They have advanced the process of disengagement quite effectively, and they often are uncomfortable when the retiree does not disengage also.

Ability and power. Many kinds of job skills require constant updating, an effort that can become increasingly frustrating in the later years. Younger workers may already be trained in the newer skills, whereas older workers may need retraining at some expense to their organization. Unfortunately for the older worker, learning these new skills is not made easier—and is often made more difficult—by lengthy experience with previous skills. Individuals choosing early retirement were shown in one study to be beset by problems in meeting work demands and by inability to control the speed and pace of their work (Barfield & Morgan, 1969).

Although the ability to perform certain specific tasks may diminish with age, competence in many jobs does not diminish at all and may actually be greater at the time of retirement. Whether work capability is actually reduced or is merely believed by the organization to be reduced, the impact is still the same: retirement at the indicated age. And imminent retirement also causes a reduction in employees' power and influence. Not only do they lack the power to retain their position—even top-management personnel are often without the power to keep themselves entrenched beyond the mandatory retirement age—but limited job future permits others to bypass them in many ways. Conversely, since employees about to retire may have begun to disengage from the organization and to adapt to aspects of the coming role as retiree, they may no longer try to exercise the power they still retain.

Meaningfulness. For some people, work provides the major source of meaning in their lives. Without the opportunity to work, life appears hollow and without challenge. When asked what he would bring to a desert island if he were stranded with a dozen others for the rest of his life, one research-oriented professor responded "My typewriter, lots of paper, and books." Some people find meaning in work because they thoroughly enjoy their jobs: given the chance to do anything they wished, they would choose to do pretty much what they are doing. For others, the meaning of work has a more religious overtone: for them, work is a given "good" and a way of fulfilling their mission on earth.

In spite of the thorough enjoyment of work for some and the mystical quality of work for others, only 8% of a sample of retired persons stipulated the loss of work itself as the most important in retirement, although—interestingly enough—19% of those interviewed who were still employed believed that this loss would be paramount (Shanas et al., 1968). Perhaps those who were retired felt less concerned about the meaningfulness of work because they had found other satisfying tasks. Or perhaps they felt that they had justified their existence through many years of work and were now entitled to relax and enjoy their leisure. Whatever the process, concern over loss of the meaningfulness that work affords may be much more valid for those who had seen their jobs as giving their lives more meaning and power.

The work itself. Relatively few people really enjoy the tasks they are required to perform on their jobs, although they do like many of the relationships, the feeling of usefulness, and the money that come with work. Given the option of having time free from onerous tasks they have been performing for 45 years, they accept, but not without concern over what they have lost. In the study by Shanas and her associates (1968), fewer than one-fifth of the retirees reported missing the work itself.

Although upper-echelon employees, managers, and professionals seem to have the greatest involvement in their work, there is little evidence as to whether they perceive their loss through retirement as greater than do other groups. Part of the difficulty in gathering conclusive evidence is that these people also have the highest retirement incomes and tend to have ongoing interests outside their previous jobs. Again we are confronted with the question of how much one's previous life history affects ability to deal with an age-related change. Are those best able to adjust to retirement the people who have lost or changed their status the least or those who have had the most successful and satisfying work lives to look back on?

Early Retirement

Do people want to continue working as long as possible? We are all familiar with the statements made by highly active older people that it is only their work that keeps them vital and excited or that not working is tantamount to being dead. However, study after study has shown these people to be a small minority. When given the option to retire early, even with reduced benefits, a very high proportion of people do so. One study of General Motors employees showed that only 2% remained until the mandatory retirement age of 70; 89% retired before their 65th birthday (J. H. Schulz, 1980).

In fact, early retirement has been consistently more popular than continuing to work until reaching the mandatory retirement age. In 1975, 61% of the men and 80% of the women who received Social Security benefits for the first time did so before the age of 65 (J. H. Schulz, 1980). A portion of these individuals undoubtedly retired because of poor health or some other physical limitation, but there is no doubt that most did so by choice.

When early retirees were compared with those who chose to remain on the job, a number of differences were found, none of them especially surprising. Early retirees were in a better financial position. They also had spent more time discussing retirement with others. Some job-related factors were also important: early retirees were more likely to have experienced recent change in the nature of their jobs, to feel that commuting was an irritation, or to find it difficult to keep up with their work demands or to control the pace of their work (Barfield & Morgan, 1969).

These data again show that, to understand a phenomenon such as retirement, we need to examine the characteristics of both the individual and the individual's situation—and, of course, the characteristics of the interaction between the two.

Mandatory Retirement

For many years work organizations had an arbitrary, mandatory retirement age, often 65, for most positions. Now, however, legislation in the United States restricts the imposition of mandatory retirement for most jobs until at least age 70, and similar legislation is now under consideration in Canada. At the same time that retirement laws have gone into effect, inflation has caused older workers to fear a drop in the purchasing power of their retirement income, and these two coinciding factors appear to have reversed the trend toward more and more early retirements. It is too soon, however, to judge the long-term effects of these factors.

The vast majority of people oppose mandatory retirement, assuming that the worker can still do a good job, but nearly two-thirds of the same survey's respondents agreed that most older people retire of their own choice, either because they no longer wish to work or because they are in poor health (Harris & Associates, 1975). These figures are supported by other data. When retirees who wanted to work were asked what was keeping them from working, well over half cited poor health; only 15% mentioned a lack of job opportunities (Harris & Associates, 1975). When we eliminate those who do not wish to continue to work and those whose health keeps them from working, only a very small proportion of older people appear to want to remain in the labor force. One analysis made in the late 1960s showed that only 10% of just-retired men both wanted to work and were capable of working; about 30% of these were able to find jobs (J. H. Schulz, 1980).

I believe that the immense fervor created by advocacy of the changes in mandatory retirement tended to represent the values of middle-aged and middle-class professional people who found their work exciting rather than the desires of the elderly themselves. Nonetheless, these changes were certainly a step in the direction of increased rights for older persons, and they will undoubtedly benefit some older individuals.

Life after Retirement

Expectations of retirement and the actualities of retirement often turn out to be quite different. Furthermore, when middle-aged people—adult children, personnel directors, social workers, or gerontologists—try to project their own retirement years, the projections do not always help them understand people who are presently retired. People with young children, with rising status and power, with increasing income and consumption, and without aches and pains on arising in the morning are likely to lack a real awareness of what retirement provides, both positively and negatively, for the retired person.

Adjusting to Retirement

For years many writers have advanced the notion that retirement is onerous, that being retired is being made meaningless, that people become bored with retirement, that the leisure time of retirement is seldom filled with worthwhile activities. Perhaps (but only perhaps) this was true for those older people who had been brought up to value the work ethic so much that any alternative was difficult to accept. My own observations lead me to believe that this is no longer the case for the majority of the elderly today.

For example, one expert on retirement has stated that most people look forward to retirement and expect to be "active, involved, expanding, full and busy" (Atchley, 1976, p. 28). This is especially true for those who anticipate a reasonable income and are in reasonably good health. By and large, the evidence shows that people adjust fairly quickly to retirement, and retirees report very little negative effect on self-esteem, depression, loneliness, or anxiety (Ward, 1979a).

According to a Swedish study, although more than half of the employees surveyed anticipated that they would miss working after they retired, only 36% of those already retired reported this to be the case (Skoglund, 1979). In 1968 a national sample of retirees in the United States responded to the question "Generally speaking, have you found your life since retirement enjoyable?" Another national sample was asked the same question in 1976. In the first interview 75% of the answers were favorable, and only 10% were unfavorable. By 1976 the mood had changed somewhat; only 56% were favorable, and 22% were unfavorable. The two major determinants of dissatisfaction were poor health and low income (Barfield & Morgan, 1978).

A recent study provides additional supportive data. A large northern California corporation distributed questionnaires to nearly 1000 of its retirees who had agreed to participate anonymously in the project; nearly 900 responses were returned sufficiently filled out to become part of the study. Most of the respondents had been white-collar employees, and their present family incomes were well above average. More than 80% had retired prior to the company's mandatory retirement age, primarily so that they could do other things they wished to do or get away from job pressures; only 11% had retired for health reasons. Only 20% of these retirees were presently working for money, either full or part time. Although this company is not typical of all corporations, the information reported is consistent with the data provided by other studies.

The most important factor determining these people's life satisfaction in retirement was the extent to which their actual participation in activities (80 activities were listed in the questionnaire) coincided with their desired participation in these activities. The less the discrepancy between the two measures, the higher the life satisfaction (Carlisle, 1979).

A number of other factors were also related to life satisfaction. The people who enjoyed their retirement were likely to be in good health, to have a higher family income, to be younger, to have retired more recently, to have wanted to retire, to have been white-collar employees, to have had more education, and to be married. It's obvious that some of these factors go together, such as being younger and having retired more recently, or being married and having a higher family income.

The respondents were also asked whether they felt limited by health, transportation, finances, lack of companionship, lack of motivation, or lack of opportunity. About 25% felt some health limitation, and 36% felt some financial limitation; an additional 26% felt some lack of motivation. However, except for financial limitations, none of these factors was cited by more than 10% of the respondents as "applies a lot." Again the evidence seems strong that older people do well in retirement if finances and health are adequate (Carlisle, 1979).

Some results of this study are shown in Table 6-2. Judging from these findings, it certainly seems that retirement can improve people's life situation in many ways. Of course, it is important to keep in mind that the participants in this study were younger, healthier, and better off financially than most retirees. Nonetheless, the available evidence indicates that many more people want to retire and enjoy their retirement than resist retirement and dislike it. And many people become so busy in retirement that they don't even have time to remember that they're retired.

Effective preretirement counseling could help to reduce the fears and misconceptions about the significance of being retired as well as improve awareness of the numerous options that retirement may provide. Although increasing numbers of organizations are providing some preretirement programs, relatively few of these programs go beyond the basic information of future income, a few health practices, and some encouragement to look into the local senior center. Very recently, however, there has been an increase in the number of more comprehensive programs, and this trend is likely to continue.

The studies of early retirement and of postretirement suggest that, of all the factors amenable to change, adequate income may well be the most important single element in providing postretirement satisfaction. Women are especially vulnerable to low retirement income because they have, on the whole, worked for briefer periods and for lower wages. I do not mean to detract from the significance of preretirement programs and senior centers, but these are of limited use to that segment of the aging population whose financial resources are extremely restricted.

Table 6-2. Changes for better or worse in retirement.

Factor in Life Satisfaction	*Much Better*	*Somewhat Better*	*Same*	*Somewhat Worse*	*Much Worse*
Health	18%	19%	47%	13%	3%
Finances	13	23	30	29	5
Marriage	20	20	57	2	2
Friendships	14	26	52	8	1
Enjoyment of Life	44	31	21	4	1

From *Accommodation to Retirement Years: Discrepancy as a Predictor Measure,* by A. E. Carlisle. Unpublished doctoral dissertation, California School of Professional Psychology, Berkeley, 1979.

Lifestyles in Retirement

Lifestyles in retirement certainly reflect earlier lifestyles, although conclusions on the exact relationships are difficult to draw. Most of those who are old today have not perceived many (if any) alternative lifestyles. They worked hard—or at least felt they should—in order to achieve certain goals, and they have often carried this orientation into retirement. Younger people have chosen among a greater range of alternatives, including the choice of rejecting the entire premise that work is necessary for personal fulfillment or income. How these younger people will eventually deal with retirement would make a fascinating longitudinal study. Lowenthal (1972) discusses this issue and then outlines nine lifestyles that influence retirement, five of which she discusses in some detail. These five are:

1. *The obsessively instrumental style.* People following this lifestyle are seen by a casual observer as highly engaged. They appear to be task oriented, driven to be involved, and, even in their leisure, compulsively active.
2. *The instrumental/other-directed style.* For these people, work provides access to satisfaction gained from interacting with others, particularly in meeting dependency needs. When these people retire, they will have to devise some alternative sources of satisfaction.
3. *The receptive/nurturant style.* Such individuals have developed "networks of close personal relationships" (Lowenthal, 1972, p. 321). Retirement seems to have little effect on these people, except to require them to develop social networks outside the work situation. Retirement may be more destructive for those for whom work provided the greatest source of interpersonal satisfaction—such as teachers, social workers, or psychotherapists.
4. *The autonomous style.* Autonomous people are often creative and are necessarily able to initiate action and establish relationships as needed. The implication of the term *autonomous* is that these people are still enjoying personal growth. Loss of work roles should cause less interference in their lives than in the lives of other groups because they can generate new roles and capacities.
5. *The self-protective style.* These people protect themselves from expressing their dependency needs, and they may well have established little engagement with life over the years. Therefore, retirement and concurrent disengagement are desired goals for them.

This list does not cover all the possible types of lifestyles in retirement; indeed, there may well be better methods of establishing categories. Nonetheless, the five types are suggestive and can be used as a foundation for understanding the varying needs of retired persons.

Leisure Time in Retirement

Like many terms that defy precise and all-encompassing definition, *work* and *leisure* can be approached in various ways. One possibility is to differentiate leisure and work activities by whether or not they are income producing; another consideration is whether or not the activity is sought for pleasure. In the final analysis, we need to recognize that the concepts are blurred around the edges. For example, since I dislike gardening, gardening is work for me, whereas it is pleasure for many people; indeed, many older persons find gardening very relaxing and seek the opportunity to garden many hours each week. What about the person who gardens for other people for a living? Is that work? Is it work even if he or she thoroughly enjoys gardening and would rather garden than do anything else?

The kinds of leisure activities available are numerous, depending on the income, health, mobility, and personal preferences of the individual. Some of the most popular leisure activities of the elderly are gardening, reading, watching television, watching sporting events, participating in social activities, visiting friends and relatives, taking walks, and pursuing creative and educational interests.

A low-income elderly man in the inner city may spend much of his time sitting on a park bench and talking with friends or visiting a neighborhood senior center. His life may appear lonely to others, and, indeed, he may very well feel lonely and isolated; on the other hand, he may have developed the role of loner many years earlier and may actually prefer this kind of life pattern. A middle-income elderly couple still living in their suburban home may be socially active with friends, participate in political action, do volunteer work in a local hospital, or take up painting or ceramics. Again, their lives may appear full and rich to the outside observer, although many such persons report that they feel lonely, especially if their spouse has died. To understand the feelings of older people, we need to know the actual nature of what they are doing, their previous life pattern, and their expectations and subjective perceptions.

While working—including doing housework and caring for children and others—an individual's time is structured by the demands of the work. In retirement the day, the week, and the year may be without external structure, so that the individual must structure his or her own time. This task can be very difficult, and time can slip away in a meaningless fashion—a disconcerting phenomenon for those who feel that time must be used *profitably* (however they define that term). Others take pleasure in unstructured time, whiling it away in casual pursuits.

My personal observations suggest that those working with the elderly are overly concerned about retired people's inability to enjoy leisure because of the work ethic and insufficiently concerned with providing adequate options for the enjoyment of leisure. However, those who work with the elderly are themselves work oriented, and perhaps they project their own views and feelings onto the elderly with whom they work. It seems entirely possible that, given sufficient income and transportation, the elderly who are in good health would willingly make use of whatever sources of leisure and entertainment available without longing for work.

The working potential of the elderly has brought forth some penetrating controversies—controversies that are moral issues as much as social concerns. For example, in a period of fairly high unemployment, particularly among unskilled younger and minority workers, how much effort should be expended to keep the older worker on the job? Does this effort serve to undermine the unions' bargaining power? Are we encouraging work for the elderly because we don't wish to provide them with adequate income through Social Security? Should there be a "right to work" that remains in effect regardless of age? To some extent, the information discussed earlier is relevant to these issues, but each person will bring his or her own value system to bear in interpreting the evidence regarding these questions.

Retirement Activities

In many ways retired people do the same things they did before they retired: they eat, sleep, play, make love, spend time with friends, go to church, participate in political and social organizations, read, garden, and watch television. However, the new time structure permits them to pursue activities that their previous work schedule did not allow.

One activity that has received considerable attention is watching television. Although public television has produced a half-hour program for and primarily about older people, virtually no other programming is aimed at them. Since some elderly people are confined to their homes because of disabilities and since many more are fearful of leaving their homes after dark, television is not only a source of information and entertainment but virtually a companion; the familiar people whom they see every week or every day on television become like friends (Davis, 1977). Interestingly enough, older viewers tend to prefer news shows to entertainment, perhaps because many of them feel isolated from what is going on in the world (Kubey, 1980).

There is a strong tendency for the general public to misperceive the kinds of activities that the elderly pursue. Table 6-3 shows how the elderly and the nonelderly spend their time and how the general public, including older people, thinks "most people over 65" spend their time.

The Physical Environment

Until the 1960s behavioral scientists ignored the influence on human behavior of the physical space within which the individual functions. Industrial studies had been made of the effects of lighting, color, and sound on behavior, but the general topic received little attention. Conversely, those who design space—architects, planners, engineers, builders—tended to ignore the characteristics of the people for whom they were designing, often emphasizing costs, efficiency of design, and their own esthetic preferences—all necessary factors for consideration, but not the whole story. Fortunately, those who design physical space and those concerned with human behavior are now sitting down and talking with one another.

Table 6-3. Participation in activities by the elderly and the nonelderly.

Activity	Percentage Spending "A Lot of Time" 18–64	Percentage Spending "A Lot of Time" 65 and Over	Percentage of the General Public Who Think "Most People Over 65" Spend a Lot of Time
Socializing with friends	55	47	52
Gardening or raising plants	34	39	45
Reading	38	36	43
Watching television	23	36	67
Sitting and thinking	37	31	62
Caring for younger or older family member	53	27	23
Participating in recreational activities or hobbies	34	26	28
Going for walks	22	25	34
Participating in fraternal or community organizations or clubs	13	17	26
Sleeping	15	16	39
Just doing nothing	9	15	35
Doing volunteer work	8	8	15
Participating in political activities	5	6	9
Participating in sports such as golf, tennis, or swimming	22	3	5

Reprinted from *The Myth and Reality of Aging in America,* a study prepared by Louis Harris and Associates, Inc. for The National Council on the Aging, Inc., Washington, D.C. © 1975.

Some kinds of physical space are used primarily to promote social interactions. Everyday experience tells us that discussion is easier when people face one another across a table, are in a circle, or are at right angles to one another. Nonetheless, seating in many settings for the elderly is arranged so that the seats are all parallel or all facing a television set. Often, to increase the amount of physical space in the center of a room, the seating is arranged along the walls, a design efficient in its use of space but inefficient for interaction. Healthy and socially aggressive younger persons might push the seats into better positions, but older people—especially those in institutions—often are too passive or lack the physical strength.

Since the design of buildings sets limits on the flexibility of interior physical space, planning for flexibility must begin early in the design process. In one high-rise apartment building for the well elderly, the mail is delivered to a centrally located counter, and the designers have created opportunities for social interaction by increasing the amount of surrounding space and placing chairs and tables and a supply of magazines at this place, where people normally congregate anyway. The result is a high degree of social interaction. Another plan for this building was to provide a small furnished space near the elevator where people could sit and talk, again making use of natural traffic patterns to encourage informal contacts. In another high-rise building, a small room set aside for reading and casual discussion failed in its purpose because people had to walk down a normally untraveled corridor to get there. Since the elderly residents had to plan ahead to go there, without knowing whether any companions would be in the room, the room was often empty.

Do older people prefer to be "where the action is" or to remain secluded and private? The obvious answer is that both options are important, and, if both are available to the elderly, their flexibility of functioning increases. In one housing project for the elderly, the main entrance opened on a lovely garden, surrounded by a wall and containing benches for sitting; the back of the building faced a moderately busy street. Although the garden benches were used, many of the elderly would take deck chairs to the back of the building, where they could view the street activity through the design of the stone fence, even though that space was cramped and not at all attractive.

The opportunity to alter physical space to suit individual needs and preferences is another necessity for the elderly. "To project one's personality upon a space, one must be able to change it" (Gelwicks, 1970, p. 155). Rooms in institutions for the elderly, and even the physical arrangements in a senior recreation center, are often designed so that the users can change them very little. The selection and arrangement of furniture, the decorations, and the color scheme are all established by professionals without involving the users in the decisions and without permitting subsequent change easily and inexpensively. Some institutions do not permit the elderly to bring in their own furniture or even to hang their pictures on the wall. Older people coming to an institution already feel that their power to influence their own lives has diminished greatly, and this inflexibility of room arrangements intensifies their sense of powerlessness and helplessness (Gelwicks, 1970).

Some special physical environmental necessities arise for the elderly whose health or strength is impaired. The most obvious ones are grip bars for the bathtub and shower, stoves that are designed so that the user does not have to lean across the burners to reach the oven or things above the oven, and doorways wide enough for wheelchairs and without risers that might trip elderly occupants. Other needs are less obvious. Arthritic hands may require special knobs on kitchen and other types of equipment; visual limitations can obscure spatial boundaries (between wall and floor, between the edge of the top step and the space beyond it), and these boundaries can be marked with contrasting paint; strength limitations may make it difficult to get up from a soft-cushioned couch that lacks rigid armrests.

Many other environmental considerations are particularly distressing for the elderly. These include high curbstones, high steps on buses, traffic lights of short duration, especially on wide streets that lack a median strip, broken sidewalks or flagstone walkways, too much glare, too little light, and institutions in which all rooms have the same shape, furniture, and location (confused older people can end up in the wrong room). I have barely touched the surface of this topic. The following sections on housing and transportation will discuss it further.

Housing

Of all heads of households over 65 years of age, 71% own their own homes (Brotman, 1981). This statistic may surprise you, but since some older persons are not heads of households, the figure does not imply that 71% of all older persons live in a home they own. Neither should this figure be interpreted to mean that older people have no housing problems. First, a high proportion of their homes are extremely old and often run down; second, many are located in high-crime areas, where older people are especially vulnerable as victims; third, rising property taxes often take a substantial portion of the older person's income, leaving no money for repairs; and, finally, the elderly often remain in these homes because they have no adequate alternative.

One apparent solution for the older homeowner is to sell the house and then rent slightly smaller facilities with the money obtained. In practice, this solution is frequently impossible. The average 1977 value of the home owned by a person over 65 was under $31,000 (Brotman, 1981). Selling costs would consume a portion of this amount, and moving expenses would take an additional portion. Even assuming, however, that the individual could net $29,000 through such a sale, by investing that amount in the bank at normal interest rates, he or she could not obtain very much in the way of housing. If the individual wished to draw from the principal to add to the interest for rent payments, the capital would eventually run out, and he or she would be in danger of having no money at all. This situation is typical of the financial conflicts that the lower-income elderly face.

In truth, most older people are satisfied with their present housing. They are especially unhappy about attempts to move them out of their neighborhoods (Lawton & Nahemow, 1973). These attempts were a great problem during the 1960s, when urban renewal forced so many elderly people, especially the low-income and non-White elderly, from their homes and neighborhoods.

Several varieties of housing are available for the elderly as alternatives to owning or renting their own home. Mobile homes are very popular among older people; more than half of the residents at some trailer courts are retired. Many of the elderly find the low cost and informality of such facilities very attractive; others are put off by the lack of privacy and the limited amount of room in mobile homes. Another alternative is the retirement hotel, usually an old hotel or apartment house, often in the downtown area of a city. It may provide limited services, such as maid service or a common meal service in the dining room. Unlike mobile-home parks, which are normally located on the outskirts of a town, the retirement hotel is located in the middle of "the action," providing the elderly access to more activities but increasing their chances of being victimized by crime.

Other older people live with family members, particularly brothers and sisters and adult children. Although most elderly people are very reluctant to live with their children, limited finances, health problems, or physical disabilities sometimes force them into such arrangements.

During the past two decades, many elderly people have moved into retirement communities, primarily established in California, Arizona, and Florida. Some of these villages restrict their residents to persons in or beyond their 50s (rules vary from village to village). Homes are purchased, normally on a very long-term payment plan, by individuals who have retired with a good income and are seeking a community offering a variety of activities for people of their own age group.

The pros and cons of living in these retirement communities have produced some very heated disagreements among gerontologists and among the elderly themselves. The controversies revolve around these communities' policies of age segregation, which restrict one's neighbors to other elderly people, and the communities' often semi-isolated location.

Although residents of retirement communities do admit to having less contact with family members than do elderly residents of the general community, they seem to have more friends available, have generally higher morale, and perceive their own health as better (Bultena & Wood, 1969). Although they miss the stimulation of mixing with younger people and children on a regular basis, older persons appear to have more social contacts and greater life satisfaction when they live in communities with high proportions of other older people (Rosow, 1967). Furthermore, extensive contact with younger adults and children is not an unmixed blessing. Not only do tensions arise over lifestyle, manners, and appropriate behavior, but the noise and sudden movements of young children are often disconcerting for the elderly. (See the discussion of intergeneration relations in Chapter Five.)

Retirement communities are certainly not for all older persons. They are often isolated from activity centers, the houses are expensive, and the pressures they exert on people to participate in activity programs are often extreme (at least they have been in the past); but they do represent a significant option for living arrangements for the elderly who can afford them.

The significance of good housing for the elderly has been acknowledged in a variety of ways: the federal government has subsidized housing for older people; church and fraternal organizations have developed their own housing; local communities have found ways to encourage such housing. It's obvious that if you don't like where you live or what you live in, your general life satisfaction is likely to be lower. And one study compared persons who had moved into a well-built new housing facility with others who had applied for the facility but did not move in; eight years later, those who had moved in were healthier and had a lower death rate (Carp, 1977).

Transportation

People need to move through their physical environment as well as reside within it, and transportation is one of the greatest needs of the elderly. Relatively few cities have adequate public-transportation systems, and even when the transportation is adequate, its design may make it troublesome for the elderly to use. Even more important, the life pattern in most parts of the United States presupposes that virtually everyone has an automobile available. Yet in 1974, 38% of the households headed by a person 65 or over had no car, a figure more than two and a half times as high as the figure for younger persons (Brotman, 1981). Limited income and physical disabilities combine to produce this low percentage of car owners among the elderly.

Although many elderly people walk a great deal, others tire quickly or have medical conditions that preclude extensive walking. Moreover, many services and activities are located too far from older people's homes to permit walking. Thus, without cars, unable to walk long distances, and lacking adequate and low-cost transportation, older people frequently find themselves physically cut off from important people and necessary services.

Some action has been taken to ameliorate these conditions. Many communities have arranged for reduced fares on public transportation, although often these fares are limited to off hours. Occasionally an agency arranges for special vehicles to pick up older persons for shopping, physician visits, nutrition or recreation programs, or pleasure trips.

Just as better housing contributes to life satisfaction, better access to transportation does also. One study found that older people with adequate transportation had increasing life satisfaction, while those without transportation had diminishing life satisfaction (Cutler, 1975).

A Last Comment

A tremendous amount of thought, time, energy, and money has been put into improving the income, work and leisure, and housing and transportation of older people. Vast programs have been developed by the federal government, and extremely modest programs have been developed by small groups of concerned persons. There is little doubt that satisfaction in these areas is vital to the general life satisfaction and feelings of well-being of the elderly.

Chapter Seven

Community Responses to Older Persons

We all live in a community, and we all are affected by the social institutions that exist in that community. We are responsive to how others view us and respond to us, to social programs that are established, to legal and educational and religious institutions, and to the effects of our own ethnic and nationality backgrounds. In the first five chapters of this book, I focused on the individual older person: numbers and definitions, psychomotor and cognitive behavior, health, personality, and family. This chapter, like the previous one, discusses what takes place in the larger community.

Attitudes toward Older People

It's easy to confuse attitudes toward older people with attitudes about becoming older oneself. The two may be related, but while few people look forward to old age, many people have a favorable attitude toward the elderly. It's also easy to confuse stereotypes about older people with attitudes toward older people, although once again the two may be related. You may believe that older people are often sick or cautious or irritable and yet not let the stereotype interfere with your relationships with individual older persons.

There is an abundance of studies—and I'll discuss a few later—that describe stereotypes, prejudices, and negative attitudes about older people, held not only by nonelderly persons but also by the elderly themselves. Yet there are many stereotypes, prejudices, and negative attitudes about adolescents and middle-aged people as well. It has often seemed to me that people working in the field of aging and the elderly themselves are eager to find evidence that older people are disliked by others. It's as though they are saying "Here, look at these poor, abused older people. I'm one of the few who can really appreciate their wonderful qualities. Now I need to persuade the rest of the world that these qualities exist."

Although it's true that many nonelderly select the later years as the worst years in a person's life, almost as many of those between 25 and 55 state that the teens are the worst period of life. It is those who are 65 and over who see the later years as distinctly the worst (Harris & Associates, 1975). Perhaps the elderly can appraise those years more accurately, or perhaps they have forgotten the stresses and fears of being an adolescent.

One author has pointed out that when people are forced to choose between older persons and other age groups, it appears that they have negative attitudes toward the elderly, but when they evaluate the elderly without making such comparisons, their responses are largely positive (Kogan, 1979). I find this an important distinction that is ignored too frequently. I certainly won't claim that older people do not suffer from stereotypes, prejudices, and negative attitudes, but I do believe that other age groups suffer in similar ways and that the actual treatment of older persons is better than one might assume based on much of what appears in newspapers, magazines, and other media.

Views of Children and Young People

When more than 200 third-graders were asked to write about "an old person," it became immediately obvious that character differentiations among adult age groups are readily made, even at this age. The most common response made by these children was that older persons are "kind"; more than 75% included that appraisal. Interestingly, the second most common evaluation was that older persons are "mean"; 25% of the children included that statement. (The analysis permitted each child's paper to be scored for more than one category, and sometimes a child would mention both "kind" and "mean" characteristics.) Loneliness, having leisure time, and eccentricities (often interpreted as "senile" behavior) were all touched upon by 10% or more of the children. Although fewer children described old people's physical characteristics, walking problems and general feebleness were each mentioned by about 15% of the group. To show the perceptiveness of some of the children, I will list a few of their comments:

> My sister and I like to walk down to the corner with old Mr. Smith, but we have to walk slower when we are with him.
>
> They always ask you to talk louder.
>
> Old people usually die, or lose a leg or an arm.
>
> Old people are mean, and they don't let you walk on their lawn.
>
> Old people are funny [Hickey, Hickey, & Kalish, 1968, p. 224].

More recent studies that included even younger children produced essentially the same results. Children between 3 and 11 years of age described the elderly as sick, tired, and unattractive; the children reacted negatively to their perceptions of the physical limitations and physical appearance of older persons. Yet the very same children also described older people as wonderful, kind, and rich (Seefeldt, Jantz, Galper, & Serock, 1977). A subsequent study of children aged 5 through 8 indicated that the elderly were seen as having fewer friends, being less healthy and less attractive, and being asked for help less often by someone who is lost than persons of other adult age groups. Yet, once again, these children selected the elderly as the most desirable to seek help from if they were hurt and as the people to whom they would most want to give help (Weinberger, 1979). However, both these studies forced the children to choose among age groups; they provided no information on how these children felt about older people on a noncomparative basis.

Studies of adolescent attitudes show comparable results. When children and adolescents at ages 8, 12, 15, and 19 were asked to evaluate adults at ages 25, 45, 65, and 85, the results clearly showed that the children did recognize age differences, that they did prefer younger adults to older adults, but that evaluations of older adults were not related to the age of the child or adolescent (Hickey & Kalish, 1968). More recently, a study of 9th-grade and 12th-grade students again showed no age differences in liking for older people but did indicate an overall favorable attitude toward the elderly (Ivester & King, 1977).

To me, the results of these studies are clear: (1) children and adolescents, like most other people, do not look forward to their own old age; (2) in most ways they prefer nonelderly adults to elderly adults, but this preference varies as a function of the particular context being discussed; (3) they like being with older people and, for the most part, like older people; and (4) gerontologists and others who work with the elderly spend too much time and effort trying to prove that older people are disliked.

Perceptions by Adults

Older people consistently view themselves much more optimistically than they are viewed by the nonelderly. However, when older people are asked about "older people in general," they use very much the same stereotypes that the nonelderly use. Once again we have evidence of the syndrome "I'm fine, but look at those poor old people over there."

Table 7-1 provides three comparisons. The first compares perceptions of "most people over 65" by the elderly and the nonelderly (columns 1 and 2); the second compares the self-perception of older people with their perception of older people in general and with the perception of the nonelderly (columns 1, 2, and 3); and the third compares how older people view themselves with how nonelderly people view themselves (columns 3 and 4). I find that each comparison makes one important point. The first comparison shows that the elderly's image of older people is very similar (except for being friendly and warm) to younger people's. The second comparison

Table 7-1. Elderly and nonelderly adults' images of older persons.

	Image of "Most People Over 65"		*Self-Image*	
Characteristic	*65 and Over*	*18–64*	*65 and Over*	*18–64*
Very friendly and warm	82%	25%	72%	63%
Very wise from experience	66	56	69	54
Very bright and alert	29	33	68	73
Very open-minded and adaptable	19	34	63	67
Very good at getting things done	35	38	55	60
Very physically active	41	43	48	65
Very sexually active	5	6	11	47

Reprinted from *The Myth and Reality of Aging in America*, a study prepared by Louis Harris and Associates, Inc. for The National Council on the Aging, Inc., Washington, D.C. © 1975.

shows that older people view themselves as individuals much more favorably on three characteristics (being bright and alert, being open-minded and adaptable, and getting things done) than they are evaluated by people in general. And the third suggests that, except for wisdom and physical and sexual activity, the self-images of older people differ only very slightly from the self-images of younger people (Harris & Associates, 1975).

There is other good evidence, shown in Table 7-2, that older people view their own situations much more optimistically than the general public does. And, as mentioned earlier, older people evaluate "most people over 65" in much the same way that the nonelderly evaluate them.

In a study of three generations of women in one family (Kalish & Johnson, 1972), Ann Johnson and I found that the middle generation, the mothers, were more negatively disposed toward older people and more fearful of the aging process than were either of the other generations; the grandmothers expressed the most favorable feelings toward aging and the aged. We speculated that middle-generation women often found themselves caring for aged parents while simultaneously noticing undesirable signs of aging in themselves. Also, mother/daughter tensions would often direct one generation toward resentment of the preceding generation, perhaps also helping promote affinity between the nonadjacent generations.

Having reviewed several dozen studies of attitudes toward the elderly, McTavish (1971) lists the stereotypes emerging from these investigations: ill, tired, uninterested in sex, mentally slower, forgetful, less able to learn

Table 7-2. Older persons' experience of "very serious" problems versus public expectations of "very serious" problems of "most people over 65."

	"Very Serious" Problem Experienced by Persons 65 and Over	*"Very Serious" Problem Attributed to "Most People Over 65"*	
		18–64	*65 and Over*
Fear of crime	23%	50%	51%
Poor health	21	50	53
Not having enough money to live on	15	63	59
Loneliness	12	61	56
Not enough medical care	10	45	36
Not enough education	8	19	25
Not feeling needed	7	56	40
Not enough to do to keep busy	6	38	33
Not enough friends	5	28	26
Poor housing	4	35	34
Not enough clothing	3	16	17

Reprinted from *The Myth and Reality of Aging in America*, a study prepared by Louis Harris and Associates, Inc. for The National Council on the Aging, Inc., Washington, D.C. © 1975.

new things, grouchy, withdrawn, self-pitying, less likely to participate in activities (with the exception, perhaps, of religion), isolated, living in the least happy and least fortunate time of life, unproductive, and defensive (p. 97). McTavish concludes that, in spite of these stereotypes, attitudes toward the elderly are not consistently negative and are often related to other variables; higher education and higher social class in the elderly, for example, are predictive of favorable attitudes.

Society's Values

Given that the latter decades of life are valued less than the earlier years, what does this say about the priority system applied to human values in Western nations? Why do we value the elderly less than their youthful successors? In response to these rhetorical questions, let me hazard a list of what I perceive to be those characteristics and conditions most respected by people in Western nations:

1. Achievement and potential for achievement.
2. Productivity of goods, services, or artistic endeavors.
3. Ability to carry on human relationships successfully.
4. Independence and self-sufficiency.
5. Past accomplishments.
6. Ability to enjoy life.

7. Knowledge and awareness, capacity for grasping technology.
8. Physical attractiveness, sexual capacity, and physical vitality.
9. Influence and power.
10. Material wealth.
11. Ability to provide nurturance to others.
12. Wisdom.
13. Desire to invest time, energy, and money in the future.

You may believe that some of these values are misperceived, and you personally may not accept many of them, but you are likely to accept the list as at least representative of the way we invest our time, money, and energies. On only two characteristics listed here are the elderly likely to hold their own: past accomplishments and wisdom. Even these are questionable, since past accomplishments often dwindle in importance as the years go by. To attribute wisdom to the aged is also questionable, since views and values considered wise at one time may later be considered outdated. It is true that the elderly have had immeasurable experience, but much of their experience was gained during a time when different values were in vogue. For example, our relatively new awareness of environmental pollution in its myriad forms has, by itself, immensely affected our general perceptions of the wisdom of economic growth.

In essence, then, the older person does not fare well when evaluated against the major criteria that our culture implicitly sets up. Let me suggest a few alternative criteria:

1. Adhering to traditional codes of Judeo-Christian morality.
2. Maintaining one marriage throughout a long life.
3. Being willing to defend one's country in a defensive war or to support one's country in a controversial involvement—or even to give one's life for it.
4. Having a large number of descendants.
5. Having experienced wars and depressions.

This list is hardly a recitation of our national value system today. Earlier in our history, many of the values on the second list would have been on the first, and many of the items on the first list probably did not discriminate so effectively against the elderly. For example, in a rural, nonindustrial society, knowledge and technological awareness are found in the older, not in the younger, members; and the senior generation retains greater control over land and business, thus controlling entrée to jobs and financial resources.

The first set of values, however, are the ones reinforced by what children and adults see and hear and read. Studies of older people in children's literature (Ansello, 1977), in women's magazines (Schuerman, Eden, & Peterson, 1977), in adolescent literature (D. A. Peterson & Eden, 1977), on television (Greenberg, Korzenny, & Atkin, 1979), and even through the history of literature (Charles, 1977) all appear to agree on certain basic findings. Older people are usually underrepresented, the roles that they perform are frequently either uninteresting or unpleasant, and stereotypes are often encouraged.

Nonetheless, older people are not critical of the portrayal of the elderly on television. In fact, the overwhelming majority feel that they are treated with respect (Harris & Associates, 1975). Some pressures have been brought to bear on publishers and television producers to change the role of older persons in their media, and, as mentioned earlier, educational television has produced at least one series for and about older people. However, television comedies in which the problems of older people are held up to ridicule and books that portray the elderly as ineffectual or peculiar seem to be just as visible as ever. Furthermore, there is an issue that has not even been addressed: it seems logical that negative and stereotyped media portrayals would damage the self-esteem of the elderly and influence the attitudes of others toward the elderly. However, we don't have good information yet on whether this actually occurs.

Ageism and Its Implications

> [Positive] attitudes toward aging may be critical for adjustment and survival. It is possible that attitudes contribute to observed maladaptive behaviors among the aged, some of which may result in premature death. Negative views of aging, life in general, and oneself may result in an old person's unwillingness or inability to seek needed services, health care, or other types of assistance. Negative attitudes of old people may affect others in their environs, who in turn may feel free to respond negatively to old people or to ignore them completely [Bennett & Eckman, 1973, p. 575].

These statements are hypotheses, not established facts. They may not fairly describe the overall picture, but they have a strong ring of truth. Even though research data do not, for example, show a reduction in the self-rated self-esteem of older persons, there is little doubt that the self-esteem of some older persons drops as a result of the process of aging and—even more—as a result of some of the disruptive forces, discussed earlier, that accompany aging in disproportionate numbers.

One obvious example of ageism—those negative attitudes toward the aged mentioned by Bennett and Eckman (1973)—that influences the survival of the elderly is the attitudes of health practitioners. Geriatric medicine, geriatric social welfare, continuing education for the elderly, psychotherapeutic services for the elderly—none of these specialized services has had an overabundance of ready recruits. Health practitioners in general seem to assign lower priority to service to the elderly than to service to any other age group.

No wonder many people resent growing old. Not only do the elderly frequently suffer significant losses in psychomotor skills, in visual and auditory sensitivity, in income, and in work opportunities, but they must also deal with the many negative and often patronizing attitudes of younger people—which undoubtedly are partial reflections of the attitudes of the elderly themselves. Older persons perceive their own declining status and, sometimes, declining abilities, and they also must begin to recognize that their personal future is limited by imminent death. Since they serve to remind others of aging and death, their very presence is often upsetting, eliciting responses from younger people that range from condescending humor to bitter anger; many of us resent having to contemplate our own finitude. Recognizing what is happening to them, feeling anger and resentment and helplessness, many elderly people fight back in the only way available to the powerless; they complain, nag, criticize, become irritable and petulant, and alternate between assertions of independence and obvious manipulations to permit dependence.

This picture is often true of unhappy elderly people. The fascinating contradiction is that so many of the elderly, even those who are financially impoverished, continue to report high life satisfaction and high morale.

Social Services and Social Programs

Have attitudes toward older people become more positive over the past 30 or 40 years? We don't really know, but if increases in funding, facilities, and programs are criteria, the answer would have to be "yes." You might, with some justification, contend that these increases have come about because vested interests—such as government workers, insurance companies, health-care and nursing-home professionals, and others—stand to gain rather than because people truly care about the elderly (Estes, 1979). Or you might chalk it all up to conscience money or to improved political power and strategies of the elderly. Whatever the causes, there are innumerable programs available for older people, ranging from the vast network of Medicare and Medicaid to the small senior center supported by a local church.

Of course, not all programs can be viewed as social-service programs. Elsewhere in this chapter and in other chapters, health programs, institutional care, financial programs, educational programs, church-supported programs, legal programs, housing and transportation programs, nutritional programs, and more are discussed. In some ways they need to be seen as a whole, as a large package of programs for older people; in other contexts it is appropriate to look at them in categories or even one at a time.

From my reading (see especially Beattie, 1976) and my observations, I have noted four trends in programming and services for older people. These trends appear to be ongoing, and I believe they will continue for the remainder of this decade.

First, there is an increasing desire to help people stay in their own homes and communities. Part of the reason is cost effectiveness: it has been found that it is less expensive to keep people out of institutions. However, part of the reason is humanitarian: for the most part, people enjoy being in their homes and accessible to their friends and family and neighbors, retaining as much autonomy as possible.

Second, there is a continued emphasis on cost containment and cost effectiveness. Although programs are expanding, careful attention is given to the costs. Government at all levels, as well as the private sector, is deeply concerned about the high costs of all social and other programs, and efficiency in financial management is seen as paramount. Part of determining cost effectiveness is that the programs prove they are doing their job effectively; this requires record keeping, sometimes evaluation research, and analysis of what is going on and who is being served. Although it seems difficult to argue with the need to consider cost effectiveness, some people who oppose programs for older persons use this concept as a basis for attacking the allocation of funds.

Third, coordination of services and programs is encouraged. Thus, if older people are going to receive a hot lunch, the site where the lunch is provided can also offer opportunities for recreation; if a senior center is available, it can provide a vast array of health and social programs rather than just being a place for enjoyable leisure activities. Coordination also means that various agencies that provide services come together to plan effective ways of delivering these services. This is an attempt, on the one hand, to avoid offering unnecessary or duplicated services and, on the other hand, to make certain that the elderly who need services get them. Although such coordination is essentially advantageous, it also requires time and effort and therefore money; and sometimes so much energy is expended in coordinating and planning that relatively little is left for direct services.

Fourth, we are moving away from viewing old age as only a decremental period and toward seeing it more as a stage of life with its own required tasks, some of which are continuations of the tasks of earlier stages and some of which are newly emerging and in need of attention during the late years of life. Among the needs that continue are the needs for personal growth, challenge, and stimulation. The continuation of these needs means that services for older people must go beyond provision of basic income, health care, housing, transportation, and nutrition; older people also need the opportunity to deal with new ideas, to learn new skills, and generally to develop themselves mentally and physically. These comments are not necessarily a call for the government to allocate more funds, although that is certainly an option; older people can plan, develop, and conduct many programs themselves with little or no outside help, while other programs and services can be supported by churches, schools, universities, and private business and industry.

The Programs Available

There is an immense variety of programs, and I'll describe only a few of them here. Others are discussed elsewhere in the book, and many can probably be described by your friends, your instructor, and your classmates (if you are using this book as a classroom text) and by people who work with the elderly in your community. If you have no resources, write or phone your local Area Agency on Aging—there are several hundred in the United States—to find out what is happening locally.

For the well elderly. The great majority of older people are healthy and mobile; they have at least a little money to spend or else can find programs that will subsidize them; and they can either get around by themselves or find transportation services that will help them get around. For these people, the options are numerous. For example, the well elderly may use the information and referral programs in their communities to locate services or activities that will keep them occupied. And if they don't know how to get in touch with information and referral sources, a telephone call to the local senior center or county or town offices will usually elicit the information.

There are numerous opportunities for important volunteer work. Some of these opportunities are provided through such groups as the Retired Senior Volunteer Program (RSVP) and the Foster Grandparent program; both programs offer expense money and sometimes a small salary in exchange for working with children or others or in nonprofit agencies that can benefit from the care, the knowledge, and the involvement of older people. Another essentially volunteer program is the Service Corps of Retired Executives (SCORE). SCORE uses older retired executives as consultants for businesses or community agencies that can profit from the counsel of older people with management experience.

Other older people volunteer in hospitals, schools, libraries, and elsewhere. They may work in a gift shop, deliver meals to patients, be responsible for an information desk, tutor or read to children, or participate in "friendly-visitor" programs. The options are endless, especially in the more densely populated urban areas, but even small towns and rural areas may have such opportunities.

Another kind of service program is modeled after the SAGE Program, launched about a decade ago. SAGE has experimented with offering older people the activities associated with what was once termed the counterculture. These include the martial arts, sensory awareness, deep breathing, dance and movement, finger painting, yoga exercises, and personal discussion groups.

Senior centers deserve a special mention. There are some 5000 senior centers in the United States (Leanse, 1977), many of which not only conduct numerous programs in a central facility but also manage coordinated services in what are termed satellite centers scattered throughout the community. The activities provided through the multipurpose senior center extend far beyond the stereotypical bridge game and carpentry or weaving class, although these are usually available. Using a paid staff, supplemented by the volunteer help of both the elderly and younger persons, these facilities are probably the single most important social program for the well elderly. The staff at these centers plan and conduct trips, provide access to legal counsel, establish programs for the elderly with hearing or vision problems, develop employment opportunities, and schedule discussion groups on personal or intellectual themes. In short, senior centers offer the well elderly an immense array of varied activities and services.

For the elderly who are not well or mobile. In addition to the 4% or 5% of older persons who are in institutions, another, somewhat larger group of older people have problems that require special attention. There are many services available for these people also. For example, those confined to their homes may be served through a "friendly-visitor" program, perhaps by a high school student or perhaps by a more active older person. There are telephone reassurance programs, in which a volunteer (often elderly) at a central location phones a number of older people at the same time every day; if the older person does not answer, a neighbor is immediately notified and asked to see if everything is all right. Many lives have been saved through this program, which operates through hospitals and other facilities all over the United States.

Other programs include home repair and maintenance for older persons who lack either the knowledge or the capacity to make simple home repairs. Homemaker programs send out aides who will cook a hot meal, do some housework, and perhaps shop or do the laundry for elderly people who are capable of living at home alone but can no longer do these tasks. Of course, the social contacts between the homemaker aide and the older person are also extremely valuable.

A recently established program shows how ingenuity can provide valuable services at virtually no cost. Elderly people living alone obtain an emblem to attach to their mailboxes indicating that they are "at risk" in some fashion. If the mail deliverer notices that the previous day's mail has not been picked up, he or she checks to see what has happened or else informs the appropriate person or agency. This program, like the telephone program, protects older people who have fallen and hurt themselves, had a stroke or a heart attack, or suffered any other health problem that has incapacitated them. Such programs can greatly reduce the fears of older people living alone.

It is often assumed that programs for older people require considerable time and money. That isn't true. Anyone who is able to make a commitment can initiate a program. For example, many older people have trouble shopping or getting to their physician's office or to church, and a group of volunteers could provide transportation. They could also spend an afternoon each week or two with an older person or take the older person to a movie or a restaurant or a local park, providing a service that many elderly would greatly enjoy. The list of possibilities is endless.

Advocacy

One additional trend in services for older people is the increase in advocacy. This means that individuals or organizations expend time and effort to support funding, legislation, and human relationships that are beneficial to older people. The advocate may be a young lawyer or an elderly social worker; advocacy may take place in a hearing held by a state legislative committee or in the board room of a large corporation or a charitable foundation.

Older people are often their own best advocates, but help from appropriately trained and experienced nonelderly is extremely useful. Advocacy in the formal sense is most important in influencing legislation that affects funding for projects for older people, that provides them with protective services when they become too frail to take adequate care of themselves, or that gives them rights of employment or other kinds of rights. In a less formal sense an advocate for older people might attempt to persuade a university to permit older people to take classes without paying or a chain of restaurants to provide the elderly with price reductions for eating meals at nonpopular times.

Another form of advocacy is to encourage store employees, bus drivers, and the public in general to pay more attention to the physical limitations of some older people and to simultaneously avoid treating them as incompetents or children.

The Edlerly and Criminal Victimization

Fear of becoming the victim of a crime is one of the greatest concerns of older people in the United States, sometimes the most frequently mentioned concern of all (Harris & Associates, 1975). Although the elderly are victims of many kinds of crime, they most commonly suffer from personal larceny (that is, purse snatching and pocket picking) and robbery, whereas younger people are more often victims of rape and assault (Antunes, Cook, Cook, & Skogan, 1977).

Although the elderly appear to fear criminal victimization more than other age groups, the data show that they fall victim least often. However, when they are victimized, their financial losses represent the highest proportion of income of any age group over 30. Similarly, although the elderly are least likely to be physically hurt when victimized, when they are hurt, they tend to sustain serious internal injuries, and the cost of medical care again represents the highest proportion of income of any adult age group (Cook, Skogan, Cook, & Antunes, 1978).

It would appear, then, that the basis for the high level of fear among the elderly is their essential vulnerability: their strength and agility are diminished, so that they realize they can neither fight back nor run away; a small financial loss in actual dollars signifies a major financial setback in terms of percentage of income; and if they are hurt, they are likely to suffer serious internal injuries.

Older people living in public-housing projects frequently reside in areas of the community that have higher-than-average crime rates. As might be expected, the elderly public-housing residents who feared crime the most were those who lived in the areas of highest crime rates and those who had already been victimized. Fear was also high among those living in large communities and those living in age-integrated facilities—that is, where there was a substantial mix of age groups in the residences. Nearly 70% of these public-housing tenants never left their homes after dark, and another 10% did so less than once a month (Lawton & Yaffe, 1980). It certainly seems that older people in public housing, who also tend to have very limited incomes, suffer the most from criminal victimization.

To help older people avoid being criminally victimized, police departments have established instruction programs that describe how to carry purses to avoid injury, how to thin out shrubbery to eliminate hiding places for robbers, how to make breaking and entering more difficult, and how to organize neighborhood surveillance systems (Younger, 1976). Some elderly people have been instructed in how to fall to minimize the possibility of injury, since it is frequently the impact of hitting the concrete sidewalk that produces serious injuries.

Robberies, purse snatching, and other crimes involving force are not the only ways in which the elderly are criminally victimized. The great majority of victims of bunco and confidence games are elderly (Younger, 1976). One such "game" involves a younger person telling his (it usually is a male, but not always) elderly victim that he is a bank security officer and that the bank suspects a teller of embezzling; the older person is told to withdraw his or her money so that the teller can be observed, to give it to the phony bank officer as evidence, and then to return home to collect the reward. Of course, neither a reward is tendered nor are the original holdings ever returned.

Medical quackery and consumer fraud are two other ways in which older people are victimized. About 70% of the victims of medical quackery that come to the attention of the district attorney's office are elderly (Younger, 1976). In one example of consumer fraud, older people are sold something, perhaps a water softener or a new surface for the driveway, for what is purported to be a very low price. After they sign the contract, however, they learn that the price is much higher. A number of older people have lost their homes to the schemers because of inability to pay off the debt.

Older people are not always victims of crime; they also commit illegal acts and occasionally more serious crimes. The most common reason for arrest of an older person is drunkenness; gambling and disorderly conduct are also common offenses. As the number of crimes committed in the United States has risen, the proportion committed by people over 55 has diminished. It's possible, however, that the very low rates of crime in this age group result in part from greater leniency that judges and police show to older people; we don't have adequate information on this issue yet to draw any conclusion (Shichor & Kobrin, 1978).

In the years to come, as the proportion of elderly in the population increases, the issue of criminal victimization is likely to receive more attention. Already senior centers and other facilities are distributing materials to older people to help them reduce the chances of being victimized or, if victimized, to minimize financial loss and physical harm.

Legal Services

Important as it may be, criminal victimization is not the only legal concern of the elderly; they frequently find that they need advice on making out wills and planning estates; some elderly people do not receive their just allocation of benefits from federal or other governmental programs; they may believe that they have been deprived of pension rights or forced to retire earlier than the present law allows.

Another legal concern of older people is that of legal conservatorship. When an older man or woman is alleged to be incompetent, his or her estate is turned over to a guardian to be managed. The guardian may also be permitted to make decisions of a personal nature regarding the older person. In effect, the legal and personal autonomy of the elderly individual is forfeited. The circumstances under which this transfer of authority is appropriate are often a matter of legal controversy.

At the same time the elderly face the same legal problems faced by the nonelderly: divorce; the legal issues of second marriages, such as property division; bankruptcy requirements; lawsuits; and so forth.

Religion and the Aging

Are older people more religious than younger people? Do people become more religious as they grow older? These two questions, interrelated but not identical, have received some preliminary answers, but final conclusions still cannot be drawn. One major impediment to conclusive answers is that the definition of *religious* is so open to debate. For example, research results are quite different if we define *religious* in terms of church attendance as opposed to belief in God.

One source distinguishes five dimensions of religiousness: religious practices, religious beliefs, religious knowledge, religious experiences, and consequences of religion for personal and social life (Glock & Stark, 1965). Rather than assuming any single dimension or any combination of dimensions to be the definition of *religious* this approach looks at each dimension separately. For example, church attendance rises with age until the later years and then gradually declines, probably due to difficulties in transportation, health, and income. Similarly, although church membership among older persons is more common than all other social-organization memberships combined, active church involvement diminishes slightly in the later years. On the other hand, listening to church services on the radio and television, praying, Bible reading, and meditating all increase steadily with age (Moberg, 1971).

If we look at all of these measures, it appears that religious practice is greater among older persons and would be greater still were it not for the limitations of income, health, and mobility. How many of these age differences result from changes that occur with age and how many arise from differences in upbringing between persons born at the turn of the century and those born later is still unknown. Perhaps both factors contribute.

The elderly also retain more traditional religious beliefs than younger persons do. For example, belief in God and in immortality has been shown to be greater among the elderly (Moberg, 1971). Studies of religious knowledge, however, provided less consistent results; the elderly are apparently better versed in certain religious matters, and younger persons are more informed on others. Since the elderly have less formal education and may also be troubled by slower reaction time (if the test is timed) or lack of test sophistication, religious knowledge is difficult to evaluate.

"Many older people experience religious feelings, emotions, thoughts, visions, and dreams and share them with clergymen, relatives, and friends" (Moberg, 1971, p. 29). Again, concrete evidence is lacking, but clinicians' impressions suggest an increase in these experiences with age.

The impact of the last dimension distinguished by Glock and Stark (1965), consequences of religion for personal and social life, is almost impossible to judge because of the difficulty in deciding what the consequences should be. For example, if you believe that the consequences should include a willingness to become a missionary serving one's religion, you will arrive at a conclusion on the impact of religion and its relationship to age considerably different from the conclusion drawn by the person who believes that the consequence should be a diminution of ethnic prejudice and discrimination.

The relevance of religion and the church to the elderly goes beyond the belief systems of individual older people. One investigator asked a carefully selected sample of older people about both their kinds of group membership (for example, service club, veterans' group, labor union, study group) and their life satisfaction. He found not only that church membership was by far the largest in the 17 kinds of groups but also that it was the only one related to life satisfaction (Cutler, 1976). We don't know, of course, whether church affiliation leads to increased life satisfaction or whether people with greater life satisfaction are more likely to attend church (or even whether people who are affiliated with a church are more likely to exaggerate their life satisfaction), but the relationship was found consistently.

I believe that the role of the church in increasing the life satisfaction and well-being of older persons has been underestimated. I see half a dozen good reasons that the church has advantages over other organizations in serving the elderly:

1. Most older people have a history with their religion and their church; both are familiar to them, and they are comfortable in church.
2. The mission of the church is to serve people without regard to their age, unlike some agencies that focus on children or younger adults.
3. Discussing personal concerns with a cleric is not an indication of "craziness" or inadequacy; rather, it is usually part of a lifelong pattern, unlike seeing a social worker or a psychotherapist.
4. Seeing a cleric about worries or anxieties isn't recorded in an official file and doesn't require an explanation to friends.
5. In the later years the universal questions of the meaning of life and death become more relevant, and the idea of spiritual well-being takes on greater significance.
6. Many older people survive highly stressful situations by drawing on their personal faith and belief in a power greater than themselves (Kalish, 1979b).

Nevertheless, not all churches do a good job of offering spiritual and practical support and programs to older people. Some still place most of their resources in programs for the young, whereas others are simply insensitive to the needs of the elderly and make only feeble or inappropriate attempts to respond to these needs.

Sanford Seltzer (1980) has outlined five steps for churches to follow in responding to the needs of the elderly in their congregations:

1. Recognize that many members of the congregation are in their later years.
2. Identify the elderly in the congregation and learn more about them: who are widows or widowers, who live alone, who have transportation needs, and so on.
3. Organize committees of older members who will meet to determine the

nature of their own needs and the ways in which the church can best respond.

4. Take action, based on the committee reports, including liaison with appropriate local agencies and educational institutions.
5. Develop educational programs for church-affiliated private schools and Sunday schools so that children can begin to learn more about aging, including the role of aging in the Scriptures.

Educational Gerontology

Not many years ago the educational system was seen as being only for young people. Slowly the idea developed that adults can also profit from formal education, but only recently has it become evident that education is appropriate for people of all ages. The concept of lifelong learning is gradually becoming more than a platitude.

As recently as 1979, about half of the elderly people in the United States had fewer than ten years of formal education, and more than 2 million older people, or somewhat less than 10% of the elderly population, had fewer than five years of schooling (Brotman, 1981). These figures will be very different in the years ahead. More than half of the people born in the decade following World War I have a high school education or more, and this proportion will increase in the years to come. By the turn of the century, there will be relatively little difference between the educational levels of the elderly and the nonelderly, assuming there are no drastic changes in who is educated in the coming years (D. A. Peterson, 1974).

There seems little question that many older people are eager for continuing education, either through a public-school adult-education program or through local community colleges and universities. However, education is not limited to the familiar institutions, nor need it occur in the classroom. Television offers credit and noncredit courses in conjunction with college extension services; senior centers put on workshops, discussion groups, and seminars; and other nontraditional educational programs are available.

A fairly recent approach to later-adult education is the *elderhostel.* This is a national program, held at many colleges and universities around the United States, in which older people can attend special courses, usually taught by the regular faculty, for two weeks (or sometimes another time period) while living in college dormitories and eating at the college cafeteria. Since these programs are given throughout the summer, some older people travel across the country taking courses at various institutions and sightseeing as they drive from college to college.

Although it is generally agreed that special educational opportunities should be made available to older people, it is not always clear what the educational needs of the elderly are. One of the foremost U.S. authorities on this topic, Howard McClusky (1971), has pointed out four types of needs:

1. *Coping needs* are needs required for functioning effectively in society. These include basic education, health education, and education in finance and legal decisions.
2. *Expressive needs* involve doing activities that are enjoyed for their own sake; these may include athletics and exercise, creative arts and writing, or the enjoyment of nature such as gardening or wilderness hiking.
3. *Contributive needs* assume that older people want to contribute to other individuals or to society in general, and may therefore need to learn, for example, how to teach reading to slow-learning children. Older people may learn how to best contribute their time and energy or their wisdom and experience.
4. *Influence needs* refer to ways in which older people can influence other persons, institutions, or the political arena to improve their own situation or for whatever other reasons they wish.

Although education for older people is now readily available in many communities for those who seek it, large numbers of the elderly pull back from participating. Researchers in Wichita interviewed more than 400 older people to learn what the barriers were to their taking college classes. Among the most frequent responses were that the cost was too high, the courses offered were not interesting enough, the respondents might feel out of place with all the young students, either the respondents' hearing or vision or both were inadequate, and transportation was lacking. In addition, a substantial number informed the interviewers that they were simply too busy (Graney & Hays, 1976).

If schools are to enroll older people as students, they will obviously have to find ways of overcoming these barriers. Improved curricular programming, geared more toward the needs of the older students, is one requirement. A second is to teach the instructors ways of reaching older students and to help them overcome their own misperceptions of older learners, as well as to start placing older students in age-integrated classes. A third requirement is to eliminate the cost of tuition as a barrier, perhaps by letting older people take classes for little or no cost on a space-available basis; and, fourth, the schools need to help provide transportation, to relocate the classes closer to where older people already are (for example, in churches or senior centers), or to hold them more frequently during daytime hours, when older people are less fearful of venturing out and when they may be able to use local transportation facilities.

Recruiting older students will be no more difficult than recruiting other kinds of students who originally did not attend college as a rule, such as ethnic minorities (D. A. Peterson, 1974). And as a few older people become accustomed to attending a particular college, others will find participation much easier.

Ethnicity and Aging

Our ethnic background helps define who we are, how we view ourselves, and how others view us. Although only one of many factors that influence us, ethnicity remains with us for our entire lifetime, and the experiences that we had early in our lives concerning ethnicity may well continue to affect us in our later years. Table 7-3 shows the numbers of middle-aged and elderly persons in several ethnic groups in the United States.

Just as I began this book by insisting that "older people" are not a single entity, though we often discuss them as such, "older members of an ethnic group" are not a single entity. The elderly Black woman living in rural Alabama has a life much different from that of the elderly Black woman who went to Detroit during World War II and stayed there. The elderly Hispanic farmer in New Mexico whose family settled there in 1720 shares some experiences with the elderly Hispanic who is a migratory worker or with the elderly Hispanic Catholic priest, but their cultural differences are often greater than their cultural similarities.

Nevertheless, some general comments can be made about the elderly of minority groups, who are sometimes said to face double jeopardy: that which comes from being elderly and that which comes from being a member of a minority group. When put together, these factors may operate exponentially to increase the plight of the elderly in minority groups. For example, in addition to facing the financial restrictions, health concerns,

Table 7-3. Demographic characteristics of selected ethnic groups.

	Number of Persons (in thousands)		*Percentage of Total Population*	
Ethnic Group	*45–64*	*65 and Over*	*45–64*	*65 and Over*
Native Americans (1970)	104	44	13.7	5.7
Chinese Americans (1970)	75	27	17.2	6.2
Filipino Americans (1970)	51	21	15.2	6.2
Japanese Americans (1970)	120	47	20.5	8.0
Black Americans (1978)	4,100	1,989	16.0	7.8
Hispanic Americans (1978)	1,590	518	13.2	4.2
White Americans (1978)	39,126	21,800	20.7	11.5

Adapted from *Minorities and Aging*, by Jacquelyne Johnson Jackson. © 1980 by Wadsworth, Inc. Reprinted by permission of Wadsworth Publishing Company, Belmont, CA 94002.

and family disruptions of old age experienced by all elderly people, older people of Mexican, Asian, Cuban, Native American, and other backgrounds often do not speak English well and may not be able to read English at all. As their memory for recent events becomes poorer, the little English they have acquired may be forgotten. Therefore, filling out forms, communicating with a harried social worker, or simply getting to the right person for the right answer to a question becomes an insurmountable task. Furthermore, since some minority groups have a high proportion of impoverished elderly, the older people of ethnic groups can indeed be said to face lives of double, or even triple, jeopardy.

Another factor to consider in discussing the elderly of ethnic groups is that most of our values have been heavily influenced by Central and Northern European cultures, in interaction with those from Southern Europe, and may therefore be unfamiliar to persons arriving from Asia or Latin America or those entering urban communities from Indian reservations. In Japan and China, for example, the elderly parents of a son are cared for by the son's wife, but many American or Canadian daughters-in-law would be very unhappy with such a role.

At the same time elderly members of minority groups must find some way of coping with the new militancy found among their young. The young people's behavior may violate the older people's long-internalized values regarding proper procedures and proper role behavior. The elderly may be accused of behaving like Uncle Tom or Tio Taco or Uncle Tomatsu when they are merely adhering to long-held values that are difficult to change. Thus, many of the ethnic elderly lead a doubly difficult life. First, they are victimized by overt or covert prejudice and discrimination or by their lack of language skills, vocational training, and opportunity. (Sometimes, as in the case of laws discriminating against Asians or customs discriminating against Blacks and Hispanics, the differential in opportunity has been both extreme and inflexible.) Second, they find themselves under attack for not having been aggressive enough at an earlier age in fighting these injustices or for not being able to alter their values sufficiently in their later years.

Each ethnic group has its own culture and its own unique history in the United States. Cuban Americans, for example, came to the United States in large numbers early in the 1960s; relatively few of those who came were elderly at the time, but in the subsequent two decades, many have become elderly. Mental-health services have been established in the Miami area for elderly Hispanics (most of whom are of Cuban descent), using *personalismo*—the personal touch—through a well-known elderly Cuban actress to encourage participation (Szapocznik, Lasaga, Perry, & Solomon, 1979). In this fashion, knowledge of the history and culture of Cuban Americans is put to use in providing services to the elderly. The extent to which it is effective with Cuban Americans who migrated to the United States 50 years ago is, of course, not known.

On the other side of the country, older Filipino Americans, largely located on the West Coast and in Hawaii, tend to be primarily men. The reason is that many years ago a number of young Filipino men migrated to the United States, and very few women accompanied them. Later, in their middle years or old age, some of these men returned to the Philippines to marry and bring their wives back, virtually always marrying much younger women (Buyagawan & Krisologo, 1974).

I've described examples from two ethnic communities that receive very little attention in discussions of ethnicity and old age. Their numbers are not great compared with Black Americans or the Mexican-American segment of the Hispanic community.

Minority groups are often lauded for "taking good care" of their own elderly. This undoubtedly occurs in part because many of these groups do have strong family feelings, but it also occurs in part because facilities for minority elderly are less adequate than for the general community (Jackson, 1980). In recent years minority-group members, both elderly and nonelderly, have developed organizations to give them greater power in improving their situations. The original minority-based organization for the elderly was the National Caucus for the Black Aged, established more than a decade ago. Since then, similar organizations have evolved for Hispanic elderly, Native American elderly, and Asian American elderly. All these organizations are, in their own ways, attempting to weld together groups that have their own unique histories, a task that is not simple. The Asian Americans and Pacific Basin people include Japanese, Chinese, Koreans, Southeast Asians, Filipinos, Samoans, Tahitians, and others; the Hispanics include people with origins in Mexico, Cuba, Puerto Rico, Guatemala, and elsewhere; Native Americans come from scores of different nations; and even Black Americans may have roots in the rural South, the urban Northeast, or the Caribbean.

Research on ethnic communities has not been well developed. Is it possible, for example, that Black Americans age differently from White Americans? We know that their life expectancies differ: Black men and women have shorter life expectancies up until about 70 and longer life expectancies thereafter. We also know that they are susceptible to different diseases, live under different conditions, and have much different life histories. Is their biological aging process different? Do they display different behavior and different performance levels when they become old? If so, why? Is it a matter of genetics? Different life experience? Different cultural expectations? All of these in combination?

But even this degree of differentiation is insufficient, because it lumps all members of one ethnic group together. Research should proceed to learn about the variation within the large and diverse community (or the many communities and individuals) of Black Americans. What kinds of parent/child relationships develop between middle-aged, middle-class Blacks and their elderly parents? In what ways do these resemble and differ from the relationships found between low-income Blacks and their elderly parents? Or among middle-income Whites? Asian Americans? Hispanic Americans? Polish Americans? Why?

The Rural Aged

There are many ways of grouping older people: by sex, by ethnicity, by health or disability, by income, by age, or by marital status. One kind of grouping that has received very little attention (although this now appears to be changing) is by urban or rural living. About one-fourth of older people live in rural communities, and about 20% of these live on farms (Youmans, 1977). Since younger people have been moving out of most rural areas, older people often constitute a high proportion of the population.

Most rural elderly have lived in rural areas much of their lives, frequently in the same community in which they are growing old. If they have moved, it is often from an outlying farm to a small town where their access to services, to friends, to shopping, and so forth is easier and where their housing is more appropriate for dealing with health and physical limitations than the more isolated homes where they previously lived and reared their families.

In some ways the rural elderly are definitely at a disadvantage compared with the urban elderly. Income, for example, is considerably lower than for the urban elderly; even though it is difficult to compare the cost of living for the two groups—housing costs, for instance, would be lower in many rural areas, whereas utility bills may be higher—there is little doubt that poverty is widespread among the rural elderly. When industrial developments or housing tracts push into rural areas, it is also unlikely that the elderly will benefit. They are likely to see prices and taxes rise, but they do not have the opportunity for employment to compensate. At the same time the increased value of their homes is not helpful, since selling would only leave them at the mercy of increased housing prices elsewhere. Nor, in spite of myths to the contrary, are the rural elderly healthier than their urban counterparts. In fact, they report a much higher rate of physical ailments than elderly urban dwellers do (Youmans, 1977).

Given their greater financial and health problems, it is logical to ask whether the rural elderly's general life satisfaction and sense of well-being reflect these problems. Overall, they do appear to have a more negative outlook on life than their urban counterparts, according to one study, and they are less satisfied with their housing, finances, health, feelings of usefulness, and opportunities for social interactions with friends and neighbors. They also appear to have lower self-esteem. However, they indicate a higher level of general happiness and better family relationships, and they are more likely to be pleased with their neighborhoods (Youmans, 1977).

Given the way that the rural elderly, whether on farms or not, are spread out over such large areas, providing services becomes difficult. For example, a senior center in a town of 20,000 people that has some 2500 elderly, about 20% of whom might want to use the facilities, has a population base to develop services and programs. However, a senior center in a rural community of 2000 people that has some 250 elderly, about 20% of whom might want to use the facilities, would have great difficulty putting together a program. Advocates for the rural elderly, however, are working diligently to improve the situation for these people.

Aging in the Future

What will the aging process be like in the future? What will it be like to be old in the future? Obviously, neither question can be answered with any certainty, but we can try out some hypotheses. For example, is it likely that life expectancy will be substantially greater 50 years from now? Or 100 years from now?

Some authorities believe that we can learn enough about the process of aging, apart from the diseases associated with aging, to increase *healthy* life span significantly (Comfort, 1969); others believe that we have sufficient information about healthier living (for example, on diet, exercise, stress, substance abuse) and about preventive medicine to increase life span significantly now (Woodruff, 1977).

If life expectancy suddenly rises to, let's say, 80 years, some important questions emerge. For example, pension programs are based on present life expectancies; if life is suddenly ten years longer, how will companies or, for that matter, Social Security find the money to pay out that much more in retirement benefits? Or what about second careers? If a 50-year-old person realizes that he or she probably has a good 30 years of health ahead, does the probability increase of wanting to move to another career rather than remaining in the same field? And if second careers become more common, what are the implications for education? Will colleges and universities need to develop courses or, perhaps, entire curricula aimed at mid-life career changes? If so, will 30-year-old faculty members be capable of teaching the courses?

Other areas for speculation include marriage and family relationships. Good marriages are unlikely to be affected, except to be enriched, but will a healthy 60-year-old be inclined to remain in a poor marriage if the marriage is unlikely to be broken by death for another 20 years? Further, some older people avoid late marriages because they believe they will not live long enough or because they are reluctant to find themselves taking care of an ailing spouse. However, if a late marriage has an excellent chance of lasting for 20 healthy years, the rewards may become worth the risks.

The second set of issues is a more immediate, less speculative matter: what will it be like to be old in the future? Are mandatory retirement-age regulations completely on the way out? If so, how long will it take before

Social Security payments are adjusted to reflect the option of working until at least 70?* And will this mean that years are going to be added to the working life rather than the retired life?

Also, what will happen to services for older persons? Will senior centers and nutrition programs be expanded? Will the health insurance of the elderly cover more or less of their health costs in the future? Will older people who have adequate incomes be required to pay for more of what they get, or will means tests be seen as both degrading and financially inefficient?

What will happen to the political power of older people? Will it increase, so that the elderly begin to vote as a bloc? Will the elderly of tomorrow, having a considerably higher educational level than today's elderly, prove to be better advocates for themselves? Will radical groups of elderly emerge? Or will the overwhelming proportion of elderly become more conservative and cautious, preferring to hold onto what they have rather than take risks to gain more? Will there be a backlash against the financial costs of programs and services for older people, so that a new form of prejudice against them will come about? Or, as the older people in the population become more powerful (if they do), will they be more respected and suffer less prejudice and discrimination?

These are all unanswered questions. I have personal suppositions on each of these matters, but there is very little data available for providing answers to any of the questions—and often there is no data at all. One prediction that I will make is that even the definition of *old* or *elderly* will be pushed back five or ten years and that a new age category, something like "the mature adult," will emerge (see also Neugarten, 1974).

We have not done an especially good job of enabling today's elderly to have a satisfying life. Will we do better when the meaning of chronological age changes and more people live longer? Will the added years of vitality permit self-fulfilling activities and involvements and give people ample flexibility to select what they wish to do from a wide range of possibilities? Or will the added years signify a longer period in which to live with low income, limited resources, and low status? Does the more conservative period ushered in by the national elections of 1980 herald reduced programs and services for older persons? Does it mark the beginning of closer intergenerational relationships?

You are reading this book at least a year after I finished writing it. That year or so gives you a much better perspective on these issues than I have. And many of you are likely to live long enough to learn the answers to some of the long-range questions posed in the preceding paragraphs. One thing I can predict with certainty: the issues and concerns of older people and the processes of aging will offer stimulation and provoke action for the rest of this century.

*Judging from political trends developing after this was written, it will not take very long. (Author's note.)

References

Anderson, B., & Palmore, E. Longitudinal evaluation of ocular function. In E. Palmore (Ed.), *Normal aging II*. Durham, N. C.: Duke University Press, 1974.

Ansello, E. F. Age and ageism in children's first literature. *Educational Gerontology*, 1977, *2*, 255–274.

Antunes, G. E., Cook, F. L., Cook, T. D., & Skogan, W. G. Patterns of personal crime against the elderly: Findings from a national survey. *The Gerontologist*, 1977, *17*, 321–327.

Arenberg, D., & Robertson-Tchabo, E. A. Learning and aging. In J. E. Birren & K. W. Schaie (Eds.), *Handbook of the psychology of aging*. New York: Van Nostrand Reinhold, 1977.

Atchley, R. C. *The sociology of retirement*. Cambridge, Mass.: Schenkman, 1976.

Atchley, R. C. *The social forces in later life: An introduction to social gerontology* (3rd ed.). Belmont, Calif.: Wadsworth, 1980.

Atchley, R. C., & Miller, S. J. Older people and their families. *Annual Review of Gerontology and Geriatrics*, 1980, *1*, 337–369.

Barfield, R. E., & Morgan, J. N. *Early retirement: The decision and the experience*. Ann Arbor, Mich.: Institute for Social Research, 1969.

Barfield, R. E., & Morgan, J. N. Trends in satisfaction with retirement. *The Gerontologist*, 1978, *18*, 19–23.

Barrows, C. H., Jr. The challenge—Mechanisms of biological aging. *The Gerontologist*, 1971, *11*(1, Pt. 1), 5–11.

Beattie, W. M., Jr. Aging and the social services. In R. H. Binstock & E. Shanas (Eds.), *Handbook of aging and the social sciences*. New York: Van Nostrand Reinhold, 1976.

Bell, B., Wolf, E., & Bernholz, C. D. Depth perception as a function of age. *Aging and Human Development*, 1972, *3*, 77–82.

Bengtson, V. L., & Cutler, N. E. Generations and intergenerational relations: Perspectives on age groups and social change. In R. H. Binstock & E. Shanas (Eds.), *Handbook of aging and the social sciences*. New York: Van Nostrand Reinhold, 1976.

Bennett, R., & Eckman, J. Attitudes toward aging: A critical examination of recent literature and implications for future research. In C. Eisdorfer & M. P. Lawton (Eds.), *The psychology of adult development and aging*. Washington, D. C.: American Psychological Association, 1973.

Bequaert, L. H. *Single women: Alone and together.* Boston: Beacon Press, 1976.

Berardo, F. M. Survivorship and social isolation: The case of the aged widower. *The Family Coordinator*, 1970, *19,* 11–25.

Beresford, J. C., & Rivlin, A. M. *The multigeneration family* (Occasional Papers in Gerontology, No. 3). Ann Arbor and Detroit: University of Michigan and Wayne State University, Institute of Gerontology, 1969.

Bergman, M. Changes in hearing with age. *The Gerontologist*, 1971, *11* (2, Pt. 1), 148–151.

Birren, J. E. *The psychology of aging.* Englewood Cliffs, N. J.: Prentice-Hall, 1964.

Blenkner, M. Social work and family relationships in later life with some thoughts on filial maturity. In E. Shanas & G. F. Streib (Eds.), *Social structure and the family: Generational relations.* Englewood Cliffs, N. J.: Prentice-Hall, 1965.

Blenkner, M. The normal dependencies of aging. In R. A. Kalish (Ed.), *Dependencies of old people* (Occasional Papers in Gerontology, No. 6). Ann Arbor and Detroit: University of Michigan and Wayne State University, Institute of Gerontology, 1969.

Blum, J. E., Fosshage, J. L., & Jarvik, L. F. Intellectual changes and sex differences in octogenarians. *Developmental Psychology*, 1972, *7,* 178–187.

Botwinick, J. Intellectual abilities. In J. E. Birren & K. W. Schaie (Eds.), *Handbook of the psychology of aging.* New York: Van Nostrand Reinhold, 1977.

Botwinick, J. *Aging and behavior* (2nd ed.). New York: Springer, 1978.

Botwinick, J., & Storandt, M. Cardiovascular status, depressive affect, and other factors in reaction time. *Journal of Gerontology*, 1974, *29,* 543–548.

Botwinick, J., & Thompson, L. W. Individual differences in reaction time in relation to age. *Journal of Genetic Psychology*, 1968, *112,* 73–75.

Britton, J. H., & Britton, J. O. *Personality changes in aging.* New York: Springer, 1972.

Bromley, D. B. *The psychology of human ageing* (2nd ed.). Baltimore: Penguin, 1974.

Brotman, H. B. The aging of America: A demographic profile. *National Journal,* October 7, 1978, pp. 1622–1627.

Brotman, H. B. *The aging society: A demographic view.* Paper presented to the National Council on the Aging, Washington, D. C., April 22, 1980.

Brotman, H. B. *Every ninth American.* Draft prepared for "Developments in Aging, 1980" for the Special Committee on Aging, U. S. Senate, 1981.

Bühler, C. Old age and fulfillment of life with considerations of the use of time in old age. *Acta Psychologica*, 1961, *19,* 126–148.

Bultena, G. L., & Powers, E. A. Denial of aging: Age identification and reference group orientations. *Journal of Gerontology*, 1978, *33,* 748–754.

Bultena, G. L., & Wood, V. The American retirement community: Bane or blessing? *Journal of Gerontology*, 1969, *24,* 209–217.

Burgess, E. Personal and social adjustment in old age. In M. Derber (Ed.), *The aged and society.* Champaign, Ill.: Industrial Relations Research Associates, 1950.

Busse, E. W. Theories of aging. In E. W. Busse & E. Pfeiffer (Eds.), *Behavior and adaptation in late life.* Boston: Little, Brown, 1969.

Butler, R. N. The life review: An interpretation of reminiscence in the aged. *Psychiatry: Journal for the Study of Interpersonal Processes*, 1963, *26,* 65–76.

Buyagawan, A. K., & Krisologo, R. B. *Culture and modification in social and health services to older Filipino Americans.* Paper presented at the annual convention of the Gerontological Society, Portland, Oregon, November 1, 1974.

Campbell, A., Converse, P. E., & Rodgers, W. L. *The quality of American life.* New York: Russell Sage Foundation, 1976.

Cantor, M. H. Neighbors and friends: An overlooked resource in the informal support system. *Research on Aging*, 1979, *1,* 434–463.

Carlisle, A. E. *Accommodation to retirement years: Discrepancy as a predictor measure.* Unpublished doctoral dissertation, California School of Professional Psychology, Berkeley, 1979.

Carp, F. M. Impact of improved living environment on health and life expectancy. *The Gerontologist,* 1977, *17,* 242–249.

Case, H. W., Hulbert, S., & Beers, J. *Driving ability as affected by age* (Report No. 70-18). Los Angeles: University of California, Institute of Transportation and Traffic Engineering, 1970.

Charles, D. C. Literary old age: A browse through history. *Educational Gerontology*, 1977, *2,* 237–254.

Chown, S. M., & Heron, A. Psychological aspects of aging in man. *Annual Review of Psychology*, 1965, *16,* 417–450.

Cicirelli, V. G. Sibling relationships in adulthood: A life-span perspective. In L. W. Poon (Ed.), *Aging in the 1980s: Psychological issues.* Washington, D. C.: American Psychological Association, 1980.

Clark, M., & Anderson, B. G. *Culture and aging.* Springfield, Ill.: Charles C Thomas, 1967.

Cohen, D., & Wu, S. Language and cognition during aging. *Annual Review of Gerontology and Geriatrics*, 1980, *1,* 71–96.

Comfort, A. Longer life by 1990? *New Scientist*, 1969, *11,* 549–551.

Cook, F. L., Skogan, W. G., Cook, T. D., & Antunes, G. E. Criminal victimization of the elderly: The physical and economic consequences. *The Gerontologist*, 1978, *18,* 338–349.

Corso, J. F. Sensory processes and age effects in normal adults. *Journal of Gerontology*, 1971, *26,* 90–105.

Craik, F. I. M. Age differences in human memory. In J. E. Birren & K. W. Schaie (Eds.), *Handbook of the psychology of aging.* New York: Van Nostrand Reinhold, 1977.

Cumming, E., & Henry, W. H. *Growing old.* New York: Basic Books, 1961.

Cutler, S. J. Transportation and changes in life satisfaction. *The Gerontologist*, 1975, *15,* 155–159.

Cutler, S. J. Membership in different types of voluntary associations and psychological well-being. *The Gerontologist*, 1976, *16,* 335–339.

Davis, R. H. The role of television. In R. A. Kalish (Ed.), *The later years: Social applications of gerontology.* Monterey, Calif.: Brooks/Cole, 1977.

De Beauvoir, S. *The coming of age.* New York: Warner, 1973.

Dennis, W. Creative productivity between the ages of 20 and 80 years. *Journal of Gerontology*, 1966, *21,* 1–8.

Denton, F. T., & Spencer, B. G. Canada's population and labour force, past, present, and future. In V. W. Marshall (Ed.), *Aging in Canada: Social perspectives.* Toronto: Fitzhenry & Whiteside, 1980.

Eisdorfer, C. Intellectual and cognitive changes in the aged. In E. W. Busse & E. Pfeiffer (Eds.), *Behavior and adaptation in late life.* Boston: Little, Brown, 1969.

Eisdorfer, C. Adaptation to loss of work. In F. Carp (Ed.), *Retirement.* New York: Behavioral Publications, 1972.

Eisdorfer, C. Personal communication, 1978.

Eisdorfer, C., & Cohen, D. The cognitively impaired elderly: Differential diagnosis. In M. Storandt, I. C. Siegler, & M. F. Elias (Eds.), *The clinical psychology of aging.* New York: Plenum, 1978.

Eisdorfer, C., Cohen, D., & Preston, C. *Behavioral and psychological therapies for the older patient with cognitive impairment.* Paper presented at the Conference on Behavioral Aspects of Senile Dementia, Washington, D. C., December 1978.

Eisdorfer, C., & Stotsky, B. A. Intervention, treatment, and rehabilitation of psychiatric disorders. In J. E. Birren & K. W. Schaie (Eds.), *Handbook of the psychology of aging.* New York: Van Nostrand Reinhold, 1977.

Elias, M. F., & Elias, P. K. Motivation and activity. In J. E. Birren & K. W. Schaie (Eds.), *Handbook of the psychology of aging.* New York: Van Nostrand Reinhold, 1977.

Engen, T. Taste and smell. In J. E. Birren & K. W. Schaie (Eds.), *Handbook of the psychology of aging.* New York: Van Nostrand Reinhold, 1977.

English, H. B., & English, A. C. *A comprehensive dictionary of psychological and psychoanalytical terms.* New York: McKay, 1958.

Epstein, L. J. Depression in the elderly. *Journal of Gerontology*, 1976, *31,* 278–282.

ERA. Study shows elderly income; 30% get Social Security only. *ERA*, October 1980, p. 7.

Erikson, E. H. *Childhood and society* (2nd ed.). New York: Norton, 1963.

Estes, C. L. *The aging enterprise.* San Francisco: Jossey-Bass, 1979.

Farberow, N. L., & Moriwaki, S. Y. Self-destructive crises in the older person. *The Gerontologist*, 1975, *15,* 333–337.

Fozard, J. L., Wolf, E., Bell, B., McFarland, R. A., & Podolsky, S. Visual perception and communication. In J. E. Birren & K. W. Schaie (Eds.), *Handbook of the psychology of aging.* New York: Van Nostrand Reinhold, 1977.

Furry, C. A., & Baltes, P. B. The effect of age differences in ability: Extraneous performance variables in the assessment of intelligence in children, adults, and the elderly. *Journal of Gerontology*, 1973, *28,* 73–80.

Gelwicks, L. E. Home range and the use of space by an aging population. In L. A. Pastalan & D. H. Carson (Eds.), *Spatial behavior of older people.* Ann Arbor and Detroit: University of Michigan and Wayne State University, Institute of Gerontology, 1970.

Giambra, L. M., & Arenberg, D. Problem solving, concept learning, and aging. In L. W. Poon (Ed.), *Aging in the 1980s: Psychological issues.* Washington, D. C.: American Psychological Association, 1980.

Glaser, B. G., & Strauss, A. L. *Time for dying.* Chicago: Aldine, 1968.

Glock, C. Y., & Stark, R. *Religion and society in tension.* Chicago: Rand McNally, 1965.

Goldfarb, A. I. Masked depression in the old. *American Journal of Psychotherapy*, 1967, *21,* 791–796.

Goldfarb, A. I. Marital problems of older persons. In S. Rosenbaum & I. Alger (Eds.), *The marriage relationship.* New York: Basic Books, 1968.

Goldfarb, A. I. Institutional care of the aged. In E. W. Busse & E. Pfeiffer (Eds.), *Behavior and adaptation in late life.* Boston: Little, Brown, 1969. (a)

Goldfarb, A. I. The psychodynamics of dependency and the search for aid. In R. A. Kalish (Ed.), *Dependencies of old people* (Occasional Papers in Gerontology, No. 6). Ann Arbor and Detroit: University of Michigan and Wayne State University, Institute of Gerontology, 1969. (b)

Gottesman, L. E., Quarterman, C. E., & Cohn, G. M. Psychosocial treatment of the aged. In C. Eisdorfer & M. P. Lawton (Eds.), *The psychology of adult development and aging*. Washington, D. C.: American Psychological Association, 1973.

Graney, M. J., & Hays, W. C. Senior students: Higher education after age 62. *Educational Gerontology*, 1976, *1*, 343–359.

Greenberg, B. S., Korzenny, F., & Atkin, C. K. The portrayal of the aging: Trends on commercial television. *Research on Aging*, 1979, *1*, 319–334.

Gubrium, J. Being single in old age. *Aging and Human Development*, 1975, *6*, 29–41.

Gurin, G., Veroff, J., & Feld, S. *Americans view their mental health: A nationwide interview study*. New York: Basic Books, 1960.

Gurland, B. J. The comparative frequency of depression in various adult age groups. *Journal of Gerontology*, 1976, *31*, 283–292.

Gutmann, D. L. *The country of old men: Cross-cultural studies in the psychology of later life* (Occasional Papers in Gerontology, No. 5). Ann Arbor and Detroit: University of Michigan and Wayne State University, Institute of Gerontology, 1969.

Gutmann, D. L. Alternatives to disengagement: The old men of the highland Druze. In R. LeVine (Ed.), *Culture and personality: Contemporary readings*. Chicago: Aldine, 1974.

Gutmann, D. L. Parenthood: A key to the comparative study of the life cycle. In N. Datan & L. H. Ginsberg (Eds.), *Life span developmental psychology: Normative life crises*. New York: Academic Press, 1975.

Hall, E. Acting one's age: New rules of old (Bernice Neugarten interviewed). *Psychology Today*, April 1980, *13*, 66–80.

Harkins, E. B. Effects of empty nest transition on self-report of psychological and physical well-being. *Journal of Marriage and the Family*, 1978, *40*, 549–556.

Harkins, S. W., & Warner, M. H. Age and pain. *Annual Review of Gerontology and Geriatrics*, 1980, *1*, 121–131.

Harris, L., & Associates. *The myth and reality of aging in America*. Washington, D. C.: National Council on the Aging, 1975.

Hartley, J. T., Harker, J. O., & Walsh, D. A. Contemporary issues and new directions in adult development of learning and memory. In L. W. Poon (Ed.), *Aging in the 1980s: Psychological issues*. Washington, D. C.: American Psychological Association, 1980.

Havighurst, R. J. Successful aging. *The Gerontologist*, 1961, *1*, 1–13.

Havighurst, R. J., & Albrecht, R. *Older people*. New York: Longmans, Green, 1953.

Havighurst, R. J., Neugarten, B. L., & Tobin, S. S. Disengagement and patterns of aging. In B. L. Neugarten (Ed.), *Middle age and aging*. Chicago: University of Chicago Press, 1968.

Hayflick, L. The strategy of senescence. *The Gerontologist*, 1974, *14*, 37–45.

Haynes, S. G., McMichael, A. J., & Tyroler, H. A. Survival after early and normal retirement. *Journal of Gerontology*, 1978, *33*, 269–278.

Herr, J., & Weakland, J. *Counseling elders and their families*. New York: Springer, 1979.

Hertzog, C., Schaie, K. W., & Gribbin, K. Cardiovascular disease and changes in intellectual functioning from middle to old age. *Journal of Gerontology*, 1978, *33*, 872–883.

Hess, B. B. Friendship. In M. W. Riley, M. Johnson, & A. Foner (Eds.), *Aging and society. Vol. 3: A sociology of age stratification*. New York: Russell Sage Foundation, 1972.

Hickey, T. *Health and aging*. Monterey, Calif.: Brooks/Cole, 1980.

Hickey, T., Hickey, L., & Kalish, R. A. Children's perceptions of the elderly. *Journal of Genetic Psychology*, 1968, *112*, 227–235.
Hickey, T., & Kalish, R. A. Young people's perceptions of adults. *Journal of Gerontology*, 1968, *23*, 216–219.
Hill, R. Decision making and the family life cycle. In E. Shanas & G. F. Streib (Eds.), *Social structure and the family: Generational relations.* Englewood Cliffs, N. J.: Prentice-Hall, 1965.
Howell, S. C. Environments and aging. *Annual Review of Gerontology and Geriatrics*, 1980, *1*, 237–260.
Howell, S. C., & Loeb, M. B. Nutrition and aging: Monograph for practitioners. *The Gerontologist*, 1969, *9*(3, Pt. 2).
Hoyer, F. W., Hoyer, W. J., Treat, N. J., & Baltes, P. B. Training response speed in young and elderly women. *Aging and Human Development*, 1978–1979, *9*, 247–253.
Iglehart, J. K. The cost of keeping the elderly well. *National Journal*, October 28, 1978, pp. 1728–1731.
Institute for Interdisciplinary Studies. *Older Americans speak to the nation—A summary* (White House Conference on Aging, background papers). Minneapolis: Author, 1971.
Ivester, C., & King, K. Attitudes of adolescents toward the aged. *The Gerontologist*, 1977, *17*, 85–89.
Jackson, J. J. *Minorities and aging.* Belmont, Calif.: Wadsworth, 1980.
Jarvik, L. F. Diagnosis of dementia in the elderly: A 1980 perspective. *Annual Review of Gerontology and Geriatrics*, 1980, *1*, 180–203.
Jarvik, L. F., & Blum, J. E. Cognitive declines as predictors of morality in twin pairs: A twenty-year longitudinal study of aging. In E. Palmore & F. C. Jeffers (Eds.), *Prediction of life span.* Lexington, Mass.: Heath, 1971.
Jarvik, L. F., Kallman, F. J., & Falek, A. Intellectual changes in aged twins. *Journal of Gerontology*, 1962, *17*, 289–294.
Jung, C. G. *Modern man in search of a soul.* New York: Harcourt Brace, 1933.
Kahana, E., & Coe, R. M. Perceptions of grandparenthood by community and institutionalized aged. *Proceedings of the 77th Annual Convention of the American Psychological Association*, 1969, 735–736.
Kalish, R. A. Suicides: An ethnic comparison. *Bulletin of Suicidology*, December 1968, pp. 37–43.
Kalish, R. A. Introduction. In R. A. Kalish (Ed.), *Dependencies of old people* (Occasional Papers in Gerontology, No. 6). Ann Arbor and Detroit: University of Michigan and Wayne State University, Institute of Gerontology, 1969.
Kalish, R. A. Of social values and the dying: A defense of disengagement. *The Family Coordinator*, 1972, *21*, 81–94.
Kalish, R. A. The new ageism and the failure models: A polemic. *The Gerontologist*, 1979, *19*, 398–402. (a)
Kalish, R. A. The religious triad: Church, clergy, and faith in the resources network. *Generations*, 1979, *3*, 27–28. (b)
Kalish, R. A. *Death, grief, and caring relationships.* Monterey, Calif.: Brooks/Cole, 1981.
Kalish, R. A., & Johnson, A. I. Value similarities and differences in three generations of women. *Journal of Marriage and the Family*, 1972, *34*, 49–54.
Kalish, R. A., & Reynolds, D. K. *Death and ethnicity: A psychocultural study.* Los Angeles: University of Southern California Press, 1976.
Kalish, R. A., & Visher, E. *Journal of Divorce*, 1981, *5*, in press.
Kaplan, H. B., & Pokorny, A. D. Aging and self-attitude: A conditional relation-

ship. *Aging and Human Development*, 1970, *1*, 241–250.
Kastenbaum, R. The reluctant therapist. In R. Kastenbaum (Ed.), *New thoughts on old age.* New York: Springer, 1964.
Kastenbaum, R. As the clock runs out. *Mental Hygiene*, 1966, *50*, 332–336.
Kastenbaum, R. Personality theory, therapeutic approaches, and the elderly client. In M. Storandt, I. C. Siegler, & M. F. Elias (Eds.), *The clinical psychology of aging.* New York: Plenum, 1978.
Kastenbaum, R., & Candy, S. E. The 4% fallacy: A methodological and empirical critique of extended care facility population statistics. *Aging and Human Development*, 1973, *4*, 15–22.
Kayne, R. C. Drugs and the aged. In I. M. Burnside (Ed.), *Nursing and the aged.* New York: McGraw-Hill, 1976.
Kelly, J. The aging male homosexual: Myth and reality. *The Gerontologist*, 1977, *17*, 328–332.
Kenshalo, D. R. Age changes in touch, vibration, temperature, kinesthesis, and pain sensitivity. In J. E. Birren & K. W. Schaie (Eds.), *Handbook of the psychology of aging.* New York: Van Nostrand Reinhold, 1977.
Kiefer, C. W. *Changing cultures, changing lives.* San Francisco: Jossey-Bass, 1974.
Kivnick, H. Q. *Grandparenthood: Meaning and mental health.* Unpublished doctoral dissertation, University of Michigan, 1980.
Kleban, M. H., Lawton, M. P., Brody, E. M., & Moss, M. Behavioral observations of mentally impaired aged: Those who decline and those who do not. *Journal of Gerontology*, 1976, *31*, 333–339.
Knight, B. Psychotherapy and behavior change with the noninstitutionalized elderly. *Aging and Human Development*, 1978–1979, *9*, 221–236.
Kogan, N. Beliefs, attitudes, and stereotypes about old people: A new look at some old issues. *Research on Aging*, 1979, *1*, 11–36.
Kogan, N., & Wallach, M. A. Age changes in values and attitudes. *Journal of Gerontology*, 1961, *16*, 272–280.
Kubey, R. W. Television and aging: Past, present, and future. *The Gerontologist*, 1980, *20*, 16–35.
Kübler-Ross, E. *On death and dying.* New York: Macmillan, 1969.
Larson, R. Thirty years of research on the subjective well-being of older Americans. *Journal of Gerontology*, 1978, *33*, 109–129.
Lawton, M. P., & Nahemow, L. Ecology and the aging process. In C. Eisdorfer & M. P. Lawton (Eds.), *The psychology of adult development and aging.* Washington, D. C.: American Psychological Association, 1973.
Lawton, M. P., & Yaffe, S. Victimization and fear of crime in elderly public housing tenants. *Journal of Gerontology*, 1980, *35*, 768–779.
Leanse, J. The senior center, individuals, and the community. In R. A. Kalish (Ed.), *The later years: Social applications of gerontology.* Monterey, Calif.: Brooks/Cole, 1977.
Lee, G. R. Children and the elderly: Interaction and morale. *Research on Aging*, 1979, *1*, 335–360.
Lee, G. R., & Ihinger-Tallman, H. Sibling interaction and morale: The effects of family relations on older people. *Research on Aging*, 1980, *2*, 367–391.
Lehman, H. C. *Age and achievement.* Princeton, N. J.: Princeton University Press, 1953.
Lewis, M. I., & Butler, R. N. Why is women's lib ignoring old women? *Aging and Human Development*, 1972, *3*, 223–231.
Lipsitt, D. A medical-psychological approach to dependency in the aged. In R. A. Kalish (Ed.), *Dependencies of old people* (Occasional Papers in Gerontology,

No. 6). Ann Arbor and Detroit: University of Michigan and Wayne State University, Institute of Gerontology, 1969.

Lopata, H. A. *Widowhood in an American city.* Cambridge, Mass.: Schenkman, 1973.

Lowenthal, M. F. Some potentialities of a life-cycle approach to the study of retirement. In F. M. Carp (Ed.), *Retirement.* New York: Behavioral Publications, 1972.

Lowenthal, M. F., & Haven, C. Interaction and adaptation: Intimacy as a critical variable. *American Sociological Review*, 1968, *33*, 20–30.

Lowenthal, M. F., Thurnher, M., & Chiriboga, D. *Four stages of life.* San Francisco: Jossey-Bass, 1975.

Maas, H. S., & Kuypers, J. A. *From thirty to seventy.* San Francisco: Jossey-Bass, 1974.

Maddox, G. Activity and morale: A longitudinal study of selected subjects. *Social Forces*, 1963, *42*, 195–204.

Marris, P. *Loss and change.* Garden City, N. Y.: Doubleday-Anchor, 1975.

Marshall, V. W. (Ed.). *Aging in Canada: Social perspectives.* Toronto: Fitzhenry & Whiteside, 1980.

McClusky, H. Y. *Education: Background and issues* (White House Conference on Aging). Washington, D. C.: U. S. Government Printing Office, 1971.

McFarland, R. A. The sensory and perceptual processes in aging. In K. W. Schaie (Ed.), *Theory and methods of research on aging.* Morgantown: West Virginia University Library, 1968.

McKain, W. *Retirement marriage.* Storrs: University of Connecticut Press, 1968.

McTavish, D. G. Perceptions of old people: A review of research methodologies and findings. *The Gerontologist*, 1971, *11*(4, Pt. 2), 90–102.

Metropolitan Life Insurance Co. *Statistical Bulletin*, September 1977, *58*, 8–10.

Miller, S. J. Will the real "older woman" please stand up? In M. M. Seltzer, S. L. Corbett, & R. C. Atchley (Eds.), *Social problems of the aging: Readings.* Belmont, Calif.: Wadsworth, 1978.

Mishara, B. L., & Kastenbaum, R. *Alcohol and old age.* New York: Grune & Stratton, 1980.

Moberg, D. O. *Spiritual well-being* (White House Conference on Aging). Washington, D. C.: U. S. Government Printing Office, 1971.

Moenster, P. A. Learning and memory in relation to age. *Journal of Gerontology*, 1972, *27*, 361–363.

Neugarten, B. L. Adult personality: Toward a psychology of the life-cycle. In B. L. Neugarten (Ed.), *Middle age and aging.* Chicago: University of Chicago Press, 1968.

Neugarten, B. L. Personality and the aging process. *The Gerontologist*, 1972, *12*(Spring, Pt. 1), 9–15.

Neugarten, B. L. Age groups in American society and the rise of the young-old. *Annals of the American Academy of Political and Social Science*, 1974, *415*, 187–198.

Neugarten, B. L. Personality and aging. In J. E. Birren & K. W. Schaie (Eds.), *Handbook of the psychology of aging.* New York: Van Nostrand Reinhold, 1977.

Neugarten, B. L., Havighurst, R. J., & Tobin, S. S. The measurement of life satisfaction. *Journal of Gerontology*, 1961, *16*, 134–143.

Neugarten, B. L., Havighurst, R. J. & Tobin, S. S. Personality and patterns of aging. In B. L. Neugarten (Ed.), *Middle age and aging.* Chicago: University of Chicago Press, 1968.

Neugarten, B. L., Moore, J. W., & Lowe, J. C. Age norms, age constraints, and adult socialization. *American Journal of Sociology*, 1965, *70,* 710–717.

Neugarten, B. L., & Weinstein, K. K. The changing American grandparent. *Journal of Marriage and the Family*, 1964, *26,* 199–204.

Nimkoff, M. F. Family relationships of older people. *The Gerontologist*, 1961, *1,* 92–97.

Oberleder, M. Psychotherapy with the aging: An art of the possible? *Psychotherapy: Theory, Research, and Practice*, 1966, *3,* 130–142.

Olefsky, J. M., Reavan, G. M., & Farquhar, J. W. The effects of weight reduction on obesity: Studies of lipid and carbohydrate metabolism in normal and hyperlipoproteinemic subjects. *Journal of Clinical Investigation*, 1974, *53,* 64–76.

Palmore, E. Advantages of aging. *The Gerontologist*, 1979, *19,* 220–223.

Parkes, C. M. "Seeking" and "finding" a lost object: Evidence from recent studies of the reaction to bereavement. *Social Science and Medicine*, 1970, *4,* 187–201.

Parkes, C. M. *Bereavement: Studies of grief in adult life.* New York: International Universities Press, 1972.

Parkinson, S. R., Lindholm, J., & Urell, T. Aging, dichotic memory, and digit span. *Journal of Gerontology*, 1980, *35,* 87–95.

Petersen, D. M., & Whittington, F. J. Drug use among the elderly: A review. *Journal of Psychedelic Drugs*, 1977, *9,* 25–37.

Peterson, D. A. Financial adequacy in retirement: Perceptions of older Americans. *The Gerontologist*, 1972, *12,* 379–383.

Peterson, D. A. The role of gerontology in education. In S. M. Grabowski & W. D. Mason (Eds.), *Learning for aging.* Washington, D. C.: Adult Education Association, 1974.

Peterson, D. A., & Eden, D. Z. Teenagers and aging: Adolescent literature as an attitude source. *Educational Gerontology*, 1977, *2,* 311–326.

Peterson, J. A. Marital and family therapy involving the aged. *The Gerontologist*, 1973, *13,* 27–31.

Pfeiffer, E. Sexual behavior in old age. In E. W. Busse & E. Pfeiffer (Eds.), *Behavior and adaptation in late life.* Boston: Little, Brown, 1969.

Pfeiffer, E. Psychopathology and social pathology. In J. E. Birren & K. W. Schaie (Eds.), *Handbook of the psychology of aging.* New York: Van Nostrand Reinhold, 1977.

Pfeiffer, E., Verwoerdt, A., & Davis, G. Sexual behavior in middle life. *American Journal of Psychiatry*, 1972, *128,* 1262–1267.

Planek, T. W., Condon, M. E., & Fowler, R. C. *An investigation of the problems and opinions of aged drivers.* Chicago: National Safety Council, 1968.

Plutchik, R., Weiner, M., & Conte, H. Studies of body image, body worries, and body discomforts. *Journal of Gerontology*, 1971, *26,* 344–350.

Reichard, S., Livson, F., & Petersen, P. G. *Aging and personality: A study of 87 older men.* New York: Wiley, 1962.

Richards, W. S., & Thorpe, G. L. Behavioral approaches to the problems of later life. In M. Storandt, I. C. Siegler, & M. F. Elias (Eds.), *The clinical psychology of aging.* New York: Plenum, 1978.

Riegel, K. F., & Riegel, R. M. Developmental drop and death. *Developmental Psychology*, 1972, *6,* 306–319.

Riley, M. W., & Foner, A. *Aging and society. Vol 1: An inventory of research findings.* New York: Russell Sage Foundation, 1968.

Robertson, J. F. Significance of grandparents. *The Gerontologist*, 1976, *16*, 137–140.

Robinson, B., & Thurnher, M. Taking care of aged parents: A family cycle transition. *The Gerontologist*, 1979, *19*, 586–593.

Rodstein, M. Accidents among the aged: Incidence, causes, and prevention. *Journal of Chronic Diseases*, 1964, *17*, 515–526.

Roff, L. L., & Klemmack, D. L. Sexual activity among older persons: A comparative analysis of appropriateness. *Research on Aging*, 1979, *1*, 389–399.

Rosow, I. Forms and functions of adult socialization. *Social Forces*, 1965, *44*, 35–45.

Rosow, I. *Social integration of the aged*. New York: Free Press, 1967.

Schaie, K. W., & Schaie, J. P. Clinical assessment and aging. In J. E. Birren & K. W. Schaie (Eds.), *Handbook of the psychology of aging*. New York: Van Nostrand Reinhold, 1977.

Schaie, K. W., & Strother, C. R. A cross-sectional study of age changes in cognitive behavior. *Psychological Bulletin*, 1968, *70*, 671–680.

Schiffman, S. Food recognition by the elderly. *Journal of Gerontology*, 1977, *32*, 586–592.

Schiffman, S., & Pasternak, M. Decreased discrimination of food odors in the elderly. *Journal of Gerontology*, 1979, *34*, 73–79.

Schuckit, M. A. Geriatric alcoholism and drug abuse. *The Gerontologist*, 1977, *17*, 168–174.

Schuerman, L. E., Eden, D. Z., & Peterson, D. A. Older people in some women's periodical fiction. *Educational Gerontology*, 1977, *2*, 327–351.

Schulz, J. H. *The economics of aging* (2nd ed.). Belmont, Calif.: Wadsworth, 1980.

Schulz, R., & Aderman, D. Clinical research and the stages of dying. *Omega*, 1974, *5*, 137–143.

Seefeldt, C., Jantz, R. K., Galper, A., & Serock, K. Children's attitudes toward the elderly: Educational implications. *Educational Gerontology*, 1977, *2*, 301–310.

Seltzer, M. M. The older woman: Facts, fantasies, and fiction. *Research on Aging*, 1979, *1*, 139–154.

Seltzer, S. Strategies for using the guidelines in congregational settings. *Theological Education*, 1980, *16*, 354–355.

Selye, H. *The stress of life* (Rev. ed.). New York: McGraw-Hill, 1976.

Shanas, E. *The health of older people: A social survey*. Cambridge, Mass.: Harvard University Press, 1962.

Shanas, E. Social myth as hypothesis: The case of the family relations of old people. *The Gerontologist*, 1979, *19*, 3–9.

Shanas, E., Townsend, P., Wedderburn, D., Friis, H., Milhoj, P., & Stehouwer, J. (Eds.). *Old people in three industrial societies*. New York: Atherton, 1968.

Shelton, A. J. Igbo child-rearing, eldership, and dependence: A comparison of two cultures. In R. A. Kalish (Ed.), *Dependencies of old people* (Occasional Papers in Gerontology, No. 6). Ann Arbor and Detroit: University of Michigan and Wayne State University, Institute of Gerontology, 1969.

Sheppard, R. Life begins at 40 and now it goes on longer. *Toronto Globe and Mail*, March 28, 1979, p. 1.

Shichor, D., & Kobrin, S. Criminal behavior among the elderly. *The Gerontologist*, 1978, *18*, 213–218.

Shock, N. W. Biological theories of aging. In J. E. Birren & K. W. Schaie (Eds.), *Handbook of the psychology of aging*. New York: Van Nostrand Reinhold, 1977.

Simanis, J. G., & Coleman, J. R. Health care expenditures in nine industrial countries, 1960–1976. *Social Security Bulletin*, 1980, *43*, 3–8.

Simić, A. Winners and losers: Aging Yugoslavs in a changing world. In B. G. Myerhoff & A. Simić (Eds.), *Life's career—Aging*. Beverly Hills, Calif.: Sage Publications, 1978.

Simon, A. *Physical and mental health* (White House Conference on Aging). Washington, D. C.: U. S. Government Printing Office, 1971.

Singer, J. W. A brighter future for older workers. *National Journal*, October 28, 1978, pp. 1722–1725.

Skoglund, J. Job deprivation in retirement: Anticipated and experienced feelings. *Research on Aging*, 1979, *1*, 481–493.

Smith, H. E. Family interaction patterns of the aged: A review. In A. M. Rose & W. A. Peterson (Eds.), *Older people and their social world*. Philadelphia: Davis, 1965.

Spencer, B. G. Personal communication, 1981.

Spieth, W. Cardiovascular health status, age, and psychological performance. *Journal of Gerontology*, 1964, *19*, 277–284.

Streib, G. F. Family patterns in retirement. *Journal of Social Issues*, 1958, *14*(2), 46–60.

Streib, G. F. Are the aged a minority group? In A. W. Gouldner & S. M. Miller (Eds.), *Applied sociology*. New York: Free Press, 1965.

Sussman, M. B. The help pattern in the middle-class family. *American Sociological Review*, 1953, *18*, 22–28.

Sussman, M. B. Relationships of adult children with their parents in the United States. In E. Shanas & G. F. Streib (Eds.), *Social structure and the family: Generational relations*. Englewood Cliffs, N. J.: Prentice-Hall, 1965.

Szafran, J., & Birren, J. E. Perception. In J. E. Birren (Ed.), *Contemporary gerontology: Concepts and issues*. Los Angeles: Andrus Gerontology Center, 1969.

Szapocznik, J., Lasaga, J., Perry, P., & Solomon, J. R. Outreach in the delivery of mental health services to Hispanic elders. *Hispanic Journal of Behavioral Sciences*, 1979, *1*, 21–40.

Teaff, J. D., Lawton, M. P., Nahemow, L., & Carlson, D. Impact of age integration on the well-being of elderly tenants in public housing. *Journal of Gerontology*, 1978, *33*, 130–133.

Thornbury, J. M., & Mistretta, C. M. Tactile sensitivity as a function of age. *Journal of Gerontology*, 1981, *36*, 34–39.

Treas, J., & VanHilst, A. Marriage and remarriage rates among older Americans. *The Gerontologist*, 1976, *16*, 132–136.

Troll, L. E. The family of later life: A decade review. *Journal of Marriage and the Family*, 1971, *33*, 263–290.

Troll, L. E., Miller, S. J., & Atchley, R. C. *Families in later life*. Belmont, Calif.: Wadsworth, 1979.

Turner, B. F. The self-concepts of older women. *Research on Aging*, 1979, *1*, 464–480.

United Nations, Statistical Office, Department of Economic and Social Affairs. *Demographic yearbook, 1978*. New York: United Nations, 1979.

U. S. Department of Health, Education and Welfare. *United States national health survey, 1959*. Health statistics, Series B, No. 9, p. 9.

U.S. Department of Health, Education and Welfare, National Institute for Neurological Diseases and Blindness. *Annual tabulations of the model reporting area for blindness statistics, 1965, statistical report*. Washington, D. C.: Government Printing Office, 1966.

U. S. Public Health Service. *Vital statistics of the United States, 1970. Vol. 2: Mortality, Part A.* Rockville, Md.: Author, 1974.

Veatch, R. M. *Life span: Values and life-extending technologies.* New York: Harper & Row, 1979.

Ward, R. A. *The aging experience: An introduction to social gerontology.* Philadelphia: Lippincott, 1979. (a)

Ward. R. A. The never married in later life. *Journal of Gerontology*, 1979, *34,* 861–869. (b)

Weg, R. B. *Nutrition and the later years.* Los Angeles: University of Southern California Press, 1978.

Weinberger, A. Stereotyping of the elderly: Elementary school children's responses. *Research on Aging*, 1979, *1,* 113–136.

Weisman, A. *On dying and denying.* New York: Behavioral Publications, 1972.

Welford, A. T. Motor performance. In J. F. Birren & K. W. Schaie (Eds.), *Handbook of the psychology of aging.* New York: Van Nostrand Reinhold, 1977.

White House Conference on Aging. *Aging and blindness* (Special Concerns Session report). Washington, D. C.: U. S. Government Printing Office, 1972.

Willis, S. L., & Baltes, P. B. Intelligence in adulthood and aging: Contemporary issues. In L. W. Poon (Ed.), *Aging in the 1980s: Psychological issues.* Washington, D. C.: American Psychological Association, 1980.

Wolff, K. *Geriatric psychiatry.* Springfield, Ill.: Charles C Thomas, 1963.

Woodruff, D. S. *Can you live to be 100?* New York: Chatham Square Press, 1977.

Youmans, E. G. The rural aged. *Annals of the American Academy of Political and Social Science*, 1977, *429,* 81–90.

Younger, E. J. The California experience: Prevention of criminal victimization of the elderly. *The Police Chief*, 1976, *43,* 28–30 ff.

Author Index

Aderman, D., 67
Albrecht, R., 87
Anderson, B. G.,81
Anderson, B., Jr., 23
Ansello, E. F., 140
Antunes, G. E., 146, 147
Arenberg, D., 35
Atchley, R. C., 86, 95–97, 99, 102, 108, 117, 125
Atkin, C. K., 140

Baltes, P. B., 31, 39, 40
Barfield, R. E., 121, 122, 125
Beattie, W. M., Jr., 142
Beers, J., 29
Bell, E., 23, 24
Bengtson, V. L., 110
Bennett, R., 141
Bequaert, L. H., 97
Berardo, F. M., 99
Beresford, J. C., 95
Bergman, M., 25
Bernholz, C. D., 24
Birren, J. E., 26, 28
Blenkner, M., 102, 112
Blum, J. E., 39, 40
Botwinick, J., 11, 28, 34–36, 39, 76–78
Britton, J. H., 76
Britton, J. O., 76
Brody, E. M., 55
Bromley, D. B., 33
Brotman, H. B., 10, 12–15, 50, 51, 95–97, 111, 115, 116, 118, 119, 132, 134, 151
Bühler, C., 84
Bultena, G. L., 10, 133
Burgess, E., 86
Busse, E. W., 21
Butler, R. N., 66, 91
Buyagawan, A. K., 155

Campbell, A., 80, 95
Candy, S. E., 60
Cantor, M. H., 108, 109
Carlisle, A. E., 125, 126
Carlson, D., 110
Carp, F. M., 134
Case, W. H., 29
Charles, D. C., 141
Chiriboga, D., 95
Chown, S. M., 77
Cicirelli, V. G. 107
Clark, M., 81
Coe, R. M., 105
Cohen, D., 21, 32, 40, 52, 53, 54, 64
Cohen, G. M., 62
Coleman, J. R., 51
Comfort, A., 19, 157
Condon, M. E., 29, 30
Conte, H., 74
Converse, P. E., 80, 95
Cook, F. L., 146, 147
Cook, T. D., 146, 147
Corso, J. F., 24, 26
Craik, F. I., 33
Cumming, E., 77, 82, 83
Cutler, N. E., 110
Cutler, S. J., 134, 150

Davis, G., 113
Davis, R. H., 129
de Beauvoir, S., 113
Dennis, W., 37
Denton, F. T., 12, 14

Eckman, J., 141

Eden, D. Z., 140
Eisdorfer, C., 38, 49, 52, 53, 54, 59, 64, 121
Elias, M. F., 113
Elias, P. K., 113
Engen, T., 26
Epstein, L. J., 55, 56
ERA, 117
Erikson, E. H., 48
Estes, C. L., 142

Falek, A., 36
Farberow, N. L., 58
Farquhar, J. W., 46
Feld, S., 72
Foner, A., 25, 28, 29, 72, 77, 119
Fosshage, J. L., 37
Fowler, R. C., 29, 30
Fozard, J. L., 23, 24
Friis, H., 100, 120–122
Furry, C. A., 39

Galper, A., 137
Gelwicks, L. E., 131
Giambra, L. M., 35
Glaser, B. G., 66
Glock, C. Y., 149
Goldfarb, A. I., 78, 96, 111
Gottesman, L. E., 62
Graney, M. J., 152
Greenberg, B. S., 140
Gribbin, K., 35
Gubrium, J., 99
Gurin, G., 72
Gurland, B. J., 55, 57
Gutmann, N. D., 77, 78

Harker, J. O., 33
Harkins, E. B., 100
Harkins, S. W., 26
Harris, L., 17, 32, 51, 73, 93, 94, 100, 107, 108, 116, 124, 130, 136, 138, 139, 141, 146
Hartley, J. T., 33
Haven, C., 109
Havighurst, R. J., 79, 82, 84, 85, 87
Haynes, S. G., 121
Hays, W. C., 152
Henry, W. H., 77, 82, 83
Heron, A., 77
Herr, J., 64
Hertzog, C., 35
Hess, B. B., 108
Hickey, L., 136
Hickey, T., 45, 136, 137
Hill, R., 101
Howell, S. C., 46, 102
Hoyer, F. W., 31
Hoyer, W. J., 31
Hulbert, S., 29

Iglehart, J. K., 116
Ihinger-Tallman, H., 107
Institute for Interdisciplinary Studies, 116
Ivester, C., 137

Jackson, J. J., 14, 155
Jantz, R. K., 137
Jarvik, L. F., 33, 36, 37, 40, 53
Johnson, A. I., 77

Kahana, E., 105
Kalish, R. A., 16, 17, 58, 66, 67, 83, 106, 107, 111, 136, 137, 150
Kallman, F. J., 36
Kaplan, H. B., 72
Kastenbaum, R., 58–60, 62, 64, 66
Kayne, R. C., 49
Kelly, J., 114
Kenshalo, D. R., 27
Kiefer, C. W., 87, 88
King, K., 137
Kivnick, H. Q., 105
Kleban, M. H., 55
Klemmack, D. L., 114
Knight, B., 64, 65
Kobrin, S., 148
Kogan, N., 72, 136
Korzenny, F., 140
Krisologo, R. B., 155
Kubey, R. W., 129
Kübler-Ross, E., 67, 83
Kuypers, J. A., 77

Larson, R., 108
Lasaga, J., 154
Lawton, M. P., 55, 110, 132, 147
Leanse, J., 144
Lee, G. R., 101, 107
Lehman, H. C., 37
Lewis, M. I., 91
Lindholm, J., 33
Lipsitt, D., 112
Livson, F., 84, 85
Loeb, M. B., 46
Lopata, H. A., 99
Lowe, J. C., 89
Lowenthal, M. F., 95, 109, 127

Maas, H. S., 77
Maddox, G., 73, 83
Marris, P., 99
Marshall, V. W., 116
McClusky, H. Y., 152
McFarland, R. A., 23, 24, 26

McKain, W., 97
McMichael, A. J., 121
McTavish, D. G., 138, 139
Metropolitan Life Insurance Co., 97
Milhoj, P., 100, 120–122
Miller, S. J., 91, 95–97, 99, 102
Mishara, B. L., 58, 59
Mistretta, C. M., 27
Moberg, D. O., 149
Moenster, P. A., 33
Moore, J. W., 89
Morgan, J. N., 121, 122, 125
Moriwaki, S. Y., 58
Moss, M., 55

Nahemow, L., 110, 132
National Center for Health Statistics, 24, 25
Neugarten, B. L., 77, 79, 82, 83, 85, 89, 105, 158
Nimkoff, M. F., 103

Oberleder, M., 63
Olefsky, J. M., 46
Palmore, E., 17, 23
Parkes, C. M., 98, 99
Parkinson, S. R., 33
Pasternak, M., 26
Perry, P., 154
Petersen, D. M., 49, 50
Petersen, P. G., 84, 85
Peterson, D. A., 116, 140, 151, 152
Peterson, J. A., 64
Pfeiffer, E., 56–58, 113
Planek, T. W., 30
Plutchik, R., 74
Podelsky, S., 23, 24
Pokorny, A. D., 72
Powers, E. A., 10
Preston, C., 62

Quarterman, C. E., 62

Reavan, G. M., 46
Reichard, S., 84, 85
Reynolds, D. K., 66, 67
Richards, W. S., 63
Riegel, K. F., 9, 40
Riegel, R. M., 9, 40
Riley, M. W., 25, 28, 29, 72, 77, 119
Rivlin, A. M., 95
Robertson, J. F., 106
Robertson-Tchabo, E. A., 35
Robinson, B., 102
Rodgers, W. L., 80, 95
Rodstein, M., 27
Roff, L. L., 114
Rosow, I., 86, 101, 109–111, 133

Schaie, J. P., 55
Schaie, K. W., 7, 35, 55
Schiffman, S., 26
Schuckit, M. A., 58
Schuerman, L. E., 140
Schulz, J. H., 116, 123, 124
Schulz, R., 67
Seefeldt, C., 137
Seltzer, M. M., 91
Seltzer, S., 150
Selye, H., 20
Serok, K., 137
Shanas, E., 27, 41, 99, 100, 120–122
Shelton, A. J., 112
Sheppard, R., 14
Shichor, D., 148
Shock, N. W., 19, 20
Simanis, J. G., 51
Simić, A., 88
Simon, A., 53, 56
Singer, J. W., 120
Skogen, W. G., 146, 147
Skoglund, J., 125
Smith, H. E., 104
Solomon, J. R., 154
Spencer, B. G., 12
Stark, R., 149
Stehouwer, J., 100, 120–122
Storandt, M., 28
Stotsky, B. A., 49
Strauss, A. L., 66
Streib, G. F., 90, 101
Strother, C. R., 7
Sussman, M. B., 101
Szafran, J., 27
Szapocznik, J., 154

Teaff, J. D., 110
Tharner, M., 95, 102
Thompson, L. W., 11
Thornbury, J. M., 27
Thorpe, G. L., 63
Tobin, S. S., 79, 82, 83, 85
Townsend, P., 100, 120–122
Treas, J., 99
Treat, N. J., 31
Troll, L. E., 95–97, 99, 101, 102
Turner, B. F., 91
Tyroler, H. A., 121

Urell, J., 33
U. S. Public Health Service, 57
VanHilst, A., 97
Veatch, R. M., 19
Veroff, J., 72
Verwoerdt, A., 113
Visher, E., 106, 107

Wallach, M. A., 72
Walsh, D. A., 33
Ward, R. A., 76, 100, 125
Warner, M. H., 26
Wedderburn, D., 100, 120–122
Weg, R. B., 45
Weinberger, A., 137
Weiner, M., 74
Weinstein, K. K., 105
Weisman, A., 67, 68
Welford, A. T., 30
White House Conference on Aging, 25
Whittington, F. J., 49, 50
Willis, S. L., 40
Wolf, E., 23, 24
Wolff, K., 64
Wood, V., 133
Woodruff, D. S., 45, 157
Wu, S., 21, 32, 40

Yaffe, S., 147
Youmans, E. G., 156
Younger, E. J., 147

Subject Index

Accidents, 27, 29–30
Advocacy, 5, 146
Age cohort, 8
  role differences in, 88–90
Ageism, 144–142
Aging:
  advantages of, 17–18
  attitudes toward, 135–142
  coping with, 40–42
  definition of, 1, 8–10
  demography of, 12–15, 95–100
  future, 157–158
  individual differences in, 10–11
  meaning of, 8–12, 21–23, 30–31, 40–42
  models of, 16–17
  problems of, 93
  reasons for studying, 3–5
  successful, 79–86
  theories of, 19–20
Aging specialists, 4–6
Aging, study of, 3–5
  geriatricians and, 5
  gerontologists and, 5–6
  personal stake in, 4
  specialists in, 4–6
  vocational stake in, 4
Alcoholism, 58–59
Alzheimer's disease, 53–54
Appearance, 73–74
Attitudes of elderly toward:
  criminal victimization, 146–147
  death, 66
  religion, 148–151
  sex, 113–114
Attitudes toward elderly, 135–142
  of adults, 137–139
  ageism, 141–142
  of children/youth, 136–137
Attitudes toward elderly (*continued*)
  in children's literature, 140–141
  of elderly, 138–139
  and social values, 139–140
  on television, 141
Audition, 25–26

Bereavement, 97–99
Biological changes, 19–23
  meaning of, 21–23
  theories of, 19–20
Body image, 73–74, 113–114

Continuum of care, 62
Creativity, 37
Criminal behavior, 148
Criminal victimization, 146–148
  fear of, 146–147
  fraud as, 147–148
Cross-sectional research, 7–8, 36–37, 39

Day health center, 62–63
Death, 65–68, 83
  causes of, 52
  fear of, 66
  stages of, 67
  trajectory of, 66–67
  and widow(er)hood, 97–99
Dementia, 52–55
  Alzheimer's disease, 53–54
  cerebrovascular brain syndrome, 54
  definition of, 52–53
  "senility," 52–59
Demography of aging, 12–15
  ethnicity, 14–15, 153
  family, 95–100
  finances, 115–117
  health, 50, 51–52

Demography of aging (*continued*)
life expectancy, 13
projections, 13–14
retirement, 119
rural versus urban, 156
sex, 14
state, 15
Dental care, 52
Dependence, kinds of, 111–112
Depression, 56–57
Diet, *see* Nutrition
Disengagement, 82–84
Divorce, 96–97, 106 (*see also* Marriage)
Driving, 29–30
Drugs, 49–50

Educational gerontology, 151–152
elderhostel, 151
needs of, 152
Epidemiology:
accident rates, 29–30
auditory problems, 25–26
health, 50, 51–52
visual problems, 24–25
Ethnicity, 14–15, 153–156
and health, 51
and values, 154
Exercise, 47
Expenses, 116–117, 118

Family, 93–108
dependence/independence, 111–112
loss of, 97–99
multigeneration, 95
as support system, 109
Filial maturity, 102
Foot problems, 52
Foster Grandparent program, 144
Friends, 108–111
Functional disorders, 56–57

"Generation gap," 110
Geriatrics, 5
Gerontology, 5–6
Grandparents, 103–107
styles of being, 104
Great-grandparents, *see* Grandparents

Health (*see also* Health care):
Alzheimer's disease, 53–54
changes in, 50–59
costs, 51
and dementia, 52–55
diseases, 51, 52
epidemiology, 50, 51–52
maintenance, 44–50
mental, 55–59
and retirement, 120–121

Health care, 44–50, 59–65 (*see also* Health, Mental health)
costs, 51
and drug use, 49–50
exercise, 47
long-term facilities, 60–63
nutrition, 45–46
preventive, 44–45
and stress, 44, 47–49
Hearing, *see* Audition
Home maintenance program, 145
Homosexuality, 114
Housing, 132–134
cost of, 132
retirement communities, 133

Income, 115–117
in retirement, 120
sources of, 116–117
and stress, 117–119
Institutions, *see* Long-term care facilities
Intelligence, 35–37
Intergenerational household, 95, 102
Intergenerational relations, 94, 95, 100–107, 109–111
as support system, 101–102
Introversion, 77–78

Learning, 34–35
abilities, loss of, 38–40
Legal services, 148
Leisure, 127–129, 130
Life expectancy, 13
Life satisfaction, 80–82, 84, 108–109
in retirement, 125–126
Life-span development, definition of, 1–3
Loneliness, 93
Longitudinal research, 7–8, 36–37, 39, 76–77, 113
Long-term care facilities, 60–63
day health center, 62–63
kinds of, 60–61
staff of, 61

Marriage, 95–100 (*see also* Divorce)
never-married elderly, 99–100
remarriage, 97, 106
Medication, *see* Drugs
Memory, 31–34
long-term, 34
meaning of loss in, 38–40
Mental health, 55–59 (*see also* Health, Health care)
alcoholism, 58–59
depression, 56–57
functional disorders, 56–57
organic disorders, 52–55
schizophrenia, 57

Mental health (*continued*)
suicide, 57–58

Nursing homes, *see* Long-term care facilities
Nutrition, 45–46

Pain, 26–27
Parenthood, 100–103
Personal growth, 15–17
Personality, 70–86
changes, 75–79
continuity in, 77
disengagement, 82–84, 85
introversion, 77–78
mastery, 77–78
personal growth, 15–17
self-concept, 71–75
self-esteem, 71–73
successful aging, 79–86
Physical space, 129–132
Pleasure, 45
Preretirement counseling, 126
Programs, 144–146
Psychomotor performance, 27–31
driving, 29–30
and health conditions, 28
Psychotherapy, 63–65

Reaction time, 27–30
Relationships, 93–114
confidant, 109
dependency in, 111–112
family, 93, 94–108
with friends, 93, 108–111
in housing, 133
independency in, 111–112
intergenerational, 94, 95, 100–107
sexual, 112–114
among siblings, 107
Religion, 148–151
church, 150–151
dimensions of, 149
Reminiscence, 66
Research, 6–8
age-cohort, 8
attrition, 7–8
cross-sectional, 7-8
longitudinal, 7-8
methods, 6-8
Retired Senior Volunteer Program, 144
Retirement, 119–129
and job ability, 121–122
adjustment to, 124–126
counseling, 126
early, 121, 123
and health, 120–121

Retirement (*continued*)
leisure in 127–129, 130
mandatory, 123–124
meaning of, 122
and money, 120
relationships, 121
styles, 127
and work, 119–120, 122–123
Roles, 70, 86–92
adult socialization, 86
age, 86–88
definition of, 86
group identification, 90
women, 90–92, 95
Rural aged, 156–157

SAGE, 52, 144
Schizophrenia, 57
Self-concept, 71–75
body image, 73–74, 113–114
self-esteem, 71–73
Senescence, 11–12
Senile dementia, *see* Dementia
Senior centers, 144–145
Sensory processes, 23–27
audition, 25–26
pain, 26–27
smell, 26
taste, 27
touch, 26
vestibular, 27
vision, 23–25
Service Corps of Retired Executives, 144
Sex, 14, 78, 90–92, 95
Sexual behavior, 112–114
attitudes toward, 113–114
homosexuality, 114
Siblings, 107
Sleep, 46–47
Smell, 26
Social Security, 117
Social services, 142–146
advocacy for, 146
for frail elderly, 145–146
future trends in, 142–143
for well-elderly, 144 145
Socialization, *see* Roles
Stress, 47–49, 117–118
avoidance of, 44
Successful aging, 79–86
definitions of, 79–80
life satisfaction and, 80–82
patterns of, 84–86
Suicide, 57–58

Taste, 27
Television, 141
Terminal decline, 40

Touch, 26
Transportation, 134

Vestibular senses, 27
Vision, 23–25

Widow(er), 97–99
Women:
  demography for, 14
  roles of, 90–92
Work, 119–120, 122–123